Voyages Out, Voyages Home
[*Mordeithiau Allan, Mordeithiau Adref*]

The St. Ives fishing fleet leaving Hayle, c. 1890
Courtesy of Jonathan Holmes and the Penlee House Gallery and Museum, Penzance, Cornwall.

Voyages Out, Voyages Home

Edited by Jane de Gay and Marion Dell

Every effort has been made to trace all copyright-holders, but if any have been inadvertently overlooked, the publisher will be pleased to make the necessary arrangement at the first opportunity.

Copyright 2010 by Clemson University
ISBN 978-0-9842598-1-6

Published by Clemson University Press in Clemson, South Carolina

Editorial Assistants: Bridget Jeffs, Christina Cook, and Charis Chapman

To order copies, please visit the Clemson University Press website: www.clemson.edu/press.

Cover : *Voyages*, Oil on Canvas (100 cm. by 60 cm.), by Suzanne Bellamy.
The painting was first exhibited in 2002 at the Virginia Woolf Conference at Sonoma State University, Rohnert Park, CA.

Frontispiece: Fishing Boats Leaving Hayle Harbour, by permission of Penlee House Gallery and Museum, Penzance, Cornwall

Contents

Jane de Gay and Marion Dell • *Introduction* vi
List of Abbreviations x

☙

Beth Rigel Daugherty • *In Gratitude: Julia Briggs's Contributions to Woolf Studies* 1
Jeanne Dubino • *Engendering Voyages in Virginia Woolf's Fiction* 15
Tara Surry • *Angel Above the Houses: Virginia Woolf's Aerial Voyages* 18
Cheryl Mares • *"The Strangled Difficult Music of the Prelude": Woolf on Identity
  and Difference* 27
Su Reid • *Walking Down Whitehall* 32
Genevieve Abravanel • *Orlando's Othello* 39
Nancy Knowles • *The Voyage Home: Peter Walsh and the Trauma of Empire in
  Virginia Woolf's* Mrs. Dalloway 43
Janet M. Manson • *Leonard Woolf as an Architect of the League of Nations* 49
Beth Rigel Daugherty • *From the Beginning: Virginia Stephen's Reading and
  Virginia Woolf's Essays* 55
Nick Smart • *'Never See Rachel Again': Virginia Woolf and the End of Domestic Fiction* 62
Diane F. Gillespie • *Into the Underworld: Virginia Woolf, the Hogarth Press, and
  the Detective Novel* 70
Leslie Kathleen Hankins • *Reel Publishing: Virginia Woolf & the Hogarth Press'
  Film Publications* 77
Loretta Stec • *Virginia Woolf and* Time and Tide: *Forays into Feminist Journalism* 84
Diana L. Swanson • *Woolf and the Unsayable: The Roar on the Other Side of Silence* 92
Urszula Terentowicz-Fotyga • *The Politics of the Borderline: the Private, the
  Public and* Between 97
Joyce Kelley • *Rachel Vinrace's and Anna Morgan's Parallel Voyages: Exploring
  the Relationship Between Illness and Modernism* 104
Kathryn Harvey • *Tradition and Individual Talents: Rebecca West's and Virginia
  Woolf's Reviews and Essays* 112
Christine W. Sizemore • *Voyaging through 'Contested Cultural Territories' in
  Virginia Woolf's* Mrs. Dalloway *and Anita Desai's* Clear Light of Day 119
Andrea Adolph • *Consumption Asunder: Woolf, Dunmore, and the Mind/Body Split* 125

☙

Notes on Contributors 130
Bibliography of Publications Arising from the Conference 133

Introduction

by Jane de Gay and Marion Dell

In her diary entry for 9 March 1920, Virginia Woolf mused on the importance of writing something to be read at a later date and in different circumstances: 'I think I shall go on with this diary for the present ... I fancy old Virginia putting on her spectacles to read of March 1920 will decidedly wish me to continue' (*D2* 24). The International Virginia Woolf Society is similarly keen to preserve a historical record of its transactions for future generations, which is why we were invited to fill a gap in the records by assembling this selection of papers from the Eleventh Annual Virginia Woolf Conference, held in Bangor, North Wales in 2001. In belatedly compiling this collection, we have been involved in the kind of time-travelling that Woolf was so comfortable with, as demonstrated in *A Sketch of the Past* which takes its shape from an understanding that our perception of the past constantly shifts depending upon the circumstances of the present from which we view it.

As we reviewed the set of manuscripts from 2001 from the safe distance of 2009, we looked back on a world that seemed very different. The events of 11 September 2001 had not yet happened: as Tara Surry's paper observes, that was an age when the World Trade Center was a symbol of the seemingly unstoppable power of capitalism and patriarchal supremacy. Much has happened within Woolf studies, too: the Bangor gathering was the first Woolf conference to be held outside the United States, but since then we have had meetings in London and Birmingham and a further six further conferences have taken place, at which some 1,600 new papers have been presented. Countless books on Woolf have been published between 2001 and now, and new voices have ventured into print. The Woolf community has sustained losses too, not least one of our keynote speakers from 2001: Julia Briggs, to whom we pay tribute in this volume.

All of this of course presented challenges for us as we were invited to become guest editors for this collection as, like Mrs MacNab and Mrs Bast, we rescued from the pool of Time that was fast closing over now one paper and now another. A key principle of the annual *Selected Papers* has always been to record for posterity a reasonable cross-section of the papers actually presented at the conference. In retaining the principle of publishing actual papers, this collection is necessarily partial, for several of the papers given at the conference have since "voyaged" into new regions in Woolf Studies or been published in other fora, hence they were not appropriate for inclusion in this collection. This volume therefore, uniquely contains a Bibliography of publications arising from the conference, which supplements the selection of pieces contained here. In particular, this collection is best read alongside *Locating Woolf: The Politics of Space and Place* edited by Anna Snaith and Michael Whitworth (organizer of the 2001 Woolf conference), for six of the ten chapters in that volume derive from papers that had originally been presented at Bangor. In exploring questions of the politics of place and space, that volume reflects very strongly the conference's theme of voyaging, as the contributors—Tracy Seeley, Linden Peach, Sei Kosugi, Leena Kore Schröder, Jane Lewty and Nobuyoshi Ota—explore various ways in which Woolf travelled physically or imaginatively, in urban and rural locations, and across racial or cultural boundaries.

The passage of time has inevitably meant that some pieces that might have been offered for consideration in the autumn of 2001 were not submitted: either because the presenters had moved on in their own work and were reluctant to revisit their scholarly past; or quite simply because some scholars had lost touch with the Woolf community and were unaware of the calls for papers and other advertisements that we circulated after being invited to edit this volume. The conference programme, published at the end of this volume, therefore gives the wider picture by providing a full listing of the papers that were delivered.

We urged our contributors to remain true to another long-established principle of the *Selected Papers:* that the pieces submitted should be the actual papers read at the conference and that no significant changes should be made. This inevitably presented the danger that some papers would not reflect more recent developments on their topics and would not draw on research published more recently – although one criterion for inclusion was that contributions should still be relevant and make a contribution to Woolf studies. We therefore gave our contributors the opportunity, if they so wished, to write an Afterword in which they could acknowledge more recent publications and debates, or indeed note how they have developed their ideas since. The Afterword was therefore a way of keeping the integrity of the original papers, whilst recognizing that scholarship has moved on.

The theme of the Bangor conference was "Voyages Out, Voyages Home," and the idea of voyaging—which can be interpreted in many ways—permeates this collection. The opening pieces all take us on voyages around and within Woolf's texts. Jeanne Dubino sets the scene in "Engendering Voyages in Virginia Woolf's Fiction" by looking at how Woolf deals with gender difference in her account of voyages in four novels. By contrast, Tara Surry in "Angel Above the Houses: Virginia Woolf's Aerial Voyages," discusses Woolf's use of the trope of flight in two lesser-known essays, "Flying over London" and "America Which I have Never Seen." Cheryl Mares looks at Woolf's voyages into Russian and American literature in "'The Strangled Difficult Music of the Prelude': Woolf on Identity and Difference."

The next set of papers revolves around the theme of "Voyages around Empire"—a theme that has continued to capture the imagination of Woolf scholars. Su Reid's "Walking Down Whitehall" combines a careful reading of Woolf's depiction of London in *Mrs Dalloway* with a close critique of the imperialism on show in England's capital; Genevieve Abravanel reflects on the interaction of race and gender in *Orlando* by examining its intertext of Shakespeare's famous Moor in "Orlando's Othello"; and Nancy Knowles (continuing the theme of Shakespeare and empire), applies O. Mannoni's theory of the Prospero/Caliban complex in "The Voyage Home: Peter Walsh and the Trauma of Empire in Virginia Woolf's *Mrs. Dalloway.*" The final paper in this set, Janet Manson's "Leonard Woolf as an Architect of the League of Nations" offers a historical slant, reminding us that Virginia Woolf lived and worked in a milieu where international affairs were very much part and parcel of daily life.

The conference title (perhaps inevitably) attracted a high number of papers on *The Voyage Out*, and there was a focus on Woolf's earlier writings (appropriately, given that Woolf conceived *The Voyage Out* at Manorbier, a village in South Wales, in 1908). Two papers in this collection represent Woolf's early voyages: Beth Rigel Daugherty's masterly study of how Woolf's early reading flowed into her creativity in "From the Beginning: Virginia Stephen's Reading and Virginia Woolf's Essays," and Nick Smart's discussion of how Woolf negotiated traditional narrative patterns in *The Voyage Out* in "'Never See Rachel Again': Virginia Woolf and the End of Domestic Fiction."

The next set of papers in this collection all explore how Woolf's work voyaged between genres, pointing out that she delved deeper than she might have admitted into the "lowbrow" work she so often castigated. Diane F. Gillespie and Leslie Kathleen Hankins look at works Woolf published at the Hogarth Press on detective fiction and film publications, respectively, and consider whether these had an impact on her own writings. Loretta Stec discusses Woolf's uneasy relationship with journalism, focusing specifically on her contributions to *Time and Tide*.

The next two pieces explore "Liminalities" or "Thresholds", identifying moments where Woolf is on the cusp of one voyage/direction and another. Diana Swanson examines Woolf's engagement with the non-human, or animal world in "Woolf and the Unsayable: The Roar on the Other Side of Silence," while Urszula Terentowicz-Fotyga shows how Woolf deconstructs boundaries between inner and outer, private and public, individual and communal in *Between the Acts* in "The Politics of the Borderline: the Private, the Public and *Between*...".

Woolf's relationships with other writers, both contemporary and subsequent, have provided a perennial field for exploration and this conference was no exception. This collection features two pieces on Woolf and other early twentieth-century writers: Joyce Kelley points to parallels between Woolf and Jean Rhys, while Kathryn Harvey compares Woolf and Rebecca West as journalists. Two papers look at Woolf's influence on more recent writers: Christine W. Sizemore compares *Mrs. Dalloway* with Anita Desai's *Clear Light of Day*, and Andrea Adolph looks at consonances between novels by Woolf and Helen Dunmore.

With its theme of "Voyages Out, Voyages Home," the Bangor conference made a significant contribution to the discussion of Woolf and internationalism that has recurred in subsequent conferences and indeed became the central theme of the 2007[1] gathering. This concept resonates throughout the papers here, and it was reflected very clearly in the keynote talks: Laura Marcus discussed Woolf and the Russians in "On Not Knowing Russian"; Andrew McNeillie (after greeting the audience in Welsh) showed that Woolf had great interest in and empathy for the America she never visited in "Woolf in America and America in Woolf"; and Jane Marcus, in "A Very Fine Negress" continued her influential postcolonial studies of Woolf by examining Woolf's views of race, and concluding that she was both attracted to and afraid of the figure the negress in *A Room of One's Own*. All these pieces are available elsewhere and so are not included here.

In counterpoint to these, Julia Briggs spoke of Woolf's view of her native culture in "Woolf and Englishness." It was inappropriate to try to recover her talk for publication, so instead we begin this volume with a tribute to Briggs's work: we are very grateful to Beth Rigel Daugherty for writing this tribute on behalf of us all. This piece does more than celebrate Briggs's contribution to Woolf studies: it also provides a useful measure of how Woolf scholarship has moved on over the past decade, providing a background to developments that bridge the 2001 conference and the present day.

Notes

1 At the time of the Bangor conference, the collection *The Reception of Virginia Woolf in Europe* edited by Mary Ann Caws and Nicola Luckhurst was in production. Eight contributors to that volume spoke at the Bangor conference: Alberto Lázaro, Laura Marcus, Katerina K. Kitsi-Mitakou, Ida Kiltgård, Carole Rodier, Catherine Sandbach-Dahlström, Urszula Terentowicz-Fotyga, Pierre-Éric Villeneuve.

Works Cited

Caws, Mary Ann and Nicola Luckhurst, eds. *The Reception of Virginia Woolf in Europe*. London: Continuum, 2002.
Marcus, Jane. "A Very Fine Negress." *Hearts of Darkness: White Women Write Race*. Piscataway, NJ: Rutgers University Press, 2004. Chapter 2.
Marcus, Laura. "The European Dimensions of the Hogarth Press." *The Reception of British Writers in Europe: Virginia Woolf*. Ed. Mary Ann Caws and Nicola Luckhurst. London: Continuum, 2002. 328-56.
—. "Introduction." *Translations from the Russian by Virginia Woolf and S.S. Koteliansky*. London: Virginia Woolf Society of Great Britain, 2006. vii-xxiv.
McNeillie, Andrew. "Virginia Woolf's America." *Dublin Review* 5 (Winter 2001-2): 41-55.
Snaith, Anna, and Michael Whitworth, eds. *Locating Woolf: The Politics of Space and Place*. New York and Basingstoke: Palgrave Macmillan, 2007.
Woolf, Virginia. *The Diary of Virginia Woolf*. Ed. Anne Olivier Bell with Andrew McNeillie. Vol. 2. Harmondsworth: Penguin, 1981.

Virginia Woolf
Standard Abbreviations
(as established by *The Woolf Studies Annual*)

AHH	*A Haunted House*
AROO	*A Room of One's Own*
BP	*Books and Portraits*
BTA	*Between the Acts*
CDB	*The Captain's Death Bed and Other Essays*
CE	*Collected Essays* (ed. Leonard Woolf, 4 vols.: *CE1, CE2, CE3, CE4*)
CR1	*The Common Reader*
CR2	*The Common Reader, Second Series*
CSF	*The Complete Shorter Fiction* (ed. Susan Dick)
D	*The Diary of Virginia Woolf* (5 vols.: *D1, D2, D3, D4, D5*)
DM	*The Death of the Moth and Other Essays*
E	*The Essays of Virginia Woolf* (eds. Stuart Clarke and Andrew McNeillie, 6 vols.: *E1, E2, E3, E4, E5, E6*)
F	*Flush*
FR	*Freshwater*
GR	*Granite and Rainbow: Essays*
HPGN	*Hyde Park Gate News* (ed. Gill Lowe)
JR	*Jacob's Room*
JRHD	*Jacob's Room: The Holograph Draft* (ed. Edward L. Bishop)
L	*The Letters of Virginia Woolf* (ed. Nigel Nicolson and Joanne Trautmann, 6 vols.: *L1, L2, L3, L4, L5, L6*)
M	*The Moment and Other Essays*
MEL	*Melymbrosia*
MOB	*Moments of Being*
MT	*Monday or Tuesday*
MD	*Mrs. Dalloway*
ND	*Night and Day*
O	*Orlando*
PA	*A Passionate Apprentice*
RF	*Roger Fry*
TG	*Three Guineas*
TTL	*To the Lighthouse*
TW	*The Waves*
TY	*The Years*
VO	*The Voyage Out*
WF	*Women and Fiction: The Manuscript Versions of* A Room of One's Own (ed. S. P. Rosenbaum)

In Gratitude...
Julia Briggs's Contributions to Woolf Studies

by Beth Rigel Daugherty

> Writing is one way of stemming a sense of human loss, a way of recovering the past, recapturing its moments of plentitude, restoring the decayed house and recalling the dead.
>
> —Julia Briggs, 'This moment I stand on': Woolf and the Spaces in Time

Julia Briggs was a vibrant alive woman whose teaching and mentoring, scholarly and intellectual work, and service to the academic institutions she loved touched hundreds and thousands of people. Julia is surely "laid out like a mist between the people she knew best, who lifted her on their branches as she had seen the trees lift the mist, [and] it spread ever so far, her life, herself" (MD 9). I cannot begin to do for her what she did so ably for Woolf—bring thought and work to life—but I hope I can begin to express the sense of debt we in Woolf Studies have to Julia.

Beyond her numerous contributions to students, curricula, institutions, and higher education in general,[1] beyond her many contributions to other fields of study,[2] Julia Briggs gave so much to Woolf Studies: her reviews of work related to Woolf; her own Woolf criticism; her editing; and too many intangible contributions to count. Fulfilling the desire many of her far-flung friends had upon learning about her illness and death, this essay attempts to express our deep gratitude for Julia's good work. Though we can no longer thank her in person, she would understand, I suspect, our need to recall her in just this way.

Reviewing

We are in Julia's debt because she helped to bring feminist literary issues and Virginia Woolf to a wider readership when certain forces in the British academic world were doing their best to erase those issues, erase Virginia Woolf, and certainly erase Woolf's contribution to literature, political thought, and feminism. Her reviews in the *Times Literary Supplement*, *The Times*, and other British venues brought a sanity to the discussion of Woolf that was sometimes missing in the UK.[3] For many years, her reviews grew out of her expertise in Shakespeare and children's literature, but a shift occurred around 1993, soon after Woolf's works briefly came out of copyright and new editions began appearing. At the time, "J'Accuse,"[4] a widely-watched TV show, had insisted that Woolf's reputation was inflated, and all things Bloomsbury were being dismissed with a sneer. Julia refused to rise to the bait.[5] Instead, she forged forward, providing facts and accessible scholarship, confronting controversies, and replacing rant and distortion with patience and integrity.

Julia accomplished a great deal in her steady, even-handed reviews. Assuming Woolf was worthy of study, she frequently slipped in certain facts (such as Virginia Stephen's contribution to the women's suffrage movement) or pointed out certain complexities (the years 1897 to 1904 may have been the "seven unhappy years" in Woolf's 1940 memory, but the journals themselves reveal happy and increasingly confident times as well). Perhaps most important, Julia made readers realize that not all academics, indeed, not all *readers*, thought Woolf should be relegated to the dust heap. Perhaps, her calm and straightforward reviews indirectly suggested, the current dismissal was just a mite too easy. Joining Gillian Beer and Hermione Lee in making Woolf's work tougher to dismiss, Julia Briggs "did a lot to encourage and solidify the revived interest in Woolf in the UK" (Gillespie)

Between 1990 and 2006, Julia reviewed Mitchell Leaska's edition of *A Passionate Apprentice* in *The Times*; Mary Beard's book about Jane Harrison in the *London Review of Books*; Mark Hussey's *Major Authors on CD-ROM: Virginia Woolf* in *Computers & Texts*; Hermione Lee's biography of Woolf in *Essays in Criticism*; B. J. Kirkpatrick and Stuart Clarke's 4th edition of the Woolf bibliography in *Review of English Studies*; Victoria Glendinning's biography of Leonard Woolf in the *New Statesman*; and for *TLS*, Suzanne Raitt's study of Vita and Virginia's work and friendship, biographies by Nigel Nicolson and Herbert Marder and Anna Snaith's *Public and Private Negotiations*, and Anthony Curtis's biography. In a brief essay for a series in the *Independent* on Building a Library, she suggests several titles in the Cross-Dressing Category, including *Orlando*.

Julia reached out, then, to various general and academic audiences in the UK through her reviews. Less frequently, she wrote reviews for the smaller Woolf world, such as her comments on Mark Hussey's *Virginia Woolf: A-Z* in the *Charleston Magazine* (where she noted its usefulness and called for an electronic edition and regular updating, something publishers have so far been unwilling to do), or her review of James Haule and J. H. Stape's collection *Editing Virginia Woolf* in *Woolf Studies Annual* (in which she praises the intentions of Shakespeare Head Press and essays by Ted Bishop and Diane Gillespie, but expresses her disappointment that the collection is just the beginning rather than the scholarly rescue of Woolfian texts she had hoped for), or her assessment of *Waves* at the National Theatre in the *Virginia Woolf Bulletin* (in which she provides a brief discussion of modernist drama, summarizes the origins of Woolf's novel, and praises Katie Mitchell's emphasis on the novel's words but criticizes her predictable use of Woolf's life to express a "sense of defeat that [Woolf's] fiction so eloquently rejects" [64]).

Interpreting

We are thankful for the strength, insight, and grace of Julia's body of interpretive work, which is inspiring in both its magnitude and its clarity. Julia's presentations were "riveting" (Silver)—lucid, witty, and engaging. Karen Kukil, for example, remembers her "Woolf and Englishness" presented at the Bangor, Wales conference this volume represents, and Hans-Walter Gabler remembers her focus on the teaching implications of a "Time Passes" electronic text at a Bavarian symposium.[6] The articles and essays based on many of these presentations bring her voice back into our midst, and they are beautifully written. Indeed, Julia has passed on a writing legacy ("Readability! Really getting to the gist of it all—and making it clear, translucent, brilliant" [Hankins]) we would do well to emulate, challenging us to set the bar high. All her criticism, a pleasure to read and accessible to students as well as to scholars (Gillespie), fulfills what she hoped her biography of Woolf would do: "lead readers back to [Woolf's] work with a fresh sense of what they might find there" (*Inner Life* xi). Over the past two decades, she steadily produced excellent work on Woolf, much of it now collected in *Reading Virginia Woolf*, but some of it existing outside that collection, for example her introduction to the Everyman edition of *To the Lighthouse*; her essay on "Novels of the 1930s" in the *Cambridge Companion to Virginia Woolf*; her piece on "Editing Woolf for the 90s" for the *South Carolina Review*;[7] her piece on "Searching for New Virginias" in *Virginia Woolf: Turning the Centuries: Selected Papers from the Ninth Annual Conference on Virginia Woolf*; her foreword to Vanessa Curtis's *Virginia Woolf's Women*; her lovely essay on Hope Mirrlees for *Gender in Modernism*; and "Virginia Woolf Meets Sigmund Freud" in the Supplement to Issue No. 27 of the *Virginia Woolf Bulletin*.

The fourteen essays in *Reading Virginia Woolf*, presented or published between 1992 and 2005, cover a wide variety of topics—reading Shakespeare, genre, *Night and Day*, Hope Mirrlees, form, time, Constantinople, revision, short stories, England—but they lightly link Woolf's publications chronologically and subtly focus on absence thematically. They reveal Julia as an "uncommonly precise...archeologist of Woolf's caves of meaning" and as a pioneer and visionary who saw "all of Woolf's texts as a long continuum, giving the same value to all words, from the earliest drafts of a novel, an essay, to its lasting version in print" (Villeneuve). They also capture Julia's ability to "synthesize new and familiar insights" (Froula), her "knack for discovering the 'little pieces' of Woolf's work that no other critics have noticed" (Reynier), and her "genius for explication that rather than being dry brings a text vividly to life" (Silver). Reading this collection is a treat because Julia's interpretations and conclusions are stunning in their logic, solid in their scholarship, persuasive in their tone, and stimulating in their implications. Her immersion in Woolf and her sensitive reading, curious spirit, and love of literature show everywhere. Julia is a joyful scholarly detective, roaming around, for example, in Woolf's invention of a spectacle maker as an "ancestral common reader," the Stephen children's reading of *Punch*, a quotation from Shakespeare linking books to spectacles, and a citation from the *OED* to arrive at the suggestion that Woolf's phrase about gig-lamps in "Modern Fiction" may refer to a picture of Tom Briggs's "spectacles 'symmetrically arranged' on trays, quite as much as—or even instead of—rows of carriage lamps" ("Reading People" 73-74). What fun! And such moments fill her essays.

Julia's *Virginia Woolf: An Inner Life* is also the biography many of us have been waiting for, "one of the best things ever written about Virginia Woolf" (Barrett), "quietly wonderful" (Dunn). Reviewers were amazed that anything more could be said about Woolf, but Julia's approach, to focus on Woolf's work—from conception through reception—without losing sight of the life or the historical, social, and cultural forces acting on that life, was simply brilliant. Using primary sources—manuscripts, typescripts, diaries, letters, autobiography, essays, and short stories—Julia reconstructs, as well as they probably can be, Woolf's creative and thinking and writing processes from Woolf's own words. The ability to pull together such abundant material (along with some memoirs and letters of Woolf's contemporaries) into a clear and readable biography is nothing short of phenomenal. Julia acknowledges her own speculations and interpretations, characteristically uses "both/and" instead of "either/or" in discussing Woolf's attitudes and behavior, and courageously confronts Woolf's blind spots. Neither condemning nor condoning Woolf, Julia's word choices and narrative allow the fluid complexity of Woolf's thought and psyche to emerge.

Because of Julia's extraordinary work in gathering together all this primary material, readers now have a detailed, tightly-woven, and intriguing narrative of the steps Woolf took as she created ten novels, a collection of short stories, two collections of essays, two extended feminist essays, a biography, and an autobiographical draft. An intellectual biography of the highest order, *Virginia Woolf: An Inner Life* is "a mesmerizing read" (Merkin) about Woolf's working life, a book teachers and scholars and students will turn to for many years to come because they can *use* it—tracing the birth, life, and publishing aftermath for each of Woolf's major texts, Julia provides us with a time-saving way to begin our own work.

Editing

Notwithstanding her judicious reviews and incredible criticism, we in Woolf Studies may ultimately be most grateful to Julia for the mark she made on the editing of Woolf's texts. She clearly outlined the work ahead of us, ably leading and pointing the way. Indeed, scattered through her work are numerous suggestions about specific projects we and the next generations of scholars and students can and should undertake.[8] Beginning with her work as general editor of the Penguin edition in Great Britain, extending through her individual editing of *Night and Day* (and her assistance with the textual editing of some other series volumes), and ending with her crucial role in the electronic projects related to "Time Passes" and "A Sketch of the Past," Julia made it her responsibility to learn about the important textual issues facing Woolf Studies and to urge us to confront them. Her drive to make us pay attention to the scholarly basics ("If our knowledge of Woolf's texts and the revisions she made to them are to keep pace with the critical study of her work and support it appropriately, we now need full collations of the various impressions and editions published by the Hogarth Press in Woolf's lifetime" ["Between the Texts" 226]) threads its way through introductions and footnotes and essays, and it underlies her approach to her intellectual biography of Woolf as well.

In a flurry of activity prior to 1991, when Virginia Woolf was to come out of copyright in the UK, several new editions were planned and ultimately published (although Woolf's time out of copyright turned out to be brief): the Hogarth Press Definitive Edition (which was not at all definitive), the Oxford World Classics edition under the guidance of Frank Kermode, the Shakespeare Head Press Edition of Blackwell Publishers under an Editorial Committee, and the Penguin Twentieth-Century Classics under Julia as General Editor. The Penguins were "the most important event to happen in Woolf studies for decades" as they stood out from the crowd: "built to last" and "conceived and carried out and edited as a feminist project" (Marcus, "Embarrassment" 18). Briggs's vision of Woolf's modernist experiment—"to rewrite the great tradition of fiction so as to set nearer its centre women's experience and their ways of relating to one another and to the wider world" (*Introductions to the Major Works*)—is a "generous" feminism, allowing contributors to "translate it in their turn as they wish. ... Such a variety of feminist responses is heartening" (Roberts). Julia was part of the decision to return to the texts of the first British edition so that errors in later editions could be discarded, but that return was made with care, and as Jeri Johnson points out, the Penguin texts *were* edited, generally in comparison with the American editions. As a result, the Penguins have "fuller textual histories" than the Oxfords, are "textually half way between Oxford and the...Blackwell edition"

(Johnson 5). Four of the thirteen volumes have separate textual editors, all the volumes have notes on the texts with clear explanations of variants, collations, and emendations or corrections made, and the texts are followed by appendices of substantive emendations. As general editor, Julia helped collate and compare many of the texts behind the scenes (Marcus, "Embarrassment" 18), but she also edited *Night and Day*. Clearly loving the novel, Julia's introduction confronts those who automatically dismiss Woolf's second piece of fiction as regressively traditional and reveals a much more complex novel, "darker and more serious...than its form might indicate," one involved in a "continuous process of self-interrogation" (xix). Perhaps most important, however, Julia's experience of editing the series taught her a great deal about how Woolf worked and revised, and her thought about Woolf's process and the effect that process had on her texts continued to evolve. As a result, Julia began to question the assumption she and others had made, that Woolf had nothing to do with changes made to her texts after publication, and she called for full collations of editions and impressions and parallel electronic texts so that we might begin to understand the full range of Woolf's revisions.

In the meantime, Woolf remained under copyright in the US and was available to Americans only in Harcourt Harvest reprints, although a few titles gained introductions in the early 1980s. The new UK editions were difficult if not impossible for American scholars to get. Thus, when the thirteen introductions to the texts in the Penguin edition were published by Virago as *Virginia Woolf: Introductions to the Major Works* and appeared in the US, great rejoicing was heard in the Woolf Studies world on the other side of the Atlantic. The venture may have seemed like "a slightly odd idea" to some readers in the UK (Abrams), but it also had the potential to "forge an alliance between feminist readers in Britain and the US" (Marcus, "Embarrassment" 18), no small feat. In addition, Julia's brilliant "'The Story So Far...': An Introduction to the Introductions," traced the history of Woolf's reputation in both countries and made it clear why a feminist edition of her works was necessary. As a result, the essay remains a marker of Woolf Studies' history up to that point.

Woolf Studies will remain deepest in Julia's debt, however, for the vision of editing embodied in the online genetic edition of "Time Passes" that launched in October 2008 at the De Montfort University Centre for Textual Scholarship site, <www.woolfonline.com>.[9] This site provides a fully searchable environment or research platform where users can explore all the stages of the composition of "Time Passes" and have access to other materials from the period, such as newspapers and documents relating to the General Strike, other Woolf materials, such as family photos, diaries, letters, essays she was working on at the time, and additional literary and scholarly content (Hussey). Exactly when Julia's most lasting legacy on the editing of Woolf became more than just a glimmer in her mind is hard to say, but Hans Walter Gabler wrote that as early as the turn of the millennium, she was attempting to find funding for a "genetic exploration of Virginia Woolf manuscripts" and asked him to be a referee for a grant proposal (Gabler "Re"). As he worked to assemble an electronic re-transcription of Susan Dick's *To the Lighthouse* transcription, she began to think about constructing a learning site on "Time Passes" that could be used for research *and* teaching, and their close professional association—he read chapter drafts of her biography and she provided him with "invaluable" knowledge and advice as he worked on an article about the two published versions of *To the Lighthouse* and a review of *Editing Virginia Woolf* (Gabler "Re") —ultimately led to Julia's grant application for the "Time Passes" project to the Leverhulme Trust and Gabler's electronic texts for the draft, typescript, proofs, and published editions that now underlie the online genetic edition. (The edition also includes facsimiles of the holograph and the typescript.)

"An Electronic Edition and Commentary on Virginia Woolf's 'Time Passes'" will revolutionize how we conceive of editing, partly because it reproduces the elements of multiplicity and indeterminacy so pervasive in Woolf's work, but also because it encourages conversation, collaboration, and hands-on work between and among all sorts of readers: scholars wanting to compare texts from holograph draft through published versions, teachers wanting to access contextual material about World War I or the General Strike, students wanting to pore over Woolf's revisions, and common readers wanting to know more about this portion of *To the Lighthouse*. Julia's ideas and aims, her drive and persistence, combined with Nick Hayward's technical expertise, have led to a site that allows users to organize their searches by page of text or day in Woolf's writing life; to focus on the big picture (historical, social, intellectual, or scholarly context) or on the very smallest (a word on the page); to scan the surface of one text or explore the depths of the creative process in various versions of the text; to work privately or share publicly; to annotate or just read; to move forward or backward in either time or space (users will be able to see, for example, what a passage looked like *before* Woolf made her revisions). Its potential is enormous—for textual scholarship, critical research, and teaching of both literature and creative writing—and it could change the relationship between textual scholarship and criticism. Julia's dream that this project function as a model for other such online projects is also possible because Hayward's framework design will be released and can be adapted (Hayward). As Brenda Silver notes, "the richness and expansiveness of this project speak to the richness and expansiveness of Julia's approach to Woolf and literature in general" (Silver), and it will surely set scholars in Woolf and Modernist Studies off on searches for new Virginias for years and years to come.

As only one example of where such visions and new electronic technologies could lead, Hans Walter Gabler is continuing the work he and Julia had done together on another online project, an "anatomy" of the drafts and typescripts of "A Sketch of the Past." Together, he writes, they "got as far as establishing genetically layered transcripts of the documents and checking them against the originals at Sussex. ... [T]he entire lot of surviving documents [was] digitally photographed...under Julia's direction" by Gabler's student assistant in the summer of 2006 (Gabler "Re"). The goal is not to establish a text, since the writing never reached full text status, nor to create a traditional edition, but to reveal "the volatility of [Woolf's] writing, the virtuoso re-writing that constantly went on both in the autograph sections themselves and in the reshaping of these into the typescript versions" (ibid.). For Julia, this unfinished and "unpublished" memoir reveals Woolf in the midst of her creative process and thus provides a wonderful text for the teaching of writing. To that end, Gabler is gradually making the digital facsimiles of the "anatomy," presented in the HYPER environment, available at http://www.woolfsource.org.

Intangibles

We are also grateful to Julia for all those contributions not so readily visible. The reviews, the articles and books, the editing—all can be quantified as her contributions to Woolf Studies, the public work of a fine intellect. But the personal work of a fine heart—the teaching, the behind-the-scenes assistance, the generosity, the mentoring, and the modeling of an academic life—cannot really be measured. Julia's legacy also resides in the hearts and minds of family and students and friends and colleagues, as can be seen in the eulogies at her funeral service (Clarke), web site testimonies (Humanities; Deegan; Fernald), and recollections in the *Virginia Woolf Miscellany* (Robin Briggs, Daugherty, Kukil, Marcus, Pawlowski). As friends groped to capture "the spirit in her, the essential thing" (*TTL* 52), they kept returning to words such as warm, generous, and open.

So Julia not only organized the Virginia Woolf: Women and Writing Conference at Oxford in 1992, which had an important influence on the teaching of Woolf in the UK (Barrett), but she had everyone at the conference to her house for dinner (Marcus, "Julia" 7). So Julia not only introduced a course on women's writing at Oxford, but she invited graduate students involved in research but without teaching positions to give lectures on a wide variety of women writers in a parallel lecture course (Foreword, Jump viii-ix). So Julia ignored the "sometimes testy relationships between British and American Woolf scholars" (Gillespie), traveled to American conferences and universities, and not only read and used American critics, but acknowledged them. So Julia, when asked what she did, not only said she was a teacher (*Times* obituary), but also had a "profound and transformative" influence on students (Gandhi) as she encouraged and nurtured their projects. So Julia, "being totally dedicated to her friends," not only drove Pierre-Eric Villeneuve to Monks House on a cold 28th of March, but also sat with him, on the high stone gates near Woolf's writing hut for the whole afternoon, where they wrapped themselves in blankets, drank a bottle of red wine, talked about John Donne, Sir Thomas Browne, and *Between the Acts*, and shared their "long lasting passion for the heretics" (Villeneuve). So Julia not only sparked the Byron chapter in Anne Fernald's book, but also gave her the "tremendous gift" of being a feminist academic who was "openly happy" in both her work and her children (Fernald).

Tears occasionally spotted this essay. "Oh, Julia," I achingly thought when I learned that as late as May 2007, she hoped she could participate in the Woolf Editing/Editing Woolf Conference planned for June 2008 at the University of Denver, thinking she would be "out of action" for just a couple of months; thus, she emailed Eleanor McNees with a "little holding note to say that I would be very interested to speak, if there was a place for me, and believe there are quite a number of very worthwhile topics associated with editing Woolf" (Briggs "Re"). But it has also been lovely meeting Julia again through her work. Passion for the subject, love of words, thoughtful and meticulous scholarship, care for the reader, and always, somewhere, that mischievous gleam—there she is, on every page, in love with Woolf and people and life.

Julia's vision, of a thinking, working, revising, and editing Woolf, will not "be rolled up and flung under a sofa" (*TTL* 182), and our vision of Julia will continue to sustain us as we teach, assist, give, mentor, model, do research, and write. Her contributions, her work in its largest public and personal sense, her *self* are a mist that lifts her up, connects her to us, and connects us all to Woolf.[10] "How then did it work out, all this? How did one judge people, think of them? How did one add up this and that and conclude . . .?" (*TTL* 28). Of course I can't conclude. Not really. How can one person add up all of Julia's contributions or summarize her gifts? But here's what I know: we owe you, Julia. And if you were still here and we were thanking you in person, you would probably reply, with that infectious grin and those sparkling eyes, "Well then, love, pass it on. Pass it on."

Notes

1. Julia was awarded the OBE for her contributions to English literature and education in 2006; she was a Fellow of Hertford College, Oxford for sixteen years, where she introduced women's studies and chaired the Oxford English faculty, leading them through the first Research Assessment Exercise; she became professor of literature and women's studies at De Montfort University in Leicester in 1995, where she was instrumental in enriching the PhD programs, developing new MAs, establishing the Centre for Textual Scholarship, hosting international conferences, and developing the undergraduate curriculum; she taught adults in day schools and workshops throughout her career; and she helped found the British Shakespeare Association (Light; St. Clair; Julia Briggs).
2. Julia wrote books about the English ghost story, Elizabethan and Jacobean drama, E. Nesbit, and children's literature. She also completed Donald Crompton's book about William Golding's later novels after Crompton died. (See list of her works below.) She continued to contribute many reviews and essays about these subjects to newspapers, journals, and edited collections even as her work on Woolf increased, and she succeeded in bringing performance studies, women's studies, and children's literature into the English curriculum.
3. See Jane Marcus, "Wrapped in the Stars and Stripes: Virginia Woolf in the U.S.A.," "A Tale of Two Cultures," and "An Embarrassment of Riches" for descriptions of UK Woolf reception at that particular time.
4. "J'Accuse: Virginia Woolf," one in a series of "J'Accuse" television programs, was broadcast on 29 January 1991, a few days after Woolf's birthday and just before her works came out of copyright in Britain. It was written by Tom Paulin and directed by Jeff Morgan.
5. Her discussion of "J'Accuse:Virginia Woolf" in "The Story So Far" is a model of understatement.
6. Woolf scholars would welcome a collection of Julia's unpublished work—presentations and perhaps even drafts of essays—if such a collection did not go against her wishes and was gathered together by her family and closest colleagues. For example, both Jane Marcus and Merry Pawlowski mention presentations in their recollections. Surprises may also continue to turn up in her published works. For example, I finally tracked down Julia's foreword to Harriet Devine Jump's collection of critical essays about twentieth-century American, African-American, Canadian, African, and Irish women writers only to discover that Julia had also contributed an essay on Willa Cather, a publication that did not turn up in any of the databases I checked. Another surprise was Julia's afterword to Norah Hoult's *There Were No Windows*.
7. An abstract of this talk/article appears in *Virginia Woolf and the Arts: Selected Papers from the Sixth Annual Conference on Virginia Woolf* edited by Diane F. Gillespie and Leslie K. Hankins.
8. To put together Julia's commentary about editing Woolf, see "Editing Woolf for the Nineties" (1996), "Between the Texts" (1999; 2006), her review of *A Bibliography of Virginia Woolf* (1999), "In Search of New Virginias" (2000), her review of *Editing Virginia Woolf* (2004), and the Aftermath sections of *Virginia Woolf: An Inner Life* (2005).
9. Peter Shillingsburg, De Montfort University, and Marilyn Deegan, King's College London, are now co-directors of the "Time Passes" project, with Nicholas Hayward as technical assistant, Mark Hussey as coordinator of scholarly content, and various others, such as Ann Banfield, Michael Lackey, Karen Kukil, Michael Whitworth, Alison Light, Marion Dell, and Hans Walter Gabler as consultants or contributors (Hussey). The Leverhulme Trust funded the project with a two-year grant.
10. I would like to thank Jane de Gay and Marion Dell for asking me to write this essay and Michèle Barrett, Christine Froula, Hans Walter Gabler, Diane Gillespie, Leslie Hankins, Mark Hussey, Christine Reynier, Brenda Silver, and Pierre-Eric Villeneuve for their willingness to share information and memories with me. They provided me with several additional pairs of eyes to "get round that one woman with" (*TTL* 201); their correspondence with me is cited throughout this essay, and I only wish I could have used more of their comments. Many thanks as well are due Stuart Clarke and the Virginia Woolf Society in Great Britain, who published a Supplement to Issue # 27 (January 2008) of the *Virginia Woolf Bulletin* that included the moving eulogies from the funeral service, an essay by Julia about Woolf and Freud, and a selected bibliography. Any errors in this essay are, of course, my own.

Works Cited

Abrams, Rebecca. "Golden Virginias." Rev. of *Virginia Woolf: Introductions to the Major Works*, ed. Julia Briggs and *Virginia Woolf: Four Great Novels*, Oxford UP. *The Guardian* 12 Apr. 1994. Lexis Nexis. Courtright Memorial Library, Westerville, OH. 21 Apr. 2008 <http://www.lexisnexis.com>.
Barrett, Michèle. "Re: Julia Briggs." E-mail to the author. 28 Apr. 2008.
Briggs, Robin. "Email and picture to *VWM* editors." *Virginia Woolf Miscellany* 72 (Fall/Winter 2007): 5.
Clarke, Stuart N., ed. *Julia Ruth Briggs, OBE*. Supplement to *Virginia Woolf Bulletin* 27 (January 2008): 1-32.
Daugherty, Beth Rigel. "I Remember Julia ..." *Virginia Woolf Miscellany* 72 (Fall/Winter 2007): 6.
Deegan, Marilyn. "In Memoriam." Woolf Online: An Electronic Edition and Commentary on Virginia Woolf's "Time Passes." 26 Jan. 2008 <http:///www.woolfonline.com/obituary.html>.
Dunn, Jane. "Biography: *Virginia Woolf* by Julia Briggs." *Sunday Times* 27 Mar. 2005. Times Online. Courtright Memorial Library, Westerville: OH. 26 Jan. 2008 <http://entertainment.timesonline.co.uk>.
Fernald, Anne. "Julia Briggs, 1943-2007." Online posting. 21 Aug. 2007. Fernham blog. 28 Apr. 2008 <http://fernham.blogspot.com/2007/08/julia-briggs-1943-2007.html>.
Froula, Christine. "Re: Julia Briggs." E-mail to the author. 14 Apr. 2008.
Gabler, Hans Walter. "Re: Questions about Julia Briggs." E-mail to the author. 8 May 2008.
———. Rev. of *Editing Virginia Woolf: Interpreting the Modernist Text*, ed. James M. Haule and J. H. Stape. *TEXT: An Interdisciplinary Annual of Textual Studies* 16 (2006): 333-43.
———. "A Tale of Two Texts: Or, How One Might Edit Virginia Woolf's *To the Lighthouse*." *Woolf Studies Annual* 10 (2004): 1-29.
Gandhi, Leela. "Being a Student of Julia." *Julia Ruth Briggs, OBE*. Ed. Stuart N. Clarke. Supplement to *Virginia Woolf Bulletin* 27 (January 2008): 10.
Gillespie, Diane. "Re: Julia Briggs." E-mail to the author. 15 Apr. 2008.
Hankins, Leslie. "Re: Julia Briggs." E-mail to the author. 20 May 2008.
Hayward, Nicholas. "Digitizing Woolf: An Electronic Edition and Commentary on Virginia Woolf's 'Time Passes'." 18th Annual Conference on Virginia Woolf. University of Denver. 19 June 2008.
Humanities faculty home page. De Montfort U School of English and Performance Studies. Julia Briggs. 26 Jan. 2008.
Hussey, Mark. "Re: Julia Briggs's contributions to Woolf Studies." E-mail to author. 25 Mar. 2008.
Johnson, Jeri. "Woolf Woman, Icon and Idol: The Canonization of a Sceptical Modernist." *Times Literary Supplement* 21 February 1992: 5-6. <http://www.dmu.ac.uk/faculties/humanities/english/jbriggs.jsp>.
Kukil, Karen. "Julia Briggs (1943-2007)." *Virginia Woolf Miscellany* 72 (Fall/Winter 2007): 6-7.
Light, Alison. "Julia Briggs." *The Guardian* 31 Aug. 2007. Courtright Memorial Library, Westerville, OH. 27 Jan. 2008 <http://books.guardian.co.uk>.
Marcus, Jane. "An Embarrassment of Riches." *Women's Review of Books* 11.6 (March 1994): 17-19.
———. "Julia." *Virginia Woolf Miscellany* 72 (Fall/Winter 2007): 7-8.
———. "A Tale of Two Cultures." *Women's Review of Books* 11.4 (January 1994): 11-13.
———. "Wrapped in the Stars and Stripes: Virginia Woolf in the U.S.A." Special issue: Virginia Woolf International. *South Carolina Review* 29.1 (Fall 1996): 17-23.
Merkin, Daphne. Rev. of *Virginia Woolf: An Inner Life*. By Julia Briggs. *Kirkus Reviews* 73.17 (1 Sept. 2005): 951. *Literary Reference Center*. EBSCOhost. Courtright Memorial Library, Westerville, OH. 26 Jan. 2008 <http://web.ebscohost.com>.
"Obituary." *The Times* 3 Sept. 2007. Lexis Nexis. Courtright Memorial Library, Westerville, OH. 26 Feb. 2008 <http://www.lexisnexis.com>.
Pawlowski, Merry. "Remembering Julia." *Virginia Woolf Miscellany* 72 (Fall/Winter 2007): 8.
Reynier, Christine. "Re: Julia Briggs." E-mail to the author. 31 May 2008.
Roberts, Michele. "Making Waves." Rev. of *Virginia Woolf: Introductions to the Major Works*, ed. Julia Briggs. *The Sunday Times* 20 Feb. 1994. Lexis Nexis. Courtright Memorial Library, Westerville, OH. 21 Apr. 2008 <http://www.lexisnexis.com.>.
St. Clair, William. "Professor Julia Briggs, English Scholar and Biographer." *The Independent* 17 Aug. 2007. Independent Online. Courtright Memorial Library, Westerville, OH. 27 Jan. 2008 <http://news.independent.co.uk>.
Silver, Brenda. "Re: Julia Briggs." E-mail to the author. 14 Apr. 2008.
Villeneuve, Pierre-Eric. "Re: Personal recollections." E-mail to the author. 28 Apr. 2008.
Woolf, Virginia. *Mrs. Dalloway*. Ed. Bonnie Kime Scott. Annotated ed. Orlando: Harcourt, 2005.
———. *To the Lighthouse*. Ed. Mark Hussey. Annotated ed. Orlando: Harcourt, 2005.

List of Julia Briggs's Work, Cited and Noted

Briggs, Julia. Afterword. *There Were No Windows*. By Norah Hoult. London: Persephone Books, 2005. 329-41.
———. "Between the Texts: "Woolf's Acts of Revision." *RVW*. 208-30.
———. "Books: Building a Library: Cross-Dressing." *Independent on Sunday* 1 May 2005. Lexis Nexis. Courtright Memorial Library, Westerville, OH 21 Apr. 2008 <http://www.lexisnexis.com>.
———. ed. with Gillian Avery. *Children and Their Books: A Celebration of the Work of Iona and Peter Opie*. Oxford: Clarendon P, 1989.
———. "The Dead at Our Mercy: Virginia Woolf and the Need to Change Human Relations." Rev. of *Virginia Woolf*, by Nigel Nicolson; *The Measure of Life*, by Herbert Marder; and *Virginia Woolf: Private and Public Negotiations*, by Anna Snaith. *Times Literary Supplement* 19 January 2001: 5-6.
———. "Editing Woolf for the Nineties." Special issue: Virginia Woolf International. *South Carolina Review* 29.1 (Fall 1996): 67-77.
———. Foreword. *Diverse Voices: Essays on Twentieth-Century Women Writers in English*. Ed. Harriet Devine Jump. New York: St. Martin's, 1991. vii-xviii.
———. Foreword. *Virginia Woolf's Women*, by Vanessa Curtis. Madison: U of Wisconsin P, 2002. 11-12.
———. "Hope Mirrlees and Continental Modernism." *Gender in Modernism: New Geographies, Complex Intersections*. Ed. Bonnie Kime Scott. Urbana: U of Illinois P, 2007. 261-303.
———. "In Search of New Virginias." *Virginia Woolf: Turning the Centuries: Selected Papers from the Ninth Annual Conference on Virginia Woolf*. Ed. Ann Ardis and Bonnie Kime Scott. New York: Pace UP, 2000. 166-76.
———. Introduction. *Night and Day*. By Virginia Woolf. London: Penguin, 1992. xi-xxxv.
———. Introduction. *To the Lighthouse*. By Virginia Woolf. Everyman's Library. New York: Knopf, 1991. v-xx.
———. ed. *Night and Day*. By Virginia Woolf. London: Penguin, 1992.
———. *Night Visitors: The Rise and Fall of the English Ghost Story*. London: Faber, 1977.
———. "Nothing Matters." Rev. of *Leonard Woolf: A Life*, by Victoria Glendinning. *New Statesman* 18 Sept. 2006: 63-64.
———. "Not What You Know, But Who." Rev. of *Virginia Woolf: Bloomsbury and Beyond*, by Anthony Curtis. *Times Literary Supplement* 20 Oct. 2006: 25.
———. "The Novels of the 1930s and the Impact of History." *The Cambridge Companion to Virginia Woolf*. Ed. Sue Roe and Susan Sellers. Cambridge: Cambridge UP, 2000. 72-90.
———. "Pen and Ink Pot." Rev. of *Virginia Woolf*, by Hermione Lee. *Essays in Criticism* 48.1 (1998): 97-104.
———. "Re: 18th Annual International Conference on Virginia Woolf." E-mail to Eleanor McNees. 3 May 2007.
———. "Reading People, Reading Texts: 'Byron and Mr Briggs'." *RVW*. 63-79.
———. *Reading Virginia Woolf*. Edinburgh: Edinburgh UP, 2006. *RVW*.
———. Rev. of *A Bibliography of Virginia Woolf*, 4th ed., by B. J. Kirkpatrick and Stuart N. Clarke. *Review of English Studies* NS 50.198 (May 1999): 266-68.
———. Rev. of *Editing Virginia Woolf: Interpreting the Modernist Text*, ed. James M. Haule and J. H. Stape. *Woolf Studies Annual* 10 (2004): 325-29.
———. Rev. of *The Invention of Jane Harrison*, by Mary Beard. *The London Review of Books* 22.18 (2000): 24-25.
———. Rev. of *Major Authors on CD-ROM: Virginia Woolf*, ed. Mark Hussey. *Computers and Texts* 14 (1997): 20.
———. Rev. of *Virginia Woolf, A to Z*, by Mark Hussey. *Charleston Magazine* 13 (Spring/Summer 1996): 43-5.
———. Rev. of *Vita and Virginia: The Work and Friendship of V. Sackville-West and Virginia Woolf*, by Suzanne Raitt. *Times Literary Supplement* 16 Apr. 1993: 24.
———. Rev. of *Waves* at the National Theatre, London. *Virginia Woolf Bulletin* 25 (May 2007): 62-64.
———. "Rites and Traces of a Mind's Passage." Rev. of *A Passionate Apprentice: The Early Journals*, ed. Mitchell A. Leaska. *The Times* 29 Dec. 1990. Lexis Nexis. Courtright Memorial Library, Westerville, OH. 21 Apr. 2008 <http://www.lexisnexis.com>.
———. "Teaching through Writing Processes." From HyperNietzsche to Hyper-Learning. Kloster Seeon, Germany. 25 Oct. 2004.
———. "'This Moment I Stand On'': Woolf and the Spaces in Time*. London: Virginia Woolf Society of Great Britain, 2001.
———. *This Stage-Play World: Texts and Contexts, 1580-1625*. 2nd ed. New York: Oxford UP, 1997.
———. "The Story So Far . . . : An Introduction to the Introductions." *VWIMW*. vii-xxxiii.
———. *Virginia Woolf: An Inner Life*. Orlando: Harcourt, 2005.

———. ed. *Virginia Woolf: Introductions to the Major Works*. London: Virago, 1994. *VWIMW*.
———. "Virginia Woolf Meets Sigmund Freud." *Julia Ruth Briggs, OBE*. Supplement to *Virginia Woolf Bulletin* 27 (January 2008): 13-28.
———. "Willa Cather: The Woman as Artist." *Diverse Voices: Essays on Twentieth-Century Women Writers in English*. New York: St. Martin's, 1991. 32-56.
———. *A Woman of Passion: The Life of E. Nesbit, 1858-1924*. 1987. Stroud, UK: Tempus, 2007.
———. "Woolf and Englishness." 11th Annual Conference on Virginia Woolf. U of Bangor, Wales. 14 June 2001.
———. *The Works of Virginia Woolf in Twentieth-Century Classics*. 13 vols. London: Penguin, 1992-2000.
Crompton, Don. *A View from the Spire: William Golding's Later Novels*. Ed. and completed, Julia Briggs. Oxford: Blackwell, 1985.

Engendering Voyages in Virginia Woolf's Fiction

by Jeanne Dubino

By the end of the nineteenth century, travel at home and abroad had become a commonplace activity for white, middle-class British men and women. Virginia Woolf joined the throng. During her lifetime, she traveled throughout Great Britain, and made a number of trips as far west as Ireland and as far east as Turkey. She also read, reviewed, and published travel books, and wrote several travel essays. [1]

It is hardly any surprise that she recounts scenes of travel in her novels. In this paper, I focus on the scenes of sea voyages in *Jacob's Room*, *The Voyage Out*, *To the Lighthouse*, and *Orlando*. In Woolf's fiction, sea voyages are gendered; they become an educational occasion in which women learn about femininity. Far from undergoing a sea change into something rich and strange, as one might expect, women characters who undertake sea voyages in Woolf's novels awaken into the straitjackets of conventional gender roles. After I briefly discuss the gendered aspects of the genre of the travelogue, I use *Jacob's Room* as a point of departure from which to contrast *The Voyage Out*, *To the Lighthouse*, and *Orlando*. I then examine the specific purpose of the voyages taken in these three novels, the significance of what happens on each voyage, and the destination of each of the major voyagers.

By its very nature, travel for reasons apart from the "necessary" (such as migration, exile, nomadism, pilgrimage, etc.) is an anti-domestic activity: it involves a flight from home. Until the end of the eighteenth century, travel as voluntary, as pleasure, as exploration and adventure, was generally not an option for women of any social class, particularly for women traveling without their families. Improved travel conditions, greater access to education and other forms of knowledge acquisition, and the emerging movements for women's emancipation led to women traveling in significantly greater numbers and writing about their experiences. However, because of the ideal of the Angel in the House that prevailed throughout the nineteenth century, when women did write about their travels, they offered, typically, greater rationalization for why they were leaving home, and demonstrated greater self-consciousness about their gender. In the nineteenth century, women tended to emphasize their femininity even as they were conscious of violating a female norm. Men, on the other hand, had the luxury to emphasize what they did, and where they went. They did not have to justify their travels nor think consciously about their gender. Certainly, though, it is easily possible for a reader attuned to gender to see how travel was often used by men as an occasion to prove and assert masculinity.

One can see the differences between men's and women's travel experiences in Woolf's novels alone. *Jacob's Room* features a six-day excursion to the Isles of Scilly, off the coast of Cornwall. Along with his friend Timmy Durrant, Jacob is sailing a little boat. Though Jacob is unconscious of the role his gender plays in this little excursion, Woolf asks us to read gender into the scene. In the same way she parodies Mr. Ramsay's envisioning himself as a sea captain "exposed on a broiling sea with six biscuits and a flask of water" in his failed quest for R (*TTL* 54), she parodies Jacob's desire to brave the elements—to float with the seaweed and a log of wood, to "tumble and lollop all across the horizon" like the waves, to face "the sky and worship" (47). Far from experiencing a sense of adventure, Jacob grows sulky with Timmy over a quarrel about the right way to open a tin of beef (47). Yet even in the midst of this quarrel, neither Jacob nor Timmy express any self-consciousness. The narrator portrays Timmy totally focused on his work at hand, sailing the boat, "with his hand on the tiller, rosy gilled, with a sprout of beard, looking sternly at the stars, then at a compass, spelling out quite correctly his page on the eternal lesson-book" (47). Timmy is blithely unaware that the display he presents "would have moved a woman" (47), such as the narrator herself. The sight of Jacob unbuttoning his clothes and sitting naked, save his shirt, which he then removes before he plunges into the waves (48), again arouses the narrator's eye as she carefully and lovingly describes the scene, but, like Timmy, Jacob is immersed only in the activity at hand. At first swimming like a fish, he loses control, gulping in water, gasping and splashing about, till Timmy hauls him in (48). Clearly, in this scene again, Woolf undermines any sense of mastery that Jacob might have, and a few pages later when the narrator describes Jacob sitting on the deck, "plunging about, half to stretch himself, half in a kind of jollity, no doubt, for the strangest sound issued from his lips as he furled the sail, rubbed the plates—gruff, tuneless—a sort of paean, for having grasped the argument, for being master of the situation, sunburnt, unshaven, capable into the bargain of sailing round the world in a ten-ton yacht, which, very likely, he would do one of these days instead of settling down in a lawyer's office and wearing spats" (50). Of course, several months later, "settling down in a lawyer's office and wearing spats" is precisely what he does.

Yet, though Woolf undermines Jacob's and Timmy's control in subtle ways, it's important to note that at least they both have some measure of it. With Timmy obviously more in charge, the young men sail the boat themselves. *Jacob's Room* includes other captains and sailors as well: Jacob's brother Archer, who is in the Navy (125); his mother Betty's companion Captain Barfoot; and Mrs. Durrant's husband, now dead, who had a keen interest in sailing, and had kept a yacht before his marriage (61). Indeed, references to and characters of sea captains and sailors dot Woolf's writing. Besides those already mentioned, there are, just to name a few, Captain Willoughby Vinrace in *The Voyage Out* and Captain North Pargiter, now retired as a farmer, in *The Years*. In *Mrs. Dalloway*, Clarissa has a momentary and impulsive vision of Peter Walsh as a captain with whom she wants to embark on "some great voyage" (70). In *The Waves*, Bernard, imagining himself en route to Tahiti, attempts to control the waste of water around him by transforming visual impressions into words (189)—in contrast to Rhoda, who dissolves her sense of self into "the foam that races over the beach" (130), an image that recalls Aphrodite, whose name may be derived from *Aphros*, or foam. In both her fiction and her essays, Woolf refers to and elaborates on navigators and maritime explorers from history, including the Renaissance adventurers John Hawkins, Martin Frobisher, Francis Drake, Richard Grenville, and Richard Hakluyt.[2]

No doubt, Woolf often undercuts or parodies the amount of control that each captain or male voyager actually wields, as we have seen in the case of Jacob and more briefly, in the case of Mr. Ramsay. With the character of Marmaduke Bonthrop Shelmerdine in *Orlando*, she in part presents a figure of fun spending his life "in the most desperate and splendid of adventures—...voyag[ing] round Cape Horn in the teeth of a gale" (252).[3]

Nonetheless, the informing assumption is that only men are entitled to be the masters of their fate, the captains of their soul, to paraphrase W. E. Henley's frequently-quoted lines from "Invictus." Women are at best passengers who think about their gender, and indeed, seem to embark on voyages for the sole purpose of learning how to fit into conventional gender roles.

Though informed by famous voyages of discovery undertaken by active men,[4] including Hakluyt's *Collection of the Early Voyages, Travels, and Discoveries of the English Nation*, Walter Raleigh's *Discovery of the Large, Rich, and Beautiful Empire of Guiana*, and Charles Darwin's *The Voyage of the Beagle* (Hussey 337-38), *The Voyage Out* is about a passive and vague young woman whose voyage is determined for her by her imperializing father, Willoughby (23).[5] She is a project, an undertaking herself, akin to the ten ships that Willoughby plies across the water (22) and the factories he owns in Hull; she is his, and the society's he represents, to shape into a young lady, or more specifically, to transform into the role of his dead wife Theresa, or someone who could host dinner parties for him (86). Though Helen Ambrose wants to remove Rachel from Willoughby's overprotective wing and provide for her a more modern socialization, one that would expose her to the ways of the world, one that would mark some lines of individuality in her "smooth unmarked... face" (25), the role of wife into which she would insert Rachel is no less conventional than that of society hostess.

The sea journey toward the marriage that never takes place becomes an occasion for Rachel to learn the truth about heterosexual relationships. "'So that's why I can't walk alone!'" she bursts out to Helen after Richard's kiss. In contrast to one of wide-open expanses and possibilities, Rachel becomes aware of her life as "a creeping hedged-in thing, driven cautiously between high walls, here turned aside, there plunged in darkness, made dull and crippled for ever" (82). This "creeping hedged-in thing" is what life becomes in a world in which woman is the victim, man the aggressor. In *The Voyage Out*, this imbalance is determined in part by the natural order. The wind itself violently stifles her—"'It blows—it blows!' gasped Rachel, the words rammed down her throat" (18)—and then shortly after throws her into Richard Dalloway's arms. Richard, on the other hand, claims that he can control the weather: he (albeit archly) boasts to Rachel, "'Are you aware...how much can be done to induce fine weather by appropriate headdress?'" (61). Though he may be joking about having a godlike ability to control the weather, Richard does play a godlike role that originates at least as early as Greek myth: Zeus in the form of a swan raping Leda. This role is suggested proleptically in the image of Rachel, "lying unprotected," from Helen's point of view,[6] "like a victim dropped from the claws of a bird of prey" (37), an image that foreshadows the aftermath of the symbolic rape that takes place when Richard swoops down on her.

The voyagers on the ship are complicit in Rachel's gender socialization. In her failure to show sympathy—instead, "belittl[ing] the whole affair" (80)—in her failure to act outraged—instead, encouraging Rachel just to "'take things as they are'" (81) and even worse, expressing jealousy over the kiss (81)—Helen proves herself as a supportive of the same violence she had earlier condemned in her brother-in-law Willoughby (24). Almost everyone on Rachel's voyage out seems to steer her toward her ultimate fate, including the seemingly helpful Clarissa, who urges the marriage plot on her in the form of Jane Austen's *Persuasion* (78). Even the name of the ship, *Euphrosyne*, one of the names of "the three

Graces, Greek goddesses who presided over social events" (Hussey 84) and who attended Aphrodite, goddess of love and fertility, suggests the fate that would have befallen Rachel had she not died.

If her voyage to the lighthouse is any indication, Cam Ramsay in *To the Lighthouse* also seems destined for a life as equally entrapping as Rachel's. Seventeen-years-old, on the brink of adulthood at the end of the novel, Cam sets sail with her father, the old salt Macalister and his son, and her brother James on a much-delayed voyage, one that James had wanted to take ten years earlier. However, James is no more inclined to go this time around than Cam (222); like his sister, he is coerced into accompanying his father. In outrage, Cam and James make a compact—"to resist tyranny to the death" (243). Initially allied with James against Mr. Ramsay's overbearing will, Cam quickly becomes caught in the middle of the struggle between her brother and her father.[7] "[T]o which did she yield" (251) she thinks. It is hard not to see how she is in nearly the exact position that Mrs. Ramsay was in at the beginning of the novel, as James himself recognizes as he predicts Cam's capitulating:

> She'll give way, James thought, as he watched a look come upon her face, a look he remembered. They look down he thought, at their knitting or something. Then suddenly they look up. There was a flash of blue, he remembered, and then somebody sitting with him laughed, surrendered, and he was very angry. It must have been his mother, he thought, sitting on a low chair, with his father standing over her. (251)

On the voyage, as Cam wrestles between the warring desires of her father and her brother, she learns to become her mother's daughter. Caught and mutilated like the fish that Macalister's boy tosses back into the sea, Cam has ahead of her a life that seems no more promising than Rachel's. For Rachel, life is "a creeping hedged-in thing"; for Cam, it is poisoned with rage, submission, and sadness (253).

For Rachel and Cam, the socialization into gender is clearly tragic; for Orlando, it is mostly comic. Just as Rachel's destiny would have been that of the name of the vessel that carried her, a Euphrosyne, so does Orlando learn that she is to become an *Enamoured Lady*. As she feels the "coil of skirts about her legs" (153) while she is sitting on the deck of the *Enamoured Lady* on her return to England, Orlando thinks about her sex. She is forced to pay attention to her flowered paduasoy in a way she had not had to when, like many real women travelers to Turkey, most famously Lady Mary Wortley Montagu, she was traveling about as a gypsy in Turkish trousers. In addition to feeling self-conscious, Orlando experiences the other meanings of the word coil: toils and trouble (as in "this mortal coil"), hampered movement, and psychic restriction. The "privileges of her [new] position" (153)—the pleasure of resisting and yielding—do not match the penalties. As a woman, she must strive to be "obedient, chaste, scented, and exquisitely apparelled"; not only do these "graces" require "the most tedious discipline," but without them, a woman "may enjoy none of the delights of life" (157). By the time Orlando finishes her reflections on what it means to be a woman, she concludes that her life will be as hemmed in as Rachel's would have been, and Cam's probably will be: it would mean "conventionality, ...slavery, ...deceit, ...denying her love, fettering her limbs, pursing her lips, and restraining her tongue." It is no wonder that she longs to "turn about with the ship and set sail once more for the gipsies" (163).

But though Orlando is returning to a time and a country that strictly prescribes gender roles, her destiny is not as circumscribed as Rachel's and Cam's; indeed, in keeping with the spirit of freedom that characterizes the rest of the novel, it is more promising. True, Orlando does marry, but her husband is as free-spirited and flexibly-gendered as she, and, moreover, he is absent much of the time. More ominously, however, Marmaduke Bonthrop Shelmerdine is a sea captain—the same occupation as the also triple-named Nicholas Benedict Bartolus, who captained the *Enamoured Lady*. Marmaduke Bonthrop Shelmerdine also fulfilled another of Orlando's fantasies—the "'pleasure of being rescued by a bluejacket'" (155)—when he swooped upon her after she broke her ankle (250), the exposure of which, on the *Enamoured Lady*, nearly makes a sailor fall to his death (157). Had Shelmerdine not arrived at that moment, Orlando might have met Rachel's fate, but she didn't. Instead, we see her, in a penultimate scene, confidently in control, driving her own car.

Why, then, is *Orlando* more hopeful than *The Voyage Out* and *To the Lighthouse*? There is no definitive answer, and to answer this question fully and satisfactorily would require another paper in itself. But, I will note that *The Voyage Out* and *To the Lighthouse*, by virtue of their autobiographical dimension, prohibited a happier destination for Rachel and Cam. Rachel represents in part the ambivalence Woolf felt at the time toward her own marriage, and Cam, in part, her ambivalence toward her childish and tyrannical father. The generic dictates of comedy require that *Orlando*, on the other hand, end on an upbeat note, of course, but then the fact that the novel ends in the present day, in 1928, the year in which women gained full voting privileges and really did have more choices available to them other than marriage and death, may also determine its final comic vision.

Given the fact that all of Virginia Woolf's novels describe characters in flux, it is surprising that critics tend to avoid the motif of travel and displacement in her writing—or even the literal fact of travel. Though this presentation has focused on the form of the voyage, other means of transportation prevail as well; from even a cursory reading of Woolf's fiction, we can see her characters perambulating about, riding in trains, driving cars, and, if not flying in planes, at least gazing upon them. As Linden Peach writes, "we should pay more attention to the tropes of travel and movement in Woolf's work" (39); then, paraphrasing Susan Stanford Friedman, he continues, "we [should] shift our emphasis from reading Woolf's texts as ethnographies of dwelling—deconstructions of family plots; revisionings of domesticity—to seeing them as ethnographies of traveling" (39).[8] To do so would lead not only to a greater understanding of Woolf's work, but to appreciate a genre—the travelogue—which has been relatively undervalued by literary critics.

Notes

1   Books she reviewed include, just to name a few, Gilbert Watson's *The Voice of the South*; Rowland Thirlmere's *Letters from Catalonia and Other Parts of Spain*; W. S. Maugham's *The Land of the Blessed Virgin: Sketches and Impressions in Andalusia, etc.*; Henry James's *Portraits of Places*; Vernon Lee's *The Sentimental Traveller. Notes on Places*; and A. von Rutari's *Londoner Skizzenbuch* (*The Essays of Virginia Woolf*, vol. 1). Those she read include, among others, Alexander Kinglake's *Eothen*; Laurence Sterne's *A Sentimental Journey through France and Italy*; Frederick Temple Hamilton-Temple Blackwood, Marquis of Dufferin and Ava, *Letters from High Latitudes*; and Gertrude Bell's *The Earlier Letters* (*The Essays of Virginia Woolf*, vol.

1). The titles of some of her travel essays include "An Andalusian Inn" and "A Priory Church" (*The Essays of Virginia Woolf*, vol. 1). The Hogarth Press published, among other works, Vita Sackville-West's *Twelve Days An account of a journey across the Bakhtiari Mountains in South-western Persia*, Michel de Montaigne's *The Diary of Montaigne's Journey to Italy in 1580 and 1581*, and Horace B. Samuel's *Unholy Memories of the Holy Land* (Woolmer).
2. See *Orlando* (59), *Between the Acts* (84), "The Strange Elizabethans" (15), "Sir Walter Raleigh" (162), "Reading" (162), and more.
3. When one examines the character of Shelmerdine alone, one can easily see how *Orlando* is a parody of a travelogue. In the twentieth century, after all the blank spots of the world had been colored in, travel for adventure-seekers became more adventurous. Thus, Shelmerdine's spending his life "in the teeth of a gale" (252) —though started in the nineteenth century—is not historically inaccurate.
4. It is interesting to note that one of the generic traits of travel writing is that it is often metatextual: it positions itself in and hails back to a tradition of other travel texts.
5. See Naremore, Neumann, Froula, and Phillips, among other critics, for a discussion on Rachel's voyage into sexual knowledge and marriage.
6. See Louise DeSalvo's more contextualized discussion of this scene (82-84).
7. See Elizabeth Abel's illuminating analysis of Cam's Scylla and Charybdis predicament between James as the embodiment of Old Testament justice and Mr. Ramsay as the figure of New Testament pity.
8. Peach is referring to p. 27 of Friedman's "Uncommon Readings."

Works Cited

Abel, Elizabeth. *Virginia Woolf and the Fictions of Psychoanalysis*. Chicago: U of Chicago P, 1989.

DeSalvo, Louise. *Virginia Woolf's First Voyage: A Novel in the Making*. Totowa, NJ: Roman and Littlefield, 1980.

Friedman, Susan Stanford. "Uncommon Readings: Seeking the Geopolitical Woolf." *The South Carolina Review* 29:1 (1996): 24-44.

Froula, Christine. "Out of the Chrysalis: Female Initiation and Female Authority in Virginia Woolf's *The Voyage Out*." *Virginia Woolf: A Collection of Critical Essays*. Ed. Margaret Homans. Englewood Cliffs, NJ: Prentice-Hall, 1993. 136-61.

Henley, William Ernest. "Invictus." 1888. *The Norton Anthology of English Literature*. Ed. M. H. Abrams et al. 6th ed. Vol. 2. New York: Norton, 1993. 1615.

Hussey, Mark. *Virginia Woolf A-Z: A Comprehensive Reference for Students, Teachers and Common Readers to Her Life, Work and Critical Reception*. New York: Oxford UP, 1995.

Naremore, James. *The World Without a Self: Virginia Woolf and the Novel*. New Haven: Yale UP, 1973.

Neumann, Shirley. "*Heart of Darkness*, Virginia Woolf, and the Spectre of Domination." *Virginia Woolf: New Critical Essays*. Ed. Patricia Clements and Isobel Grundy. Totowa, NJ: Barnes and Noble, 1983. 57-76.

Peach, Linden. *Virginia Woolf*. New York: Palgrave Macmillan, 2000.

Phillips, Kathy. *Virginia Woolf against Empire*. Knoxville: U of Tennessee P, 1994.

Woolf, Virginia. *Between the Acts*. 1941. New York: Harcourt, 1969.

———. "The Elizabethan Lumber Room." *The Common Reader*. 1925. New York: Harcourt, 1953. 40-48.

———. *The Essays of Virginia Woolf*. Ed. Andrew McNeillie. Vol. 1. New York: Harcourt, 1986.

———. *Jacob's Room*. 1922. New York: Harcourt, 1950.

———. *Mrs. Dalloway*. 1925. New York: Harcourt, 1953.

———. *Orlando*. 1928. New York: Harcourt, 1956.

———. "Reading." *The Captain's Death Bed and Other Essays*. New York: Harcourt, 1950. 151-79.

———. "Sir Walter Raleigh." *Granite and Rainbow*. New York: Harcourt, 1958. 162-66.

———. "The Strange Elizabethans." *The Second Common Reader*. 1932. New York: Harcourt, 1960. 3-16.

———. *To the Lighthouse*. 1927. New York: Harcourt, 1955.

———. *The Voyage Out*. 1920. New York: Harcourt, 1948.

———. *The Waves*. 1931. New York: Harcourt, 1959.

———. *The Years*. 1937. New York: Harcourt, 1965.

Woolmer, J. Howard. *A Checklist of the Hogarth Press 1917-1946*. Revere, PA, 1986.

Angel Above the Houses: Virginia Woolf's Aerial Voyages

by Tara Surry

This paper examines aerial voyages performed by Woolf in two comparatively little-known essays, "Flying over London" and "America which I have never seen."[1] Both essays employ the trope of flight to explore spaces of modernity and the spaces of subjectivity, and the relationship between the two. I use these texts as a taking off point for a consideration of a constellation of Woolfian themes and narrative strategies. My reading discusses the ways in which Woolf uses digressive maneuvers to explore the politics of embodied female subjectivity, and her own relationship with London in particular. It also discusses flying in relation to walking the city, and in comparison to other modern modes of travel. I also look at the trope of the winged figure or angel, the conventions surrounding it, and the ways in which Woolf plays with these conventions, investigating and interrogating gendered technologies of modernity and mobility. The essays revise the conventional travel narrative through a series of shifting perspectives and a self-conscious, playful use of language which constantly undermines the male-centred journey paradigm, with its emphasis on heroism and conquest, and appropriates and adapts it for women.

The essays are a form of *flânerie* through flight; they escape the limitations placed on women in urban space and enact what Gillian Rose has called a "paradoxical geography" (155). They are thus both a spatial practice and a textual tactic, part of a project of renegotiating and remapping space by destabilizing the border between public and private coded and gendered space. The imagined space above London and New York allows Woolf to observe and critique her own society—an angel above the houses who remains politically grounded and engaged, situated yet mobile. Woolf is not in flight from the real world, but is instead negotiating a space within it: between the room of one's own and the city outside and actively engaging in both.

"Flying over London" is a lyrical portrayal of a voyage by an aeroplane over "London," a shifting and mutable narrative space. The aeroplane is a metaphor and a literal metaphorai (de Certeau 115)—a vehicle bearing ideas. It transports the reader through the narrative and provides an alternative perspective from which to view the city. Aeroplanes are a recurrent and multivalent motif in Woolf's work (Beer 1990): for example, the famous skywriting plane in *Mrs Dalloway* and, more menacingly, the planes which appear overhead in *The Years* and *Between the Acts* and the military planes in "Thoughts on Peace in an Air Raid." They represent both the possibility of connection and communication and potential destruction and chaos.

"Flying over London" is also connected to Woolf's reading about scientific theories (Beer 1996). Time as represented in "Flying" is cyclical and fluid rather than strictly linear. Layers of the modern city and of primeval England are seen as coterminous, and the fields seen from above are like waves, "made and remade perpetually" (187), like subjectivity itself. As the plane leaves the ground at the beginning of the essay, both the body and the world it has left behind seem to dissolve and transmogrify:

> As the sky pours down over one, this hard little granular knob, with its carvings and frettings, dissolves, crumbles, loses its domes, pinnacles, its firesides, its habits, and one becomes conscious of being a little mammal...nothing permanent but melting at the touch of each other without concussion, and the fields that are with us meted into yards and grow punctually wheat and barley are here made and remade perpetually ...One could see through the Bank of England; all the business houses were transparent; the River Thames was as the Romans saw it, as paleolithic man saw it...England was earth merely, merely the world. (186-87)

Woolf chooses the vantage point of a flight over a proto-London to challenge cultural assumptions and arrangements ("Everything changed its values seen from the air" [192]). For example, she demonstrates that institutions such as the Bank of England are not immutable but rather the product of a comparatively recent culture. The image of the city as a palimpsest of civilizations also suggests that modernity is not an endpoint, a culmination of a march towards progress. History, like the subject, is instead shown to be contingent and in continual process. Consequently, it can be re-imagined and re-mapped: a traditional patriarchal institution such as the Bank of England, mischievously rendered transparent so that it can be "see[n] through," is open to (potentially feminist) reinscription. The description of an England without boundaries can also be read as anti-imperialist; it strips away the reasons for patriotism along with the trappings of civilization because it denaturalizes the existence of the nation-state and challenges its borders as a fiction, a cultural construction. Woolf interrogates territories and boundaries—spatial markers with great significance for the movement of women. She suspends these divisions and calls into question their immutability.

Woolf employs metaphors of travel because women's ability to travel had historically been limited and their experiences of travel under-represented and understood differently to those of men travelling. She unsettles the paradigm in which men journey and women wait (Barthes 13-14). Woolf frequently and significantly linked figures of exploration to the lives of women. By putting women in flight, she re-inserts them into the narrative and presents alternative models for both literal and literary exploration. "Flying over London" takes up a hybrid, interstitial position, implicitly challenging gendered spatial constructions. What Deleuze and Guattari have called Woolf's "line of flight" (277) leads her to examine her position in society and to describe her own embodied subjectivity.

The self in the essay is shown to be fissured and under threat. The narrator conveys a sense of dissolution ("extinction has become now desirable. For it was odd in this voyage to note how blindly the tide of the soul and its desires rolled this way and that, carrying consciousness like a feather on the top" [188]) as well as anxiety about the corporeal and visceral: "ribs, entrails, and red blood belong to the earth" (186). A tension is revealed between the "contamination" of the world below ("we rose again like a spirit shaking contamination from its wings, shaking gasometers and factories and football fields from its feet" [188]) and the purer zone of the skies. The earth is presented as immanent, the sky as transcendent: "one becomes conscious of being a little mammal, hot-blooded, hard boned, with a clot of red blood in one's body, trespassing up here in a fine air; repugnant to it, unclean, antipathetic" (186). This description, as Woolf was well aware, is saturated with gendered constructions which associate women with the earth and the body. The narrator is transgressive by "trespassing up here." Woolf alludes to this coding throughout the essay, and the final descent from the rarefied zone is represented as a fall back into the body (190). However, she also complicates these representations: "in spite of our vertebrae, ribs and entrails, we are also vapour and air, and shall be united" (188). Woolf's flight path is an escape from the association of femininity with the bodily and earthbound and a challenge to the association of masculinity with the intellect.

Woolf also engages with the winged figure of the angel, traditionally associated with transcendence and incorporeality—qualities mapped on to "high" space, the aerial zone. This is complicated by the frequent representation of women as angels. The angel is a contradictory presence within Woolf's work. Most famously, in "Professions for Women" she is the ideologically imposed Victorian supposed ideal of female domesticity and self-censorship—the "Angel in the House" who must be killed by the woman writer, and by extension by all women seeking to escape the domestic sphere. However, it may be possible to recuperate certain aspects of the angel (cf. Gualtieri 148). I suggest that Woolf is challenging some of the stultifying aspects of the angel, for example by drawing attention to its hybridity and lack of defined gender status and thus to a repertoire of possible identities. The winged figure becomes an alternative form of voyager; one who employs the tropes of travel narratives, but adopts an alternative type of gaze.

The gaze from far above is generally seen as exerting a power relationship over the scene beneath, as we shall see in my discussion of "America…" However, the narrator's viewpoint does not lead to a sense of detachment or superiority. Woolf's perspectives shift, and operate otherwise. In contrast to the panoramic, mastering gaze, the narrator takes up binoculars to "zoom in" along Oxford Street and focus on one particular inhabitant:

> it was odd how one became resentful of all the flags and surfaces and of the innumerable windows symmetrical as avenues…and wished for some opening, and to push inside and be rid of surfaces. Up in Bayswater a door did open, and instantly, of course, there appeared a room, incredibly small, of course, and ridiculous in its attempt to be separate, and itself, and then—it was a woman's face. (191-2)

Rather than imposing from above a rationalizing and homogenizing order, Woolf elects to focus sympathetically on one particular woman: "the power that buys a mat, or sets two colours together, becomes perceptible" (192). Woolf individuates and unfixes; she stresses the individual over flags and over order and symmetry and celebrates the random, nonlinear and transient. Her focus on the woman demonstrates against the mythos of the heroic, uninvolved male aviator. Her winged observers are not ethereal but engaged:

> Personality was outside the body, abstract. And one wished to be able to animate the heart, the legs, the arms with it, to do which it would be necessary to be there, so as to collect; so as to give up this arduous game, as one flies through the air, of assembling things which lie on the surface. (192)

The narrator rejects the abstract and returns to the body and the sphere of action; she gathers together the fragments of the city she sees beneath her, but wants to animate them as well as integrate them, to combine them into a new kind of body. Despite Woolf's aerial perspective, she remains grounded in a materialist and feminist consciousness which particularizes the city and draws attention to the spatialized politics of women's lived experience. Rather than simply surveying the city she is, as de Certeau would say, practicing it, transforming the possibilities of urban space.

Woolf's relationship with London is refracted and reconsidered through the trope of the aeroplane flight. Travelling is shown to break up the perceived unity of the self. Journeys by railway or motor car make available imaginative access to new ways of understanding space and the self (Minow-Pinkney 1998, 2000; Cuddy-Keane 1996b), but aeroplane flight was the quintessentially modern experience (Stein 59-60) and thus a productive site for modernist and feminist experimentation. As the flight moves toward its conclusion, Woolf performs another inversion of expectations:

> And then the field curved round us, and we were caught in an eddy of green cloth .... We had landed, and it was over. As a matter of fact the flight had not begun; for when Flight-Lieutenant Hopgood stooped and made the engine roar, he had found a defect of some sort in the machine.... So we had not flown after all. (192)

This twist in the tale has a tactical purpose. By negating the 'real' existence of the experience just described, Woolf refuses closure and adds another level of uncertainty to the destabilization of identity and society already portrayed. She creates an aporia, an irresolvable blockage in the text, an expression of doubt which undermines its own suggested meanings. It also undoes the impasse faced by Mrs Thornbury in *The Voyage Out* (122), by playfully making flight available to women. The substitution of a radical open-endedness for a safe landing to her flight invites the reader to re-engage with the text and to re-imagine a feminist geography.

Woolf's non-conclusion does not appear in the manuscript version, which breaks off after the aeroplane lands.[2] This reinforces the sense that the stratagem was selected not simply to subvert readers' expectations but also to disrupt more general structures. Melba Cuddy-Keane has discussed the significance of Woolf's turns in narrative direction, arguing that the "twists" deliberately privilege the conversational mode rather than univocality and didacticism and open up a more dynamic mode of reading which offers an alternative to patriarchal discourse (1996a, 137). The text is shown to be provisional and therefore (like the landscape seen from the aeroplane) open to change. Paradoxically, Woolf's non-flight frees the reader for other voyages. The twists and turns constitute a methodology, a form of stunt piloting. Woolf disrupts conventional narratives of aerial voyages, introducing a social critique and a vision of her own. Exploration is both her topic and her technique. In "America...," she abandons the aeroplane altogether in favour of wholly self-guided flight, and further develops her exploration of modernity and subjectivity.

"America..." was written as a somewhat tongue-in-cheek response to the question "What interests you most in the cosmopolitan world of today?" It follows the flight of a winged woman that the narrator refers to as "Imagination" over a New York City which is both real and imagined, both a literal space and a literary one. "America..." shares with "Flying over London" its aerial motif and sense of playfulness. However, it announces its status as a fantasia from the beginning; the flight is unassisted and quasi-magical. "America is the most interesting thing in the world today" (21) Woolf claims, and then deputes Imagination (a winged figure personified as female) to fly over to America and report back. We are warned from the outset that "imagination, unfortunately, is not an altogether accurate reporter, but she has her merits; she travels fast; she travels far" (21). The essay is set up as a conversation, with Imagination in the role of a narrator and the listener, situated "on a rock on the coast of Cornwall" (21), interrupting with questions. The narration emphasizes America's modernity:

> The city of New York, over which I am now hovering, looks as if it had been scraped and scrubbed only the night before. It has no houses. It is made of immensely high towers; each is pierced with a million holes. Coming closer in I see in every hole—they are windows—a typewriter and a desk. Down below in the streets long ribbons of traffic move steadily, on and on and on. Bells chime; lights flash. Everything is a thousand times quicker yet more orderly than in England. (21)

"America…" also shares with "Flying" a fascination with the layering of civilizations:

> There are no Saxon burial grounds, Roman camps, Norman churches, Georgian rectories with rose gardens and owls one on top of one another as in England. But there is, running along one side of us, a river. Or is it the sea? It is as broad as the English Channel, but smooth and waveless. The borders are stained every colour you can imagine.[3]

Woolf replaces a literally stratified society with a vision of a fluid, shifting one: "It is a primeval country; a country before there were countries" (144). As in "Flying," travelling emphasizes the sense of the dissolution of boundaries of nationality and subjectivity.

Imagination's report focuses largely on the idea of the luxuries and conveniences of American life. The extravagance and opulence of this fantasized lifestyle is both celebrated and satirized:

> A spring is touched; a refrigerator opens; there is a whole meal waiting to be eaten; clams on ice; ducks on ice; iced drinks in very tall glasses; ice creams all colors of the rainbow. The Americans never sit down to a square meal. They perch on steel stools and take what they want from a perambulating rail. (21, 144)

The very excessiveness of the language undermines and parodies itself. Woolf also points to the detritus left by such excessive consumption. Yet the ease of life and, paradoxically, the lack of servants ("Everybody is equal" 21) is rejoiced in and becomes a covert comment upon class relations in England. Notably, the world described is apparently without domestic drudgery. The narrator also emphasizes the openness of American life and homes: "You can see right in. The rooms are light and airy.… There are no dark family portraits hanging in shadowy recesses" (21). This sense of transparency is implicitly contrasted with such houses in England. The "America" produced here functions as a discursive space in which Woolf could experiment with some of the representations of America as the New World and thereby critically examine some of the conventions of her own society. From her vantage point above an imaginary New York, Woolf has a fresh triangulation on London. The America she chooses to present, with its energy, spontaneity and flexibility of social relations, appears to offer greater freedom to the individual, and perhaps especially to women. Woolf's writing of "New York" is intimately caught up with how she experienced London. It is deeply concerned with issues of movement and identity.

"America..." moves across generic boundaries, and is characteristically self-deconstructing. Like "Flying" it is a travel narrative that refuses to define or fix the cartography of the scenes it maps, emphasizing instead the shifting perspective of the observer. In both essays Woolf negotiates a way to perform a voyage of exploration that (unlike her first novel) does not end in the death of the heroine and which refuses to re-enact narratives of conquest of the New World. These flights offer what Foucault calls a heterotopia: the aeroplane, like the ship, is a place of contestation of dominant discourses and of potential reversal. "America..." is not merely "an obviously mercenary and populist exercise" (Brosnan 85), but rather is part of a serious investigation of the *idea* of America as a liberating textual space. America is represented as an opportunity for personal metamorphosis, and as especially transformative for women: a space in which to play with and shift identities. "America" is a tissue of quotations, continually in process and with its boundaries undefined and unfixed. This makes it available as a metaphor within Woolf's poetics of space.

Time in the essay is complex and multilayered. At least three Americas exist simultaneously: prehistory (represented by Woolf's favored figure of a mammoth), the sixteenth and seventeenth century, and the modern age, represented by an "immense building" of "stainless steel" which is a treasure house of Old World literature: "Shakespeare's folios, Ben Jonson's manuscripts, Keats' love letters blazing in the light of the American sun" (144). This hybrid cultural space, made up of the shards of European cultures, is simultaneously celebrated and mocked. Yet Woolf was well aware that such pastiche is a sign of (post)modernity and as such is not confined to America (compare, for example, the buildings in "Oxford Street Tide"). She also recognized the positive aspects of heterogeneity, including the sense in this building of a spirit of democracy and openness. In contrast to the strict surveillance of the colleges and libraries in *A Room of One's Own*, there are "no sentries; the doors are open to all" (144). The essay presents a vision of a space which would be more welcoming to and inclusive of women.

In the narrator's initial description of New York, the confusion, energy and multiplicity represented by the skyscrapers, the Babel of voices they suggest, gesture toward the prospect of greater diversity and freedom. The skyscrapers are also seen to contain possible scenes of writing: through every window can be glimpsed "a typewriter and a desk" (21). These can be read as rooms of one's own, set in a specific modern urban scene. It is significant that the first sight that Imagination chooses to report is the Statue of Liberty "clothed in radiant silver" (21). However, this vision is satirically undercut: the figure is "lighted up, whether with electric light or the light of reason I am not at this moment certain" (21). The essay destabilizes its own assertions with regard to the splendour and freedom of American life, yet overall Woolf suggests that America is building something new with its fragments of other cultures and developing its own unique form. Imagination portrays Americans as moving into the future ("while we have shadows that stalk behind us, they have a light that dances in front of them" [145]) thus flattering her audience while also implying that England is trapped in the past, including the "shadows" of imperialism. In the tradition of satires such as *Gulliver's Travels*, Woolf is commenting on her own society through the medium of a fantastic travel narrative. The essay concludes with the caveat: "imagination with all her merits is not always strictly accurate" (145). The unreliable narrator undercuts her own claim to veracity, thus throwing into doubt the authenticity not only of her assertions about America but also about England. This leaves identity open to experimentation and negotiation anywhere.

Woolf's aerial perspective is in direct contrast to that described by de Certeau, looking down from the 110th floor of the World Trade Center, in which the male spectator is positioned as omniscient and omnipotent: "he leaves behind the mass.... His elevation transforms him into a voyeur" (92). This panoramic gaze emphasizes the desire to subject and own the city, to reconquer the New World. Woolf's partial and shifting perspective is the opposite of this totalizing viewpoint. Instead of insisting on rendering the city legible and legitimate, authorized by the dominant discourses of power, she suggests a different kind of conquest of the city, one which leaves it available for other possibilities. Her America is a dialogic space in which the reader (like the listener in the essay) is able to interrupt with questions. Rather than imposing a narrative from above, Woolf creates a fractured and multiple narrative space, continually drawing attention to its own artificiality and leaving it open to further interrogation. Her approach is thus the opposite of the panoramic, panoptic gaze, which operates from a position of power. Writing from the margins yet refusing marginalization, Woolf unfixes and unsettles, leaving spaces on the map for new representations.

Woolf's flights are feminist tactics. Hélène Cixous, for example, sees flight as a strategy for women. Playing on the ambiguity of the "*vol*" of theft and the "*vol*" of flight, she suggests that "To fly/steal is woman's gesture, to steal into language to make it fly" (96). Woolf's flight, as Cixous says, "proceeds by lapse and bounds" (96). "Flying" and "America" move digressively and paratactically; the advantage of an imaginary flight is that it need not follow a linear train of thought. The voyages above the houses choose an anecdotal and mobile narration rather than an authoritative and thus closed one. Woolf's desire to "invent a new critical method—something swifter and lighter and more colloquial yet intense...more fluid and following the flight...to keep the flight of the mind and yet be exact" (*D5* 298) is accomplished through destabilization. Flying is both an inspiration and a methodology: her opportunities are what de Certeau calls "seized 'on the wing'" (ix). The flights enable her to contemplate and critique her own society, and work to create a continually shifting, mutable space, open to reinscription through further flights of imagination.

Afterword

I was later able to explore these issues in much greater detail in two separate chapters on these essays in my thesis, *Opening the Door and Flying Over the City: Re-Writing London in Virginia Woolf's Essays* (University of Western Australia, 2004). Issues also looked at included: different forms of modern travel and their effects on perception and on modernist writing, women and metaphors of exploration, women aviators, the uncanny elements of "Flying over London," and early travel narratives and their influence on Woolf's writing—as well as her relationship with London and with urban space more generally. I also discussed the history of Woolf's fascination with America and the American language, and particularly her re-imagining of America as a space of emancipatory play with language and identity. Writing this now, the paper would have had less on the figure of the angel, and more on these topics. My reference to the World Trade Center would also have been somewhat different to that in the summer of 2001. My central point, however, remains the same: in both "Flying over London" and "America…," Woolf's view from above is the opposite of the panoramic, panoptic gaze and narratives of conquest. She focuses on individual, shifting perspectives and emphasizes connection rather than detachment, weaving together and creation rather than disassembly and destruction.

Notes

1. "Flying over London," in *The Captain's Death Bed and Other Essays* (London: Hogarth Press, 1981 [1950]), 186-92. "America which I have never seen…" in *Hearst's International Combined with Cosmopolitan* (April 1938): 21, 144-5. "America…" has now been republished in *The Dublin Review*, no. 5, (Winter 2001-2): 56-60, with an essay by Andrew McNeillie (41-55).
2. "Flying over London," MS, Berg Collection, New York Public Library.
3. This passage appears in the typescript of "America…," (M44, Berg Collection, New York Public Library) but is not in the article as published in *Hearst's* (or *The Dublin Review*).

Works Cited

Barthes, Roland. *A Lover's Discourse*. New York: Farar, Straus and Giroux, 1978.
Beer, Gillian. "The Island and the Aeroplane," *Nation and Narration*. Ed. Homi K. Bhabha. London: Routledge, 1990, 265-290.
———. *Virginia Woolf: A Centenary Perspective*. New York: St Martin's, 1984.
———. *Virginia Woolf: The Common Ground*. Ann Arbor: University of Michigan Press. 1996.
Brosnan, Leila. *Reading Virginia Woolf's Essays and Journalism: Breaking the Surface of Silence*. Edinburgh: Edinburgh University Press, 1997.
Cixous, Hélène. *The Newly Born Woman*. Minneapolis: University of Minnesota Press, 1986.
Cuddy-Keane, Melba. "Virginia Woolf and the Trope of the Twist." *Ambiguous Discourses: Feminist Narratology and British Women Writers*. Ed. Kathy Mezei. Chapel Hill and London: University of North Carolina Press, 1996a.
———. et al. "The Heteroglossia of History, Part One: The Car." *Virginia Woolf: Texts and Contexts: Selected Papers from the Fifth Annual Conference on Virginia Woolf*. Ed. Beth Rigel Daugherty and Eileen Barrett. New York: Pace University Press, 1996b.
de Certeau, Michel. *The Practice of Everyday Life*. Berkeley and Los Angeles: University of California Press, 1984.
Deleuze, Gilles, and Felix Guattari. *A Thousand Plateaus: Capitalism and Schizophrenia*. Minneapolis: University of Minnesota Press, 1987.
Foucault, Michel. "Different Spaces." *Aesthetics, Method and Epistemology*. Ed. James D. Faubion. London: Allen Lane; Penguin, 1998.
Gualtieri, Elena. *Virginia Woolf's Essays: Sketching the Past*. Houndmills: Macmillan; New York: St Martin's Press, 2000.
Minow-Pinkney, Makiko. "Flânerie by Motor Car." *Virginia Woolf and Her Influences: Selected Papers from the Seventh Annual Conference on Virginia Woolf*. Ed. Laura Davis and Jeanette McVicker. New York: Pace University Press, 1998.
———. "Virginia Woolf and the Age of the Motor Car." *Virginia Woolf and the Age of Mechanical Reproduction*. Ed. Pamela L. Caughie. New York and London: Garland, 2000.
Rose, Gillian. *Feminism and Geography: The Limits of Geographical Knowledge*. Minneapolis: University of Minnesota Press, 1993.

Stein, Gertrude. *Picasso*. London: B.T. Batsford, 1938.
Woolf, Virginia. "America which I have never seen...." *Hearst's International Combined with Cosmopolitan* (April 1938): 21, 144-5.
The Diary of Virginia Woolf. 5 vols. Ed Anne Olivier Bell. London: Hogarth Press, 1977–1984.
——. *The Essays of Virginia Woolf.* 4 vols to date. Ed. Andrew McNeillie. London: Hogarth Press, 1986–.
——. "Flying over London." *The Captain's Death Bed and Other Essays.* London: Hogarth Press, 1981 (1950), 186-192.
——. *A Room of One's Own* (1929). London: Penguin, 1992.
——. *The Voyage Out* (1915). London: Penguin, 1992.

"THE STRANGLED DIFFICULT MUSIC OF THE PRELUDE": WOOLF ON IDENTITY AND DIFFERENCE

by Cheryl Mares

In her 1925 essay "American Fiction," Virginia Woolf explicitly compares the experience of reading the literature of another culture to the experience of traveling in a foreign country (*E4* 269). But there are different types of readers and, as she notes in her 1925 essay on Montaigne, different types of travelers. Some "travel only to return home" ("Montaigne," *E4* 76), while others travel in an effort to escape. Some try to do both at once, to hold onto the comforts of home while seeking signs that they really are elsewhere. Ideal travelers, according to Montaigne, view travel as an end in itself, without fixed notions of home or preconceived destinations. "Accept endlessly, scrutinize ceaselessly, and see what will happen" ("Tchehov's Questions," *E2* 246). This philosophy, which Woolf gleaned from her reading of Chekhov, might serve to guide Montaigne's ideal traveler as well as Woolf's ideal reader and critic of contemporary work.

As Pamela Caughie reminds us, "Woolf acknowledges in 'The Narrow Bridge of Art' that one of the critic's duties is to prepare us for new literary forms to come" (182-83). Yet, to do so requires remarkable receptivity as well as a searching and skeptical mind. It is very difficult, Woolf notes in 1918 in "Mr Howells on Form," to identify new forms, let alone to determine which may be truly significant (*E2* 325). For her own generation, she observes in "How It Strikes a Contemporary" (1923), being "sharply cut off from our predecessors" (*E3* 357), with no great critics to exercise "a centralising influence" (354), "the risks of judging contemporary work" may be "greater than ever before" (359).

When that work is also from another country and perhaps is being read in translation, the risks, Woolf writes in 1925 in "The Russian Point of View," are even greater (*E4* 182). The reader/critic is then a foreigner, a tourist, and "the tourist's attitude," she remarks in "American Fiction," is noted for "its crudity and one-sidedness" (*E4* 269). Besides the danger of distorting the other culture's values, there is the danger of self-alienation, of being overwhelmed (*E4* 183), of "los[ing] our bearings" (*E4* 187-88) —the danger of going native, as it were, or of trying to.

At times when Woolf claims, as she does in "How Should One Read a Book?" (1926), that "we cannot sympathize wholly or immerse ourselves wholly" as we read, she seems to mean that we should not, because that is tantamount to self-suppression (*CR2* 243). It is one thing to broaden one's sensibility and "train [one's] taste"; it is quite another to silence "the demon in us who whispers, 'I hate, I love'" (243). At other times, when Woolf says that we cannot "sink our own identity" (243), she means just that: it cannot be done. "The mind takes its bias from the place of its birth" ("The Russian Point of View," *E4* 189).

Can the French and the Americans understand English literature? Woolf has her doubts. Can the English understand Russian literature? Her doubts are even graver. Nevertheless, in "The Russian Point of View," she defends the potential value of the outsider's perspective: the "special acuteness and detachment...the foreigner will often achieve" may enlighten even the insider, at least "momentarily" (*E4* 182). Here Woolf suggests that, at least in some cases, this limited reciprocity may be due to the indifference or insularity of the insiders, rather than to "the crudity and one-sidedness" of the outsiders.

Moreover, even though the outsider cannot understand the other culture from an insider's point of view, he or she still may experience an encounter with the new, an encounter in which, as Derek Attridge describes it, the *subject's* modes of understanding undergo change as the subject registers and "affirms the singularity of the other" (24). In this process, "the other is transformed from other to same, but the same is not the same as it was before the encounter" (24).

Evidence of Woolf's encounters with the new in this sense among the works of her contemporaries and near contemporaries can be found in her readings of Proust and of the great Russian writers. Since I have discussed her reading of Proust elsewhere, to clarify this point about encounters with the new, I will quickly review her responses to Chekhov, Tolstoy, and Dostoevsky. Granted, they were not her contemporaries, but the Maude and the Garnett translations of them were, and Woolf clearly recognized their importance.

Woolf's 1918 essay "Tchehov's Questions" provides a striking example of the kind of encounter with the new that Attridge describes:

> The choice of incidents and of ending produces at first a queer feeling that the solid ground upon which we expected to make a safe landing has been twitched from under us, and there we hang asking questions in mid air. It is giddy, uncomfortable, inconclusive. But…we come to feel that the horizon is much wider from this point of view; we have gained a sense of astonishing freedom….Away fly half the conclusions of the world at once. (*E2* 245-46)

Woolf considers Chekhov "a modern," and her description of the effect of his work in her 1920 review of *The Cherry Orchard* also applies to much of her own: "we seemed to have sunk below the surface of things and to be feeling our way among submerged but recognizable emotions" (*E3* 248).

Woolf's descriptions of her experience of reading the other great Russian writers are even more dynamic and dramatic. Tolstoy, she suggests in "The Russian Point of View," is the writer "who most enthralls us and most repels" (*E4* 189). Re-reading him in 1940, she recalls what "a revelation" *War and Peace* was to her in 1910: "the shock" of his "genius" was "like touching an exposed electric wire" (*D5* 273). In 1917, she attests to Dostoevsky's "extraordinary power" ("More Dostoevsky," *E2* 83). Several years later, in "The Russian Point of View" (1925), she describes how, in reading his work (even in translation), we find ourselves "holding on by the skin of our teeth"; we are "rushed through the water; feverishly, wildly…now submerged, now in a moment of vision understanding more than we have ever understood before." In short, she asserts that "[o]ut of Shakespeare there is no more exciting reading" (*E4* 186).

The force of Woolf's encounters with Tolstoy, Dostoevsky, and Proust also makes itself felt in "The Art of Fiction," where she states bluntly that "[i]n England…the novel is not a work of art. There are none to be stood beside *War and Peace*, *Brothers Karamazov*, and *A la Recherche du Temps Perdu*" (*E4* 603). This profound sense of excitement, this particular affective intensity, is unmatched in Woolf's comments on other modern writers, including the Americans.

Taken as a whole, Woolf's comments over the years on American literature are much more diffuse and equivocal. In "American Fiction," she states that she found "all modern literatures…simpler to sum up and understand than this new American literature" (*E4*

276). This may be surprising, given all that the two cultures have in common, but that turns out to be part of the problem.

Woolf does compare her experience of reading Sherwood Anderson's stories to that of her initial reading of Chekhov, but her tone is different. Neither writer gives us a conventional short story, she observes; neither provides "familiar handles to lay hold of" ("American Fiction," *E4* 271). Anderson's stories are baffling at first; like "chastened schoolchildren," she suggests, we have to go back and reread them (272). This sounds more like chagrin followed by submission than, as with Chekhov, bewilderment followed by exhilaration. "How much of your mental furniture remains entire" after reading Chekhov, she asks in "Tchehov's Questions" (*E2* 247). It is not a question that Anderson's work would prompt, nor Ring Lardner's, though she notes that Lardner's work "provides something unique," "a trophy" for "the traveller" to take home to prove that America actually is "a foreign land" (*E4* 276). She praises both writers, but it seems unlikely that reading either of them somehow transformed Virginia Woolf.

If in reading works by modern American writers, Woolf was never jolted by "the shock of the new" (Attridge 26), perhaps that is because they seemed to her to be either essentially more of the same or else different, but not sufficiently compelling as works of art. What she wanted was "something *shapely* of a new kind" ("An American Poet," *E3* 170; emphasis mine). She continued to hold out for a new, "real American literature" ("American Fiction," *E4* 277), one that would not keep defining itself in relation to the English, whether through deference or defiance. In 1920 in "An American Poet," she admits that "it may well be unfair" (*E3* 170) to consider "the real American" the "simpler and cruder" type. It is "so fatally easy for the English of the present day to do," she writes, "worshipping vitality, divesting himself of culture, trying to get away, to get back, to forget, to renew" (*E3* 167). "It may well be unfair," she concedes, to describe Vachel Lindsay's traits as a writer as "proof of his American birth," but "rightly or wrongly," that is what she proceeds to do. His "typically American" traits include "a primitive love of rhythm," "vitality," "simplicity," and "an enviably fresh" use of common speech (*E3* 170). She knows that this construction of "the real American" as a foil or an antitype to the world-weary, overcivilized European is a primitivist fantasy. Yet, she herself sometimes seems to be caught up in it.

For example, in "A Real American," an essay written the previous year, Woolf claims that Dreiser gives us a sense of "America herself, gross, benevolent, and prolific"—which sounds more like Whitman's America than Dreiser's (*E3* 87). She is happy to report that Dreiser is not writing to suit European taste: "his taste seems to be bad" (87). But "he has genuine vitality." He gives us a sense of "real American men and women." And what are they like? Well, actually, they seem rather "childish," but "their animal spirits are superb" (88).

"Typically American" traits do not in themselves add up to great literature, and Dreiser is not a great writer, in Woolf's judgment. Still, she speculates, he "may be the stuff from which, in another hundred years or so, great writers will be born" ("A Real American" *E3* 88). That is a long time to wait, and occasionally Woolf's patience seems to wear a bit thin. "There is every reason to believe America can bring something new to literature," she writes in "An American Poet." And "[i]t is high time," she adds, "that America did" (*E3* 167).

By 1925 she has decided that both types of American writers—"the simpler and cruder [ones], like Walt Whitman, Mr. Anderson, and Mr. Masters," as well as the "more sensitive or at least the more sophisticated" ones, like James and Wharton—are in the way ("American Fiction," *E4* 276). They "only delay the development of the real American literature itself" (277). Somewhat tentatively, Woolf presents as examples of "real American" writers Ring Lardner (whom she praises for seeming to be utterly unaware that the English exist), Willa Cather (cultured, but not excessively so), and Fannie Hurst (admirably independent). Yet, Woolf says so little about the work of any of these writers that they too seem to be at best mere harbingers.

Perhaps Woolf needed America to stand for the prospect of the new in the abstract, to serve as a permanent placeholder for the indefinite, for "something evermore about to be" (Wordsworth, *The Prelude*, 6 542). As a result, whatever American writers presented could never be "the real American literature," or at least not for long. By not allowing "the real American" to be identified and reified, Woolf seems at times even to be mocking the whole project of national self-definition, the paradoxical attempt, as Vincent Cheng puts it, to *invent* an "authentic" identity (243). At times she seems to be trying to keep the path clear for the development of the heterogeneous, open-ended, inclusive forms she felt were necessary for modern literature in general, not only for this new mongrel culture.

Yet, by participating in the discourse of authenticity, Woolf's own arguments tend to get caught in its logic. In effect, they imply that generations of American writers before 1925 (and after?) are somehow illegitimate, unreal, un-American. For, as Cheng remarks, "the concept of authenticity implies and mandates the existence of its opposites, the inauthentic, the fake, the nonauthorized" (249). "It is here," Cheng reminds us, "that the violence of discourse (in Derrida's sense) takes place" (249).

Although Woolf noted as early as 1909 that Americans do not like to be reminded by their elders of their "tender age" ("Oliver Wendell Holmes," *E1* 293), she ends "American Fiction" on a quaintly maternal note, comparing America to a child "exposed by its parents three hundred years ago upon the rocky shore"—a peculiar reading of early American colonial history—and only now, "by its own exertions," coming into its own (*E4* 278). This final note may sound patronizing, but she does make it clear in the course of this essay that the "acute self-consciousness" she associates with American writers is actually typical of many writers who are "otherwise poles asunder," including women writers in general (271).

In this sense, Woolf identifies with American writers, implicitly forging connections between them and other outsiders, underdogs, and newcomers struggling to free themselves so as to bring the new into existence; they are all "working...in the interest of a greater writer who is not yet born" ("How It Strikes a Contemporary" *E3* 359). In this respect, they inhabit the "common ground" she invokes in 1940 in "The Leaning Tower," one that "is not cut up into nations" (*CE2* 181). "The strangled difficult music" she hears coming from America's rocky shores in 1925 ("American Fiction," *E4* 278) seems to mingle with "the sound of...axes," of "breaking and falling; crashing and destruction" that she describes a year later in "Character in Fiction," the sounds of fellow modernists at work around her, "a vigorous and stimulating sound in [her] ears" (*E3* 434-35).

This idea of commonalities among authors who are writing out of positions or collective histories of asymmetrical power relations may be an earlier, more inclusive version of the Society of Outsiders that Woolf defines in *Three Guineas*. However strained and problematic the concept, it at least keeps alive the memory of our world's "violence, inequality, exclusion, and...oppression" (Jacques Derrida, *Spectres of Marx*, 84-85; quoted. in Li 33), which, as Victor Li points out, the current "master term—'globalization'" all too often occludes (9). Arguably, in time to come, the discourse of globalization may prove to be the triumph, in all its "crudity and one-sidedness," of what Woolf called "the tourist's attitude" ("American Fiction," *E4* 269), the "recto to colonialism's verso" (During 393), a vision more "class-specific" (Li 26), "parochial, even ethnocentric " (Li 17) than any that she could ever have imagined or would ever have endorsed.

Afterword

This paper was my initial attempt to explore some of the complexities of Woolf's views on "all things American." Here I focus on the affective differences between her responses to works by various modern American writers and, for example, by the great Russian novelists, and at length conclude that what mattered most to her was not so much American literature in practice, nor any particular American works or writers (not even, finally, Whitman, whom by 1925 she groups with the "simpler and cruder" American writers holding back the development of American literature as surely as are "more sensitive or at least more sophisticated" (*E4* 276) writers like James and Wharton). Rather, the essay concludes, the sense of affinity that drew Woolf to the Americans, at least in the abstract, stemmed from her being a modernist committed to formal experimentation, from her status as an outsider, in some crucial respects, and from her political sympathies. These factors continually reinforced her attachment to the idea of America and to the idea of an American literature that would be an open-ended experiment in expressing the new realities of the radical social experiment that the idea of America represents. My sense is, though, that Woolf was much more ambivalent toward even the idea of America than was suggested in either Melba Cuddy-Keane's paper or Andrew McNeillie's keynote speech at the Wales Conference (both of which were, needless to say, brilliant and memorable). Exploring these ambivalences gave rise to two other papers, "Woolf and the American Imaginary" and "The Making of Woolf's America," that I presented at the Thirteenth and the Fifteenth International Woolf Conferences at Smith College and at Lewis and Clark College, respectively. These papers were later published in *Woolf and the Real World*, ed. Karen V. Kukil, Clemson University, 2005 and *Woolf and the Art of Exploration*, ed. Helen Southworth and Elisa K. Sparks, Clemson University, 2006.

Works Cited

Attridge, Derek. "Innovation, Literature, Ethics: Relating to the Other." *PMLA* 114.1 (January 1999): 20-31.

Caughie, Pamela L. *Virginia Woolf and Postmodernism: Literature in Quest and Question of Itself.* Urbana: U of Illinois P, 1991.

Cheng, Vincent J. "Authenticity and Identity: Catching the Irish Spirit." *Semicolonial Joyce.* Ed. Derek Attridge and Marjorie Howes. Cambridge: Cambridge UP, 2000. 240-61.

During, Simon. "Postcolonialism and Globalization: Towards a Historicization of Their Inter-Relation." *Cultural Studies 14.3/4 (2000): 385-404.*

Li, Victor. "What's in a Name?: Questioning 'Globalization.'" *Cultural Critique* 45 (Spring 2000): 1-39.

Woolf, Virginia. *Collected Essays.* 4 vols. Ed. Leonard Woolf. Vol. 2. New York: Harcourt Brace, 1967.

———. *The Diary of Virginia Woolf.* 5 vols. Ed. Anne Olivier Bell. Vol. 5. New York: Harcourt Brace Jovanovich, 1984.

———. *The Essays of Virginia Woolf.* 4 vols. to date. Ed. Andrew McNeillie. London: Hogarth, 1986-.

———. *The Second Common Reader.* 1932. New York: Harcourt Brace, 1960.

Walking Down Whitehall

by Su Reid

I am interested in the functions of "real" places in fictional narratives, and in what might happen when a reader visits the "real" place and compares it with the fiction. By "real" places I mean named places that we can actually visit, such as Westminster, Whitehall, Piccadilly and Regent's Park in *Mrs. Dalloway*.

Such named places can, of course, carry histories into the fiction without being visited by the reader. A reader does not herself have to walk up Whitehall, for example, in order to construct an understanding of Peter Walsh by referencing the monuments he sees when he does it in *Mrs. Dalloway* (43-44). Peter walks (actually, "marches") up Whitehall, past the Cenotaph and towards the "exalted statues" in Trafalgar Square (Nelson on his column, Havelock, Gordon). As he walks he observes the "very fine training" given to the "weedy" boys who have laid their wreath at the "empty tomb"—the Cenotaph—and who march past him as if "life, with its varieties, its irreticences, had been laid under a pavement of monuments and wreaths and drugged into a stiff yet staring corpse by discipline"; and he thinks that the statues in Trafalgar Square have achieved their own "marble stare" after undergoing "the same renunciation." He claims "a great renunciation" for himself too, though rejecting the military stare, and thinks that the marching boys "don't know the troubles of the flesh yet," as he does. He then moves closer to one of the statues: "all that I've been through, he thought, crossing the road and standing under Gordon's statue, Gordon whom as a boy he had worshipped…poor Gordon he thought."

This brief episode focuses some of the complexity of Peter. It is not just that he, who missed the War by being in India, admires the military discipline imposed on the "weedy" boys in uniform, carrying guns. This alone would place him as a culpably naïve figure alongside the suffering of Septimus Warren Smith. The figure of Gordon adds more. General Charles Gordon, who died in 1885 at the end of the siege of Khartoum, was hailed in Victorian London as a national Christian martyr; but Lytton Strachey's *Eminent Victorians*, published in 1918, reconstructed him as a romantic ditherer saved, by an explosion in the palace whose cellar he had filled with gunpowder, from having to decide between being taken prisoner and being heroically martyred in close combat (Strachey 315-16). When Peter, revisiting London in 1923, thinks "poor Gordon," and pities himself too, he claims failure as tragic, or at least sad, rather than merely culpable. Admiring military suppression of emotion, he nevertheless admires emotion.

This scene, then, uses historical knowledge about the real place to focus the narration on Peter. But this kind of knowledge is accessed through other texts, not through visiting Trafalgar Square—where, indeed, the statue of Gordon no longer stands. David Bradshaw's excellent Oxford World's Classics (2000) edition of *Mrs. Dalloway* provides a great deal of valuable information about the London buildings and streets that the characters are to be imagined to have occupied in June 1923. In doing so it draws on two principal printed sources: Weinreb's and Hibbert's *The London Encyclopaedia* published in 1993, and *The Post Office London Directory with County Suburbs for 1923 (Mrs Dalloway* ed. Bradshaw 166). Jeremy Tambling's stimulating essay "Repression in Mrs Dalloway's London" is grounded in this kind of reading of the named landscape of *Mrs Dalloway*. It maps the novel against the buildings of London as they were in June 1923, when the novel is set; and deploys the new Cenotaph in Whitehall, the new tomb of the unknown soldier in Westminster Abbey, the recently reconstructed façade of Buckingham Palace, and the barely finished Victoria Monument, as knowledge that would have been shared by the author and her contemporary readers in 1925 when the novel was published. Using this knowledge, it reads the novel as a dramatisation of a repressive imperialist society that medicalises both suffering and difference—especially sexual difference—so as to deny them.

Visiting these places and buildings in London today does not, of course, enable a reader to visit the scenes of the novel as they are imagined to have been in 1923. Indeed, such a visit does not of itself bring about any detailed *historical* input, like Tambling's, into a reading at all. But instead, such a visit will involve movements and directions and distances which a reader might try to import into his or her continuing experience of the novel; and these, too, can enrich that reading.

I have argued elsewhere (Reid, 1997) that no visitor to St. Ives can doubt that *To the Lighthouse* employs specific places in the Cornish landscape alongside its weak Hebridean disguise. Early in the novel Mrs Ramsay walks with Charles Tansley "to the town," and they come out "on the quay" to confront a view any walker from Talland House (Woolf's family's holiday home, now holiday flats) down into St. Ives will see: the Lighthouse in the middle of the bay—"the great plateful of blue water"—and "on the right…the green sand dunes with the wild flowing grasses on them" (*TTL* 19-20). The phrase "on the right" represents exactly the distinctive layout of the dunes in relation to Godrevy Lighthouse, on its island very close to a promontory, as seen across St. Ives Bay. Even more strikingly, in the third part of the novel an island is described by Cam, to herself, as "shaped something like a leaf stood on end" (254). This improbable observation does in fact very accurately describe the appearance of Godrevy island with the lighthouse in St. Ives Bay as seen from Talland House or the beach below it—Porthminster Beach.

But here the visitor's recognition of a "real" place is disconcerted by the novel: while the tourist matches the leaf shape to the lighthouse's island in the bay, Cam is looking in the opposite direction, away from the lighthouse towards the land she is sailing from, the fictional island on which the family's house in the novel stands. Elizabeth Abel has persuasively linked Cam's musing about the island "shaped something like a leaf stood on end" with her memories of, and longing for, her mother. Abel shows that Cam repeatedly associates Mrs. Ramsay with a leaf, and that in the first part of the novel, "The Window," the leaf is contrasted in Cam's consciousness with the crackling newspapers and tidy gardening she associates with Mr. Ramsay and "the old gentlemen smoking." Here in the third part, Abel argues, Cam sees the leaf-like island, with its "dent in the middle and two sharp crags" as an image of her mother's body from which she is being drawn inexorably away (Abel, 61). If this reading is accepted, the visitor to St. Ives will understand that the remembered shape of Godrevy Island has been transformed by Woolf from the "real" place into an imagined place with a metaphorical function. This understanding will detach the idea of the lighthouse to which Cam and James and Mr Ramsay are sailing from any "real" place. After all, it does appear differently to different characters at different stages of the novel.

With all this in mind, I recently, on a warm late spring day, set out to retrace some of the steps of the characters in *Mrs Dalloway* in modern central London—which I know only as a visitor. It quickly became clear that, as with St. Ives and *To the Lighthouse*, I would experience both a recognition of the novel in the "real" place and a sense of distortion. The narration of *Mrs. Dalloway* creates a space bearing the names of real places in London, and the characters' movements can indeed be mapped in terms of modern streets, as in David Bradshaw's edition (lx-lxi). But the distances do not fit the narrative. As Bradshaw himself points out (xiv), the times "really" needed for the characters to walk from one named place to another make it impossible for a reader to re-enact their walking. Septimus and Lucrezia Warren Smith are in Bond Street near Clarissa when the car backfires (12). Almost immediately (18) they are in Regent's Park, watching the sky-writing aeroplane like everyone else in London, it seems, and including people still watching the car (17). Bond Street to Regent's Park is quite a long way. I got a taxi.

Another person in the Regent's Park Broad Walk that morning, of course, is Peter Walsh. He has visited Clarissa, back from Bond Street and in her house in Westminster, at about 11.00, and left as the clocks—Big Ben and St Margaret's—strike half past eleven. His route is mapped. He walks up Whitehall, past the Cenotaph and the marching boys in uniform, to Trafalgar Square. Then he pursues a pretty girl up Cockspur Street, across Piccadilly, up Regent Street, across Oxford Street and Great Portland Street, and loses her when she goes into a house "with hanging flower-baskets of vague impropriety" (46). He walks on to Regent's Park—not far now, but this is an impossible walk from Westminster if he is to be there, as he is, in time to have a snooze on a bench and then be awake at 11.45 (60) to see the Smiths, in their distress, move off towards their twelve o'clock appointment with Sir William Bradshaw!

Having got this far in an attempt to move about in the novel's space, I retreated into an idea of symbolism, as Abel does when she describes the displaced leaf-like island as a metaphor for the lost mother's body: I began to argue (to myself) that when the actions of the characters in *Mrs. Dalloway* are placed in "real" places by the novel, those real places work more as indicators of emotional or social and political states than of characters' movements, and that physical distances between them are simply irrelevant. I began to construct Regent's Park as a setting in which the Smiths and Peter Walsh are placed together to articulate a distress and disintegration forbidden elsewhere in London. Septimus (who fought for "an England which consisted almost entirely of Shakespeare's plays and Miss Isabel Pole…" (73)) goes to the Park between the authority of the royal car and the authority of Sir William Bradshaw. In the Park he knows he is free of his marriage because Rezia's ring has come off (57); he sees music in columns, he sings an immortal ode to time when the word "time" "splits its husk," and he sees dead Evans returning, as in a second coming, from Thessaly among the orchids (58-59). Peter, meanwhile, goes to the Park after leaving Clarissa and walking up Whitehall past the Cenotaph and Gordon's statue, and before visiting a lawyer in pursuit of a divorce. Between these two alignments with the public world he sleeps freely in Regent's Park; and there disappears beyond our normal understanding of him as a character in a novel because the narrative space of his sleep is occupied by the passage about the solitary traveller and the giant figure (48-50). This passage describes a state of consciousness in which no consistent rational transaction with surroundings, physical or social, is manageable by the individual. It employs similar terms to Septimus's when delineating moments of "extraordinary exaltation" which reveal men and women as "pigmies" from whom the mind seeks relief, believing that "nothing exists outside us except a state of mind." A "giant figure at the end of the ride" is pursued through unmappable branches and leaves and waves, but is embodied, like England perhaps, only as an absence in the shape of a person—here becoming an unknown and impersonal landlady who leaves the traveller still solitary.

As Peter wakes he exclaims "[t]he death of the soul," but believes he has been reliving, in a dream, the day long ago at Bourton when he lost Clarissa—the day when Clarissa both met Richard Dalloway and demonstrated, to Peter anyway, a fear of sexuality (50-55). Both Peter and Clarissa have been remembering this day all through the present time of the novel so far, but here, while readers are located with the characters in Regent's Park, Peter's dramatic version of its events is made more explicit. The conjunctions with Septimus become unavoidable: Peter and Septimus, romantic idealists in youth, have failed marriages, failed loves, marginal identities in London in 1923, and in Regent's Park they become would-be fugitives not unlike the animals in the zoo.

At this point I, like the sane Rezia, walked as far as the drinking fountain. (This, again, is a long walk for the time allotted in the novel.) Here in the middle of Regent's Park is a deeply ambiguous memorial, which reinforced my idea of the Park as a symbolic space which encloses distress. Its inscription honours the British Indian Empire for its defense of a minority. It reads:

THIS FOUNTAIN
ERECTED BY THE
METROPOLITAN DRINKING FOUNTAIN
AND CATTLE TROUGH ASSOCIATION WAS
THE GIFT OF SIR COWASJEE JEHANGIR
(COMPANION TO THE STAR OF INDIA)
A WEALTHY PARSEE GENTLEMAN OF BOMBAY AS A TOKEN OF
GRATITUDE TO THE PEOPLE OF ENGLAND FOR THE PROTECTION
ENJOYED BY HIM AND HIS PARSEE FELLOW COUNTRYMEN UNDER THE
BRITISH RULE IN INDIA, INAUGURATED BY H.R.H. PRINCESS MARY,
DUCHESS OF TECK, 1869

The Parsees are here, in Regent's Park, where one of them paid in gratitude for this memorial. But in its physical presence, a piece of mid-Victorian public art with a humourless citation denying its own irony, this fountain acts out the cultural imperialism that exacts loyalty from a threatened Bombay minority.

All this was, in a sense, my pursuit of the author's intentions—arguing that *Mrs. Dalloway* subordinates real physical distances to the demands of Woolf's supposed aim of dramatising failed romantic idealism and suppressed misery. I also began to think that the novel enacts in landscape terms the speed of the narration's movement among memories. As J Hillis Miller (1982) has argued, the narration of *Mrs Dalloway* resurrects Clarissa's and Peter's acts of memory within its own remembering of the day in June 1923, and the reader re-enacts that narrative's *remembering* as she or he reads. I had found that Clarissa's walk to the flower shop and back at the start of the novel includes at least one detour—to Hatchard's, and then "back" to Bond Street; and that parts of it are unnamed and entirely absent from the narration. Perhaps, I thought, the dislocated movements embody the narrative's jumping about in time.

But all this is not enough. I am interested in reading as a performance by the reader, as well as in the text as a trace of the author. Visiting a place named in a novel is, obviously, a trigger for a reader to revisit the novel, whether by remembering it or by rereading. At the same time it defines the place too—perhaps in a private way, differently from the constructions of landscape in terms of public history discussed, for example, by Simon Schama (Schama 1995). Can I ever again visit Regent's Park, with its drinking fountain, and, more alarmingly, its populace of mobile phone users muttering into the bushes, without thinking of Septimus? I have argued (Reid 1997) that when the "real" leaf-like Godrevy island is transformed into a memory of Mrs. Ramsay, the sand dunes, which are "on the right" in relation to the lighthouse, represent Mr. Ramsay; and that my own sense of St. Ives, which I visit often, is repeatedly constructed on this confrontation of masculine with feminine in the landscape.

I can reconstruct Whitehall in a similar way. In *Mrs. Dalloway*, Peter marches "*up*" Whitehall, as do the "weedy" boys. Indeed he "marched...as if there rolled down to him, vigorous, unending, his future" (43). But in *A Room of One's Own* we are bidden to imagine "walking *down* Whitehall" and in the process making a choice between two gender-differentiated readings of the place:

> ...if one is a woman one is often surprised by a sudden splitting off of consciousness, say in walking down Whitehall, when from being the natural inheritor of that civilisation she becomes, on the contrary, outside of it, alien and critical. (88)

In her diary for 10 December 1936 (*D5* 42-43) Woolf tells a story about the news of the abdication of Edward VIII. She describes herself taking a bus to "the top of Whitehall" and wandering "down the yellow brown avenue" with Ottoline Morrell, a figure who appears before her like one of the visions before the solitary traveller in *Mrs. Dalloway*. Ottoline confidently identifies a window in a government building as the one through which Charles I, an earlier ex-king, walked to his execution, and Woolf writes "I felt I was walking in the 17th Century with one of the courtiers." Ottoline refers to Edward as the "poor silly little boy" about to "throw it all away" and the diary represents "it" by means of the buildings:

> "It" seemed then, looking at the curved street, & at the red and silver guards drawn up in the courtyard with the Park and the white government buildings behind, very stately, very lovely, very much the noble and severe aristocratic Stuart England.

But nothing seems to happen so they get into a taxi and drive away *up* Whitehall, and return to ordinary tea time.

Moving *up* Whitehall, then, involves moving on and away into the many doings of individual lives—in Peter's case perhaps "vigorous" and "unending," but certainly involving his fantasy pursuit of the girl and his sleep in the Broad Walk. But walking *down* Whitehall signifies acknowledgement of a singular choice about claiming or not claiming power. Ideas about power which Woolf explores much more directly in gendered terms in *A Room of One's Own* and *Three Guineas* are here embedded more tentatively in geographical terms.

The problem which remains is: how can I theorise this kind of reading so as to develop a more detailed understanding of the relationship between movement and narrative?

In his book *Topographies,* Hillis Miller proposes and investigates the idea that "landscape provides grounding for novels" (9); that "novels ground themselves on the landscape" (10-11); or that "a novel arises from the landscape in which the action takes place" (19). The "Introduction" to his book argues that places are given existence and identity only by naming; that before they are named and mapped they do not exist as places, and what we think of as their "physical features" are incomprehensible or invisible to us (1-8). He also argues, in essence, that novels construct places by naming them.

This book does not, however, address my sense that a novel provokes a sense of *dislocation*, not of grounding, when it distorts the physical dimensions of the visited place; and that that sense of physical dislocation can itself stimulate new understandings both of the novel and of the place.

The belief that reading a novel is a dialogue, in a reader's mind, between narratives in time and physical objects in space conflicts with notions of the author's "ownership" of the text that are still familiar, and persuasive for most readers. To this extent, some of Miller's earlier work is directly helpful. In 1982 and 1983 he published three essays on Woolf, one each on *Mrs Dalloway, Between the Acts,* and *To the Lighthouse,* in that order. All three proposed that the characters and events of each novel are held simultaneously within a single mind or consciousness, which is constructed by the narration of each novel and is re-enacted afresh by the reader each time she or he reads. All these essays saw reading as a performance, an action. Nevertheless, the reader was still thought of as second at best in a series of actions, and certainly as dependent on, rather than equal to, the text. Then, in 1987, Hillis Miller published a short book, *The Ethics of Reading*, in which he sought to demonstrate that the interpretation of a text is always driven by laws or imperatives in the act of reading itself, not by the author's intentions. In his final chapter, Miller cited Henry James's Preface to the New York edition of *The Golden Bowl*, a text to which he referred again in his later book *Illustration*, published in 1992. This Preface articulates James's anxieties about the use of visual images as additions to writing, and of photographs as illustrations to his novels. To a reader now, used as we very much are to filmed or televised "adaptations" of novels, this Preface is remarkable for its fear that the visual illustration will substitute in the reader's mind meanings that are not the author's or the text's. But James goes on to argue, and to Hillis Miller this was the most striking thing about his discussion, that illustrations are acceptable if they represent the "type or idea of this or that thing," not a "particular thing in the text," and are therefore in dialogue with it (James, 11-14). Miller's proposal was that James demonstrates, here and in his re-readings of all his own novels in his Prefaces to the late New York edition of his work, that reading is always an act in itself, and indeed that a re-reading even by the author is another, separate, act in a chain of events. Miller's central argument in *The Ethics of Reading* is that an act of reading is always subject to an imperative, to what he calls an "ethical moment," to the reader's sense of what the text "must" mean (8-10).

This "must" does perhaps adequately recognise the sense of discomfort experienced by a reader comparing a "real" space to a representation of it in a fiction. That discomfort might be resolved by attributing deliberate symbolic intentions to the author. But perhaps it can be used more productively. Perhaps we can, after all, assert with Hillis Miller that all spaces are created within language, and so are endlessly replaced within successive texts, so that readers' imaginative reconstructions of places they visit are legitimate objects of study. More simply, we must acknowledge that readers do deploy immediate personal consciousnesses in their readings of both texts and places, and that while this can lead to wildly idiosyncratic readings it can also generate readings which last. The problem that still remains is that of knowing when such readings are justifiable and when they are not, and by whom they might be justified.

Afterword

In 2001, I wrote this paper as a request for ideas about how best to think coherently about physical space alongside narratives. Recently I have read with interest Eric Bulson's account of mappings of narrative space, and especially of the proliferation of "literary maps" to accompany novels in the twentieth century, in *Novels, Maps, Modernity: The Spatial Imagination, 1850-2000*, New York and London: Routledge 2007; for Bulson sees such maps as an attempt to manage a sense of spatial dislocation that he observes in many narratives. For myself, I am working instead on a closer study of confined and owned spaces—specifically parks and gardens—in narratives from Jane Austen onwards. This paper's thinking about Regent's Park in *Mrs. Dalloway* was my starting point.

Works Cited

Abel, Elizabeth. *Virginia Woolf and the Fictions of Psychoanalysis*. Chicago and London: University of Chicago Press, 1989.
James, Henry. *The Golden Bowl*, 1904, New York Edition 1907. Harmondsworth: Penguin, 1966.
Miller, J Hillis. "*Mrs. Dalloway*: Repetition as Raising of the Dead." *Fiction and Repetition. Seven English Novels*. Oxford: Basil Blackwell, 1982. 176-202.
———. "*Between the Acts*. Repetition as Extrapolation. *Fiction and Repetition. Seven English Novels*. Oxford: Basil Blackwell, 1982. 203-31.
———. "Mr Carmichael and Lily Briscoe. The Rhythm of Creativity in *To the Lighthouse*." *Modernism Reconsidered*. Ed. Robert Kiely and John Hildebidle. Cambridge Mass. and London: Harvard University Press, 1983. 167-89.
———. *The Ethics of Reading*. New York: Columbia University Press, 1987
———. *Illustration*. Cambridge Mass. and London: Harvard University Press, 1992
———. *Topographies*. Stanford, Ca.: Stanford University Press, 1995
Reid, Su. "Reading and Virginia Woolf." *Cornwall: the Cultural Construction of Place*. Ed. Ella Westland. Penzance: Patten Press, 1997. 88-98.
Schama, Simon. *Landscape and Memory*. London: Harper Collins, 1995.
Strachey, Lytton. *Eminent Victorians*, 1918. Harmondsworth: Penguin, 1948.
Tambling, Jeremy. "Repression in Mrs. Dalloway's London." *Essays in Criticism* 39 (April 1989): 137-55.
Woolf, Virginia. *The Diary of Virginia Woolf*. Ed. Anne Olivier Bell and Andrew McNeillie. Vol. 5. London: Penguin, 1984.
———. *Mrs. Dalloway*, 1925. Ed. David Bradshaw. Oxford: Oxford UP, 2000.
———. *A Room of One's Own*, 1929. Ed. Michele Barrett. London: Penguin, 1995.
———. *To the Lighthouse*, 1927. Ed. Margaret Drabble. Oxford: Oxford UP, 1999.

ORLANDO'S OTHELLO

by Genevieve Abravanel

I'd like to open this paper with a pair of questions about *Orlando*. Either might be taken on its own, but, I'll suggest, the two may also benefit from being taken together. First, I'll ask, "How should we read the intertextual display of *Othello*—which is described in performance, quoted, and mentioned in the metatextual index—in a work which opens with its principal character 'slicing at the head of a Moor' (*O* 13)?" At the same time, I'd like to connect this inquiry into *Othello* to a question that has long interested Woolf's readers: that is, "Why does Orlando change sex away from England?"

In order to attend to the first question, it may bear revisiting the well-known opening line of *Orlando*: "He—for there could be no doubt of his sex, though the fashion of the time did something to disguise it—was in the act of slicing at the head of a Moor which swung from the rafters" (*O* 13). As Rachel Bowlby and others have noted, the disavowal of doubt, in nicely Freudian fashion, throws Orlando's sex into doubt from the outset. Yet this doubt is mitigated by Orlando's apparently masculine act of lunging after the dangling head of an African. While Bowlby lingers on Woolf's comparison of the Moor's head to a "football" as an invocation of manly games, others such as Kathy Phillips note that Orlando's masculinity here is shored up by his participation in what resembles the imperial game of Woolf's own cultural moment. As the text makes clear, Orlando's swordplay with the severed head of an African follows precisely from his lineage as an English nobleman, passed down to him from his "father, or perhaps his grandfather" (*O* 13). Orlando's inheritance is thus the performance of masculinity as cross-cultural violence. Such inheritance could be said to prepare Orlando for his arrival at the court at Greenwich where, as the biographer sets the scene, "soldiers planned the conquest of the Moor and the downfall of the Turk in striped arbours surrounded by ostrich feathers" (*O* 35). By opening with the ironized image of boyish swordplay, *Orlando* establishes aristocratic English masculinity through violence against the racial metonym swinging from the rafters.

This opening scene of Orlando swinging at the head of a Moor sets up a relationship to the iconic Moor of English literature who appears shortly thereafter. Having met the Russian princess, Sasha, at Greenwich, Orlando stops with her at the performance of a play which Woolf's index assures us is none other than *Othello*. As the biographer relates:

> The main press of people, it appeared, stood opposite a booth or stage something like our Punch and Judy show upon which some kind of theatrical performance was going forward. A black man was waving his arms and vociferating. There was a woman in white laid upon the bed. (*O* 56)

Orlando and Sasha join the audience precisely at the scene of Desdemona's murder. Orlando, who has cause to suspect Sasha's unfaithfulness with a Russian sailor, finds himself identifying with Othello. As the narrator relates, "The frenzy of the Moor seemed to him his own frenzy, and when the Moor suffocated the woman in her bed it was Sasha he killed with his own hands" (*O* 57). Whereas the opening scene presents the young Orlando mimicking the violence of his forefathers toward Moors in general, here Orlando identifies with the iconic Moor's own violence. In this latter scene, Orlando momentarily escapes the strictures of English propriety—for he can't actually kill Sasha—by imagining himself in the place of the violent Othello. In this way, identification with the Moor is presented as a kind of therapy for masculine jealousy. Whether through actual swordplay or phantasmatic identification, cross-cultural violence helps to produce and define Orlando's masculinity.

Yet of course, this identification with Othello is not really identification with a cultural other, but rather with a specifically English fantasy of cultural otherness as embodied in England's master text of race and masculinity. Othello is as "English" as Hamlet, Lear, or Juliet. As presented in *Orlando*, *Othello* provides a space where fantasies of violence can display themselves without ever disturbing English propriety. In this use of the play and its tropes, Woolf is quite canny. By bringing *Othello* and the image of the Moor into her novel at various key points—the opening scene, the spasm of jealousy and rage—she is demonstrating the extent to which English masculinity depends upon conceptions of the racial other. Woolf's use of Shakespearean intertext suggests that Orlando's various engagements with violence, whether in act or imagination, are in fact scripts and Orlando largely a player, caught up in his true inheritance of cultural narratives of race and gender.

Woolf might well have chosen another play for Orlando's brief aesthetic encounter; in her initial draft she left space for, as she noted, "a masque by one of the popular Elizabethan poets—Jonson, Shakespeare, or another" (*Original Holograph* 38). Yet in a work that introduces its principal character in combat with a relic of English relations with Africa, and which contains at least seven references to the "Moor" as well as references to "gypsies," "turks" and a "blackamoor," the late addition of *Othello* seems almost overdetermined. Even when Orlando decides to furnish his estate, he meets up with Othello. That is to say, as the narrator dutifully recounts, Orlando's shopping expedition consists in part of an "adventure with a Moor in Venice of whom he bought (but only at sword's point) his laquered cabinet" (*Orlando* 110). While not precisely Shakespeare's "Moor of Venice," this Moor in Venice, like his beheaded counterpart, is defined through his encounter with the English sword. Here the transaction is at once violent and commercial, a gesture toward the global economic exploitation that sustained English ancestral estates in Orlando's day.

While shopping methods in *Orlando* may rely on the sword and imperial domination, the novel also describes gender relations at their most intimate in terms that recall Shakespeare's Venetian Moor. As rationale for Orlando's failed romance with the Archduchess Harriet, the narrator offers a string of metaphors. "For Love," explains the narrator:

> has two faces: one white, the other black; two bodies; one smooth, the other hairy. It has two hands, two feet, two tails, two, indeed, of every member and each one is the exact opposite of the other. Yet so strictly are they joined together that you cannot separate them. (*O* 117)

Here the narrator's image rests on antimonies of color to describe what one might call, with Iago, the "beast with two backs" (*O* 70). In fact, this fanciful image of love is capable of recalling the "old black ram tupping [the] white ewe" (*O* 69) as much as "the beast with two backs"; both are phrases capable of frightening Brabantio out of bed at night. Woolf had read *Othello* as early as 1909 and reread it after finishing her first draft of *Orlando*. The narrator's tribute to Love, as well as the dangling Moor's head, can be found in the holograph draft before the explicit addition of *Othello*, revealing the extent to which the text was already relying on metaphors of color to explain the vagaries of gender.

During Orlando's first thirty-odd years as a man, his relations with Africa and the East range from aggression to diplomacy. Yet when Orlando changes sex, she dons Turkish trousers and assimilates for a time in the hills near Broussa. The question of why Orlando changes sex away from England in Constantinople is crucial to the interdependence of gender and culture in the work. Potential answers to such a question might focus on the importance of Constantinople to Vita, who enjoyed cross-dressing in Turkish trousers, or on the vogue of turbans and harem pants in modern England. Somewhat less frequently noted in relation to *Orlando*, but nonetheless an important biographical connection, is Woolf's participation in the Dreadnought Hoax in 1910, in which she impersonated an African ambassador in a turban, dark makeup, and a beard. It tends to be understood that as the only woman among her brothers and their friends, Woolf dressed as a man in order to pass as an African, but perhaps it might also be said that she dressed as an African in order to pass as a man. Stepping outside one's culture in order to step outside one's gender, or performing another culture in order to perform the other sex, was thus familiar to Woolf long before she met Vita, and more than 17 years before writing *Orlando*.

Yet as far as the work itself is concerned, there is a cruder answer to the question of why Orlando changes sex away from England. Quite simply, it is to demonstrate the extent to which she doesn't. While Woolf locates the biological metamorphosis in Constantinople, she takes care to guard Orlando from its effects until Orlando reaches the English socius, in this case, a ship aptly named *The Enamoured Lady*. Directly after her sex change, Orlando puts on "those Turkish coats and trousers which can be worn indifferently by either sex" and joins what Woolf calls a "gipsy tribe." Once Orlando trades her trousers for "a complete outfit" of women's clothes, she experiences what the narrator calls "the penalities and privileges of her position" (*O* 153), a position that refracts class and gender through the lens of English culture as defined against Africa and the East.

The flexibility of gender in *Orlando* relies consistently on narratives of culture and with surprising frequency on the specific narrative of cultural difference that serves as Shakespearean intertext. Not only does Orlando as a man identify with Othello, safely displacing his passion and rage, but at least via Woolfian wordplay, the female Orlando seems momentarily to embody Desdemona. Having stumbled to the ground outside her home in England, the prostrate Orlando murmurs, "I have found my mate . . . it is the moor" (*O* 248). Here, in a tribute to the English landscape, it is possible to hear the echo of the cultural otherness that helps to constitute English identity. While the force of the homonym here remains conjectural, it is worth noting that the holograph draft, to which Woolf had not yet added *Othello*, also lacks this aside. Orlando's moment outside of the economy of English gender roles suddenly ceases with her engagement to a properly imperial Englishman: Marmaduke Bonthrop Shelmerdine, who passes his days sailing around Cape Horn. As Orlando puts it, "I am a woman...a real woman at last" (*O* 253). For Orlando to come to such a conclusion precisely after imagining the voyage around Cape Horn of a man who passes his time, as Orlando later divines, "kissing a negress in the dark," reveals the extent to which the epistemology of woman, or at any rate of a "real," woman, rests on fantasies of masculine behavior toward what Gayatri Spivak would call the South (*O* 258).

Orlando's reliance on the iconography of the Moor thus serves precisely to display the dependence of gender roles not only on cultural construction but specifically on racial and cultural difference. For if Woolf in *Orlando* demonstrates that gender is historical, as many have noted, then her use of *Othello* reveals the extent to which gender is specifically scripted and performed along racial lines. As intertext, then, *Othello* is overdetermined by literary history. It is an intertext that not only complements *Orlando*'s dangling metonyms and imaginary Moors, but may also have helped to establish the fantasies of race that inform Woolf's understanding of the English body. From this perspective, *Orlando* appears to be acting out *Othello* from the start. It does so not in its plot or particulars, but in its reflection of *Othello*'s place in English heritage. Specifically, Woolf's novel presents *Othello*'s picture of the interdependence of race and gender as part of Orlando's English inheritance. In so doing, *Orlando* both critiques and participates in the legacy of Western fantasies of race and gender. That is to say, Orlando may change sex overseas, but as far as literary history is concerned, the work's own voyages abroad don't travel far from the English literary imagination.

Works Cited

Bowlby, Rachel. *Feminist Destinations and Further Essays on Virginia Woolf.* Edinburgh: Edinburgh University Press, 1997.
Phillips, Kathy J. *Virginia Woolf against Empire.* Knoxville: University of Tennessee Press, 1994.
Shakespeare, William. *Othello.* Ed. Norman Sanders. Cambridge: Cambridge University Press, 2003.
Woolf, Virginia. *Orlando: A Biography.* London: Hogarth, 1990.
———. *Orlando: The Original Holograph Draft.* Ed. Stuart Nelson Clarke. London: Clarke, 1993.

The Voyage Home: Peter Walsh and the Trauma of Empire in Virginia Woolf's *Mrs. Dalloway*

by Nancy Knowles

In his well-known study *Prospero and Caliban: The Psychology of Colonization*, O. Mannoni describes the relationship between colonizer and colonized in psychological terms. Mannoni argues that colonialism resembles a psychological disease wherein the colonizer's unresolved infantile complexes result in "a grave lack of sociability combined with a pathological urge to dominate" (104, 102). This neurosis leads the colonizer to create a fantasy society by subjugating others (101). Peter Walsh in Virginia Woolf's *Mrs. Dalloway* suffers from such neurosis, so much so that even after the voyage home, he continues to exhibit the misanthropy and need for domination characteristic of the disease.

However, the example of Peter Walsh demonstrates that the colonial neurosis is more complicated than Mannoni implies: the complexes formed in infancy that permit colonial behavior are not individual but cultural. We can see this cultural quality in the myths of masculine power that underlie British nationalism. Such myths assume that dominance is the British gentleman's duty, they create a need in men to fulfill that duty, and they also cause insecurity when men's imperfect attempts at dominant displays fall short of the mythical ideal. By thus promising and withholding power, patriarchal institutions like the British Empire oppress not only native peoples but also their own loyal subjects. We can observe the cultural nature of such complexes by comparing Peter Walsh with the shell-shocked Septimus Smith. While Peter doesn't actually die as Septimus does, Peter becomes a walking corpse, "the dead man in the grey suit" (*MD* 70), perpetrator *and* victim of empire, whose voyage home indicates not his recovery but the mortal infection of his society.

This paper will first explore Peter's colonial neurosis and then compare it with Septimus's battle trauma. The conclusion will comment upon such diseases as a means of retaining institutional power.

I.

I'm going to use a disagreement between Mannoni and Frantz Fanon as a springboard for discussing Peter's colonial neurosis as specifically patriarchal in origin. Mannoni makes two related arguments about the colonial situation:

- Before they ever begin to colonize, European colonizers possess unresolved infantile complexes that enable colonization, complexes without which the European "would not in the first place feel the urge to go to the colonies" (98). Thus, the European colonizer is "predestined" (98) to take satisfaction from dominating others.
- The corollary of this predestination for Mannoni is that prior to colonization, the situation of the colonized also is predetermined. He argues that a "latent" inferiority complex exists prior to colonization among the soon-to-be-colonized that allows domination to occur (40).

Frantz Fanon legitimately objects to the idea that the colonized possess a natural inferiority (85, 93), arguing instead that colonization causes the colonized's sense of inferiority (93).

I would like to make a slightly different argument. I would argue that the inferiority complex both scholars locate among the colonized, whether before or after colonization, can actually be found first *within* the patriarchal institutions that govern most of the colonizer *and* colonized cultures. I propose that the predestined quality of colonization results from the patriarchal hierarchy that plants in a man the expectation of power over others, others who can be defined as somehow unlike himself. Given both colonizer and colonized cultures possess patriarchal structures, the difference between the colonizer and the colonized becomes a matter of logistics: the colonizers have the opportunity to exercise their need for dominance over another culture, while the colonized peoples do not. Because under patriarchy a man is *supposed* to be powerful, and because human beings cannot always *be* powerful, especially when that power is defined through others who may not appreciate being used to define someone else's power, the patriarchal man must forever reassure himself he fulfills the patriarchal myth of masculine power. Those capable of dominating at a particular time and place must continue to do so in order to avoid a sense of inferiority; those not capable at that particular time and place become increasingly insecure in their failure to fulfill the myth. Thus, neither Mannoni nor Fanon is exactly correct; the precolonial inferiority complex *does* exist prior to colonization, but it does *not* belong solely to the soon-to-be-colonized. Instead, the inferiority complex occurs in patriarchy on *both* sides, instigating both the need for dominance and the stigma of being dominated.

Peter Walsh, an administrator of British India, exemplifies the dialogic movement between insecurity and aggression that characterizes the colonizer both as misanthropic, fearing and therefore despising the world that can challenge his masculinity, and as needing to dominate others to erase this insecurity. Peter's insecurity is clear: like many middle-aged men, he is sensitive about his age (*MD* 43, 50) and what he sees as his failure to make anything out of his life. He thinks, "he had never done a thing that they [he and Clarissa] talked of" (*MD* 8), and he is concerned that "[Clarissa] would think me a failure, which I am in their sense, he thought; in the Dalloways' sense…he was a failure!" (*MD* 43). His sense of failure centers primarily on his work in India. For him, India represents a difficult responsibility he has to shoulder alone (*MD* 48), not the site of masculine accomplishment. The colony has resisted his power to deal with it, its size and diseases giving him a sense of defeat no matter what he does (*MD* 48). In particular, he recalls the failure of one of his innovations: "For he had a turn for mechanics; had invented a plough in his district, had ordered wheel-barrows from England, but the coolies wouldn't use them" (*MD* 49). Notice that in this example Peter's failure constitutes not only a failure of innovation but also a failure of dominance; he has failed to force people, people over whom he "should" have power, to accept his work as valuable. In claiming these failures, Peter measures his life experience against his patriarchal culture's myth of masculine power, which employs entrepreneurial success and dominance over others as means to demonstrate power. Peter's sense of failure challenges his sense of himself as man.

This combination of insecurity and need for masculine dominance appears when Peter confronts his embarrassment using the masculine symbol of his pocket-knife (*MD* 40). This phallic symbol represents the way Peter deals with his failures: he turns to sexual relationships with women to recoup his masculinity. For example, to reassure himself, Peter frames his thoughts of failure in India with thoughts of love: "All India lay behind him; [...]he, Peter Walsh; who was now really for the first time in his life, in love" (*MD* 48-49). Because dominance over women has historically reinforced patriarchal power, Peter's behavior seems a likely solution to his inferiority problem; an intimate relationship with a woman could provide the opportunity to dominate *somebody*. However, the colonizer attitude itself, rooted in patriarchy and combining misanthropy with the need to dominate, precludes Peter's acquiring the intimacy he so desperately desires.

Peter's misanthropy, born from fear of others, appears in his shallow relationships with women. Although he would like to achieve intimacy enough to dominate women, he cannot risk his masculinity in order to establish intimacy in the first place. For example, "he [...] married a woman [he] met on the boat going to India!" (*MD* 8). We know only that Peter plans to divorce this woman to marry another man's wife with whom he claims to be in love (*MD* 45). This lack of information suggests that Peter himself knows nothing about his wife either, not having taken the time to develop intimacy before marrying. Moreover, the married woman he purportedly loves and hopes to marry may fall into the same category, merely a new infatuation. The fact that Peter seems increasingly less interested in divorce (*MD* 79) attests to the shallowness of his feelings. These flimsy relationships represent Peter's desperate need for intimacy and his lack of sociability, both of which characterize the colonizer. Because he wants to dominate and won't risk himself by accepting true intimacy, his relationships always fail.

Perhaps the best example of the misanthropy and need for dominance that preclude intimacy for Peter is the scene where Peter follows a young, attractive woman through the streets. Because he has never met her, "[...] she became the very woman he had always had in mind" (*MD* 52). Peter "prefers a fantasy character" (Phillips 16), a relationship that obstructs sympathy (Hawthorne 58), because, in fantasy, he possesses total intimacy and total control, the epitome of masculine power, without risking its loss. The fantasy love affair represents another version of the fantasy the British attempt to establish in creating colonies. The fact that Peter envisions this woman revealing herself "veil after veil" (*MD* 52) like a Dance-of-the-Seven-Veils Orientalist stereotype, aligns his need for sexual dominance with his role as a colonizer. The fantasy woman perpetuates the myths of masculine power by which Peter lives, but because she is an illusion, she will never fulfill his needs.

The source of Peter's misanthropy and need for domination is not his role as a colonizer. While perhaps reinforced by the attempt to exercise power over others, these behaviors *predate* Peter's voyage to India and therefore were learned at home. We can see this in Clarissa's explanation of why she can't marry Peter: "For in marriage a little license, a little independence there must be between people living together day in and day out in the same house [...]. But with Peter everything had to be shared; everything gone into. And it was intolerable [...]" (*MD* 7-8). For Peter, the expression of dominance in intimate relationships becomes policing Clarissa's experience. He cannot allow her any privacy. His need for dominance causes his intrusion on Clarissa and Sally's moment of passion to feel "like running one's face against a granite wall in the darkness!" (*MD* 36). The unwillingness to allow privacy also implies the distrust and lack of respect for Clarissa as a person that indicates misanthropy. When Clarissa realizes that this kind of patriarchal relationship, where one partner needs to dominate and fears being dominated, will ruin them both (*MD* 8), she resists Peter's colonizing urge by marrying Richard Dalloway instead. Because Peter's colonizer mentality *predates* his involvement in colonization, his behavior must be a product of the imperial center, patriarchal British culture itself, possibly what Mrs. Lynn-Jones in *Between the Acts* labels the "something [...] 'unhygienic' about [...] home" (174). Thus, the psychological disease of colonization that Mannoni identifies is not natural to human psychology but rather is produced culturally.

II.

This idea that the imperial mentality is learned at home can be further demonstrated by comparing Peter with the shell-shocked Septimus Smith, who, like Peter, has recently returned home to England. Although Septimus's difficulties reintegrating with British society result from post-traumatic stress, the symptoms of his trauma bear remarkable similarities to the disease of colonization we see in Peter. These similarities indicate that Peter's disease can be associated with trauma and that such traumas are context-specific. In other words, trauma results in part from the patriarchal context in which it occurs. The traumas of both men result not only from their experiences outside England but also from the failure of cultural myths of masculine power that are central to British nationalism. By comparing Septimus and Peter, we can see Peter as not only the perpetrator of oppression against others but also the victim of a patriarchal system that expects displays of dominance as evidence of manhood.

It may sound strange to think of a colonizer as traumatized by his actions. First of all, given Judith Lewis Herman's well-known definition of trauma as resulting primarily from powerlessness confronting atrocity (33), how can the colonial oppression epitomized by Peter's attempt to force Indians to use ploughs compare with Septimus's experience of battlefield violence? One answer might be to suggest that where battlefield violence is quick and intense, oppression is long-lasting and uncomfortable. Where battlefield violence takes many lives in a short span of time, oppression also takes many lives but over a longer period, making life less fulfilling and ultimately reducing the lifespan (Brock-Utne 8). In this sense, oppression shares many of the qualities of torture and can be considered a kind of indirect violence. Therefore, it would seem likely that exposure to oppression might also cause psychological trauma.

Even though we might admit that trauma can result from oppressive circumstances, why would we expect Peter, the person with power in the colonial situation, to experience trauma? While it may seem unlikely to propose that perpetrators of violence can experience trauma, Herman provides one reason why this might occur. She writes, "The violation of human connection, and consequently the risk of a post-traumatic disorder, is highest of all when the survivor has been not merely a passive witness but also an active participant in violent death or atrocity" (54). Thus, someone who may not technically be a victim of the violence enacted can become a psychological victim both as a witness to violence and from a sense of guilt in participating in it.

So, we might assume from the above discussion that Peter's and Septimus's experiences abroad have caused their trauma. However, one aspect Herman has omitted from her discussion of trauma is cultural context. I would argue the fact that men living under patriarchy are expected to be brave in battle affects their psychological reaction to battlefield terror. Rather than scrapping patriarchal myths, terrified soldiers feel they have betrayed their own masculinity, a feeling that heightens the trauma they experience. A similar argument might be made for the expectations of British imperialists to dominate almost by birthright. Any failure of power triggers feelings of inadequacy that make the colonial experience more complex. In this way, patriarchal culture contributes to trauma.

The argument for trauma as at least partially resulting from culture is further demonstrated by the similarities between Peter's psychological disorder and Septimus's shell-shock. In particular, the colonizer's neurosis, characterized by a lack of sociability and a need for domination, closely resembles Herman's description of the effects of trauma. She writes, "Trauma impels people both to withdraw from close relationships and to seek them desperately" (57). This paradoxical behavior also characterizes the need for and fear of intimacy associated with masculine domination that causes an oscillating, interrelated cycle of insecurity and aggression. Such resemblance links imperialism and trauma.

We can see this "dialectic of trauma," to use Herman's term (47), in Septimus. Septimus's dialectic of trauma is characterized by, on the one hand, misanthropic paranoia, the sense of others including Holmes threatening him (*MD* 66), and, on the other hand, the desire to dominate evinced in a sense of awesome power where he becomes "the lord of men" to whom truth is now to be given (*MD* 67). This dialectic mirrors Peter's rebounding from failure to love. Septimus's relationship with his wife also resembles Peter's relationships with women: Septimus marries Rezia on the spur of the moment to escape the panic he feels about not feeling (*MD* 86), and yet he cannot bring himself to love her. He thinks, "Love between man and woman was repulsive to Shakespeare" (*MD* 89). Like Peter, Septimus desperately needs intimacy, but real intimacy represents too great a risk. The urge to dominate compels the need for others, while paradoxically the misanthropy propels the hasty escape from real relationships.

The fact that both men share similar proclivities in sexual relationships, and that these proclivities participate in the dialectic shared by imperialism and trauma, suggests that this dialectic may be context-specific. Part of Septimus's problem is cultural: his distress is infused with patriarchal issues of power. For example, although Septimus's dialectic of trauma may seem to result from guilt over *success*—he survived while buddies like Evans were killed (*MD* 86)—this success itself represents a *failure* of masculine myths of power, the assumption that success derives logically from manliness. What Septimus discovers when he volunteers "to save an England which consisted almost entirely of Shakespeare's plays and Miss Isabel Pole in a green dress walking in a square" is that the "manliness" that he initially believes results in his own promotion and the affection of Evans cannot guarantee his friend's life (*MD* 86). Rather, death in war is indiscriminate, a matter not of manliness, "the letters of a legend written round the based of a statue praising duty, gratitude, fidelity, love of England" (*MD* 51), but of luck. The shock of this realization, of the loss of patriarchal myths, combined with the violence witnessed, causes Septimus's trauma.

This loss of myths also undergirds the reason he lives, like Peter, primarily in fantasy. Both men's fantasies relate to issues of control, control both promised and withheld by patriarchal institutions. If these men cannot have the complete control over their own lives promised to men under a patriarchal system, they will create themselves as powerful by keeping step with boy soldiers (*MD* 51), preferring fantasy women to real ones, or by throwing themselves "on to Mrs. Filmer's area railings" (*MD* 149). Such illusory displays of power repeatedly fail to satisfy the patriarchal need to establish dominance, resulting ultimately in at least spiritual annihilation.

Although Peter, unlike Septimus, survives his fantasies, he *is* the man in Regent's Park whom Septimus mistakes for Evans, "the dead man in the grey suit" (*MD* 70). Peter is doomed to a living death caught between misanthropy and need for intimacy. He desperately needs love and yet cannot allow himself to be vulnerable. He is as numb as Septimus who marries to assuage his numbness and then cannot see love as anything but repulsive (*MD* 89). Thus, the lies of empire victimize not only the colonized but also the colonizers. These lies are rooted in English society itself.

III.

By way of conclusion, I would like to speculate about the parallel I've drawn between the colonizer mentality and trauma. It seems to me that patriarchy lays the foundation for masculine trauma in a particular way: the myths associated with masculinity, by their unachievable nature, set men up for failure. This failure causes anxiety, which perpetuates the patriarchal system. In other words, by promising but never delivering the ideal masculine domination, patriarchy dooms men to attempt and fail to achieve that ideal and to hide that failure in further attempts. Anxiety about such failure causes a greater investment in the myths, thus perpetuating the insecurity that keeps participants from seeing their Sisyphus-like place in the system. Even when the voyage home provides perspective from which to view these myths, the myths themselves are too strong for men like Peter and Septimus to jettison. This constant anxiety exacerbates the trauma associated with any moment where the myth itself might be perceived as such. And, if the individual cannot ultimately reject the myth, the myth can deaden or kill him. Thus, in a Foucauldian way, patriarchy hides the mechanisms of its power (Foucault 86), threatening even those who seem to have power in the system and rendering them blind to the source of their victimization.

In providing these two developed male characters, Peter and Septimus, as counterparts to the survivor Clarissa Dalloway, Woolf encourages us to recognize the deadly role masculine trauma plays in maintaining the patriarchal, imperialist status quo.

Works Cited

Brock-Utne, Birgit. *Feminist Perspectives on Peace and Peace Education*. New York: Pergamon P, 1989.
Fanon, Frantz. *Black Skin, White Masks*. Trans. Charles Lam Markmann. New York: Grove P, 1967.
Foucault, Michel. *The History of Sexuality: An Introduction*, vol. 1. Trans. Robert Hurley. New York: Random House, 1978.
Hawthorne, Jeremy. *Virginia Woolf's Mrs Dalloway: A Study in Alienation*. London: Sussex UP, 1975.
Herman, Judith Lewis. *Trauma and Recovery*. US: BasicBooks, 1992.
Mannoni, O. *Prospero and Caliban: The Psychology of Colonization*. Trans. Pamela Powesland. London: Methuen, 1956.
Phillips, Kathy J. *Virginia Woolf against Empire*. Knoxville: U of Tennessee P, 1994.
Scarry, Elaine. *The Body in Pain: The Making and Unmaking of the World*. New York: Oxford UP, 1985.
Woolf, Virginia. *Between the Acts*. San Diego: HBJ, 1941.
———. *Mrs. Dalloway*. San Diego: HBJ, 1925.

LEONARD WOOLF AS AN ARCHITECT OF THE LEAGUE OF NATIONS

by Janet M. Manson

I will demonstrate in this study that it is not really possible to examine one member of Bloomsbury without exploring his or her work with fellow members. This is especially true of Leonard S. Woolf and his political and literary activities in relation to the League of Nations. Even before prominent Fabian Socialists Sidney and Beatrice Webb recruited Leonard in late 1914 to early 1915 to write a report on international government for the Labour Party, he had put his talents as a political writer and liberal activist to good use working alongside Margaret Llewelyn Davies in the Women's Cooperative Guild (L. Woolf, Letters 384; see also Wilson 62-3; Winkler, The League, 7). As Sybil Oldfield points out in her essay on Woolf and Llewelyn Davies in Women in the Milieu of Leonard and Virginia Woolf, Leonard favorably impressed the Webbs with an article for the Guild about the working conditions of female mill workers that appeared in The New Statesman in 1913. Indeed, Llewelyn Davies not only became an important mentor to Leonard by introducing him to important Labour Party leaders such as Keir Hardie and Ramsay MacDonald, but she also cared for both Woolfs during Virginia's first breakdown after their marriage (see especially Oldfield 5-6; see also Wilson 50-54).

Leonard notes in *Beginning Again* (*BA*) that the Webbs also liked another piece that he wrote for the *Manchester Guardian* in 1913. They "thought as well of [him] as they had thought of [his] article [on the Newcastle Congress of the Women's Guild] and they got [him] to join the Fabian Society" in early 1913. He says that "this led...to [his] doing work for the Fabians and for the *New Statesman...*" (*BA* 114). As Leonard observes in retrospect, his work on the causes of World War I and ways to prevent future war began with a report for the Fabians. He says: "What started me on this was that in 1915 Sidney Webb asked me whether I would undertake a research into this vast question for the Fabian Society and write a report on it, which might or might not be published as a book" (*BA* 183). Despite the advice of friends, including John Maynard Keynes, who thought that the project was pointless, Leonard agreed to write the report in conformity with Fabian Society procedure which required that it be submitted to a committee for review (*BA* 184). Thus, Woolf began his work for the Fabian Society Research Bureau and its organ the *New Statesman*, which was created under the auspices of the Webbs and George Bernard Shaw in 1912-13 (Wilson 58, 62; Pugh 126-70). Sidney Webb oversaw the project as committee chair, and G. B. Shaw, who was the chairman of the Research Department, John C. Squire, and others served as committee members (*BA* 184; L. Woolf, Letters 384-5). However, Leonard was assured that "the committee would be a mere formality; [he] should be completely free to proceed in [his] own way, say exactly what [he] liked, and, if the book were published, it would be over [his] name" (*BA* 184). Moreover, the Fabians agreed to pay Leonard £100 for his work—a sum donated for the study by the Quaker Joseph Rowntree at the request of Beatrice Webb (Wilson 62; Pugh 129). It's obvious from Duncan Wilson's account of Woolf's work on the report that the Fabian committee members, especially the Webbs, took their work very seriously, too (especially 60-3). Sidney Webb shared his views with Woolf in several letters (Wilson 63 n10). Woolf recalled that he "worked like a fanatical or dedicated mole" on the report (*BA* 185); these efforts were rewarded with the committee's acceptance of the first draft in April 1915 (Wilson 63).

Indeed, the Research Department's satisfaction with the report was such that in May it hosted a conference to examine an international judicial system based on Woolf's blueprint. Among the numerous attendees were leaders in the new league of nations movement such as Leonard's Cambridge University mentor G. Lowes Dickinson, John A. Hobson, E. Richard Cross (a Quaker and business manager for the *Nation*), and Raymond Unwin. Woolf apparently drew on conference discussions to revise his first report for the Fabian Society entitled "An International Authority and the Prevention of War" (Winker, *The League* 7-8). He then collaborated with Sidney Webb in writing another commissioned report for the Fabians, a draft treaty designed to prevent war (Chapman, "L's Dame" 36). As was the case with many projects from the Fabian Society Research Department, these reports were destined to become Special Supplements of the *New Statesman,* and they were published as such by about mid July 1915 (Cole 157; Chapman 36). According to Henry Winkler, G. B. Shaw edited the supplements (*The League* 8). After minor revisions, both reports were transformed into parts I and III of Woolf's book *International Government* (*IG*) which was published by the Fabians in 1916. Part II of the book covered a wide range of international issues including health, labor, and commerce. Indeed, Virginia assisted with the project by gathering material on labor and commerce (Chapman 36).

When on July 23, 1915, Clifford Sharp, the editor of the *New Statesman* contacted Woolf to request that he write an article on foreign affairs for the journal, Woolf realized that this meant that he had become recognized as an authority on the subject, which was, in fact, the case (*BA* 186. See also Pugh 126-7). *International Government* emphasized the importance of cooperation within the international community to prevent war—a fundamental goal of human society since antiquity. Woolf's proposal for international government used the long-established history of cooperation within the international community, especially in matters of trade and finance, to make the point that this tradition could not be preserved unless nation states adopted an international collective security organization to deal with rogue states that use force as an instrument of foreign policy and thereby threaten world peace (*IG* 82-3). This organization would maintain international peace, in part, by referring all justiciable disputes to an international court of justice that would have the authority to enforce its decisions through a range of penalties including economic and political sanctions and, as a last resort, the use of military force by member states against a "recalcitrant state." It's clear that Woolf intended the court to have far-reaching powers because a majority of member states could refer cases to the court, and it would decide the scope of its own jurisdiction (*IG* 247-50, 53-55). As an extensive proposal for an international collective security organization, *International Government* was the first work of this kind to be widely read and to receive the close attention of the British Foreign Office (Egerton 16; Winkler, *The League* 14-15). Woolf was surprised to learn that Fabian Research Department Chairman G. B. Shaw, on his own initiative, had written a preface for the American edition of the book. Leonard wanted to establish himself as a political writer without being cast in the shadow of Shaw's literary reputation, so the book was published in England without the preface. Still, Shaw not only had his American publisher, Brentano, print this edition with his preface, praising Woolf's work, but Shaw even paid for some of the production expenses. Because of its importance at the time, *International Government* quickly appeared in French and German editions, too (*BA* 123; Chapman 36).

Also in early 1915, Leonard worked with G. Lowes Dickinson, John A. Hobson, Willoughby H. Dickinson, Raymond Unwin, and H. N. Brailsford to establish the League of Nations Society in order to publicize the importance and need for a League (*BA* 190-91). An early proponent of the League of Nations, Lowes Dickinson possibly gave the organization its name (Forster 163-4; Winkler, *The League* 16). League of Nations Society members included pacifists Lowes Dickinson, Woolf, Hobson, W. H. Dickinson, and H. G. Wells, as well as Lord Shaw of Dunfermline (Thomas Shaw, a lawyer who served in various judicial appointments, including appointments in the House of Lords and the Privy Council). Indeed, pacifism was such an important element in the Liberal Party when the war broke out that it split Prime Minister Herbert Asquith's coalition government to the point where radical Liberals, particularly Arthur Ponsonby and Edmund Dene Morel (the editor of *Foreign Affairs*), took the lead in establishing the Union of Democratic Control (UDC) alongside Norman Angell (the intellectual nucleus of *War and Peace* which promoted the UDC agenda). Labour Party members Ramsay MacDonald and Sir Charles Trevelyn, Hobson (a pacifist) and Brailsford (an International Labour Party member) were other founding members of the UDC (Wilson 58, 160; Egerton 5, 53; Winkler, *The League* 23). Thus, UDC founders were primarily Liberals and Labourites. Woolf's political activism also included membership in the UDC, which adopted a peace program that provided for a post-war collective security organization to maintain peace and boundary settlements determined by popular sovereignty. Although the UDC never did gain broad support for its objectives through its public education campaign, its members helped lay the ground work for subsequent peace proposals that provided for a league of nations (Egerton 6-7; Winkler, "Emergence" 249; Winkler, "Development" 106). Shortly after he joined the UDC, Lowes Dickinson decided to build broad support for a league by forming a study group that not only included UDC members such as Ponsonby and Hobson, but others including educators, journalists, and politicians, most notably the well-known diplomat, Lord James Bryce. And thus, the group became the Bryce Group in order to lend prestige to the cause (Egerton 8; Winkler, *The League* 16). Lowes Dickinson, the most active member of the group, conferred frequently with his good friend Leonard Woolf on issues discussed by its members, and so this information proved useful to him as he drew his own league blueprint (Wilson 82-83).

As a member of these various organizations, particularly the Fabian Society and the League of Nations Society, which promoted the league concept, Woolf participated in crucial discussions and conferences with intellectual and political leaders to hammer out what became the British position on the League of Nations. Leonard reports that he served on the executive committee of the League of Nations Society with the other founding members (*BA* 191). He also corresponded with Theodore Marburg, a member of the League to Enforce Peace, the American counterpart of the League of Nations Society.[1] Both organizations were particularly effective pressure groups because they successfully impressed their agenda on their respective governments. And the organizations consulted and conferred with one another to coordinate their proposals at critical points (Manson, "League of Nations" 52). (LEP members included Hamilton Holt, William Short,

Marburg, former president William Taft, and professors Theodore Woolsey, and George Grafton Wilson.)

Undoubtedly, Leonard's close friendship with key officials in the British Foreign Office brought his book, *International Government,* to the attention of the Undersecretary of Foreign Affairs during the war, Robert Cecil, who was a close friend of the Stephen family; Virginia affectionately dubs him "Lord Bob" in her letters *(L6* 87). Not only were Lord Bob and his wife, Nelly, close friends of the Woolfs, but Cecil's close associates, his long-time friend Philip Noel-Baker, who served on Cecil's secretarial staff at the Versailles peace conference in 1919, and Sydney Waterlow who worked for the Foreign Office and their wives were also friends of the Woolfs (Cecil 66, 105; V. Woolf, *D1* 6; L. Woolf, *Letters* 281). In *Beginning Again,* Leonard notes how Waterlow "discovered" *International Government:*

> The two reports which I had written and our draft treaty were published by me in a book, *International Government,* in 1916. It had, I think, some effect; it was used extensively by the government committee which produced the British proposals for a League of Nations laid before the Peace Conference, and also by the British delegation to the Versailles Conference. My authority for this statement comes from Sir Sydney Waterlow, Philip Noel-Baker, who was secretary, and Lord Cecil, who was head of the League of Nations Section of the British Delegation. Sydney Waterlow was in the Foreign Office and in 1918 he was instructed to draw up a confidential paper on "International Government under the League of Nations" for use by the British Delegation at Versailles. He gave me a copy. In the prefatory note he said: "The facts contained in Part I are taken almost entirely from 'International Government', by L. S. Woolf (1916). Where a mass of facts has been collected and sifted with great ability, as is the case with Mr. Woolf's work, it would be folly to attempt to do the work over again, especially as time presses. My detailed descriptions of the various existing organs of international government are therefore for the most part lifted almost verbatim—with slight abridgements, from Mr. Woolf's book. (188-89)

Waterlow's Prefatory Note and his condensation of some of the main points of *International Government* are in the Leonard Woolf Papers at the University of Sussex Library. Waterlow's confidential paper primarily outlines the League structure as set forth by Woolf in his book. In a special obituary for Woolf that was published in the London *Times,* Philip Noel-Baker pays special tribute to his friend's contribution to the birth of the League and corroborates Waterlow's account of events:

> Waterlow's enthusiasm [for *International Government*] was aroused; he condensed the book into a brilliant F.O. "print," laying emphasis on Woolf's vision of the scope for international cooperation over labour conditions, public health, transport, economic and social policy, etc. Lord (Robert) Cecil, the head of the section, was deeply impressed by the "print", and incorporated virtually the whole of Woolf's ideas into the British Draft Covenant which he gave to [American president] Woodrow Wilson in Paris. Woolf thus played an impor-

tant part in giving concrete form to the general ideas about a League. (21 August 1969, 8 f)

Noel-Baker also mentions the influence that Woolf's work had on the formation of the United Nations and its agencies (*Times,* 21 August 1969, 8 f). Of course, Noel-Baker knew that the United Nations was modeled after the League and that Woolf supported the creation of that organization, as well.

Thus, Leonard's early political activities with Margaret Llewelyn Davies and with Sidney and Beatrice Webb drew him into work that ultimately led him into Labour Party politics; this is particularly true of his role in the creation of the League of Nations and a new world order after World War I. Woolf acknowledges that his entry to Labour Party politics resulted, in part, from an invitation, in the latter years of World War I, to join the editorial board of Norman Angell's monthly magazine *War and Peace* (*BA* 223-26; Chapman and Manson, "Carte and Tierce" 64). Woolf also joined forces with Lowes Dickinson and others to establish the League of Nations Union, an influential organization formed across party lines in 1918; Robert Cecil became the chairman of the organization (Forster 168-70; Cecil 104; Egerton 90-92). And when the Seven Universities Democratic Association invited Leonard to represent that constituency in the parliamentary elections of 1918-22, he agreed to do so once Sidney Webb assured him of Labour Party support (Wilson 129-30; L. Woolf, *Downhill* 34-36; V. Woolf, *L2* 435). (Leonard was also pleased that his candidacy was sure to annoy the incumbent Herbert [H.A.L.] Fisher, a first cousin of Virginia's who did not put his Liberal principles into practice in his role as M.P.). At this point, Leonard began his twenty-year tenure as the secretary of the Labour Party Advisory Committee on International Questions, a key position that assured that he would continue to be an important force in shaping Labour Party foreign policy in the postwar world (Spotts chronology in L. Woolf, *Letters*; Winkler, "Emergence" 248).

Note

1   Theodore Marburg to Leonard S. Woolf, 28 September 1917. Marburg requested that the Fabians critique an enclosed 13 page document on proposals for a league of nations. University of Sussex Library, Manuscript Section, Leonard Woolf Papers, I.F.4. The Woolf Papers contain a couple of letters detailing some aspects of Marburg's correspondence with Woolf on a league proposal.

Works Cited

Cecil, Robert. *A Great Experiment: An Autobiography*. New York: Oxford University Press, 1941.
Chapman, Wayne K. and Janet M. Manson. "Carte and Tierce: Leonard, Virginia and War for Peace," *Virginia Woolf and War: Fiction, Reality, and Myth*. Ed. Mark Hussey. New York: Syracuse UP, 1991. 58-78.
Chapman, Wayne K. "L's Dame Secretaire: Alix Strachey, the Hogarth Press and Bloomsbury Pacifism, 1917-1960." *Women in the Milieu of Leonard and Virginia Woolf: Peace, Politics, and Education*. Eds. Wayne K. Chapman and Janet M. Manson. New York: Pace UP, 1998. 33-57.
Cole, Margaret. *The Story of Fabian Socialism*. London: Heinemann Educational Books, Ltd., 1961.
Egerton, George W. *Great Britain and the Creation of the League of Nations: Strategy, Politics, and International Organization, 1914-1919*. Chapel Hill: U North Carolina P, 1978.
Forster, E. M. *Goldsworthy Lowes Dickinson*. 1934; reprint, New York: Harcourt Brace Jovanovich, Inc., 1973.
Manson, Janet M. "League of Nations." *The Encyclopedia of U.S. Foreign Relations*. Eds. Bruce W. Jentleson and Thomas G. Paterson. 4 vols. New York and Oxford: Oxford University Press, 1997. 3: 51-54.
Marburg, Theodore. Letter to Leonard S.Woolf. 28 September 1917. University of Sussex Library, Manuscript

Section, Leonard Woolf Papers, I.F.4.

Noel-Baker, Philip. "Mr. Leonard Woolf: Vision of International Cooperation." *London Times*. 21 August 1969: 8f.

Oldfield, Sybil. "Margaret Llewelyn Davies and Leonard Woolf." *Women in the Milieu of Leonard and Virginia Woolf: Peace, Politics, and Education*. Eds. Wayne K. Chapman and Janet M. Manson. New York: Pace UP, 1998. 3-32.

Pugh, Patricia. *Educate, Agitate, Organize: 100 Years of Fabian Socialism*. 1984; reprint, London: Methuen & Co. Limited, 1987.

Wilson, Duncan. *Leonard Woolf: A Political Biography*. New York: St. Martin's P, 1978.

Winkler, Henry R. "The Development of the League of Nations Idea in Great Britain, 1914-1919." *The Journal of Modern History* 20 (June 1948): 95-112.

———. "The Emergence of a Labor Foreign Policy in Great Britain, 1918-1929," *The Journal of Modern History* 28 (1956): 247-58.

———. *The League of Nations Movement in Great Britain*. 1952; reprint, New Jersey: Scarecrow Reprint Corporation, 1967.

Woolf, Leonard. *Beginning Again: An Autobiography of the Years 1911-1918*. 1964; reprint, London: The Hogarth Press, 1972.

———. *Downhill All the Way: An Autobiography of the Years 1919 to 1939*. London: The Hogarth Press, 1970.

———. *International Government: Two Reports by L. S. Woolf Prepared for the Fabian Research Department, Together with a Project by a Fabian Committee for a Supernational Authority That Will Prevent War*. London: The Fabian Society and George Allen and Unwin, Limited, 1916.

———. *Letters of Leonard Woolf*. Ed. Frederic Spotts. New York and London: Harcourt Brace Jovanovich, 1989.

Woolf, Virginia. *The Diary of Virginia Woolf*. ed. Anne Olivier Bell. Vol.1, *1915-1919*. New York: Harcourt Brace Jovanovich, 1979.

———. *The Letters of Virginia Woolf*. Eds. Nigel Nicolson and Joanne Trautmann. Vol. 2, *1912-1922*. New York: Harcourt Brace Jovanovich, 1976. Vol. 6, *1936-1941*. New York: Harcourt Brace Jovanovich, 1980.

From the Beginning:
Virginia Stephen's Reading and Virginia Woolf's Essays

by Beth Rigel Daugherty

In the note Virginia Stephen wrote for Frederic Maitland's biography of her father, she says that when the Stephen children were old enough, Leslie spent an hour and a half each evening "reading aloud to us. I cannot remember any book before *Tom Brown's School Days* and *Treasure Island*" (*E1* 127-28). Eight years earlier, in her 1897 journal, she writes on January 5th, "Got up at half past 10, and stayed in and read the whole morning. [...] Finished vol I of Three Generations of English Women, and began vol 2," and on January 7th, she continues, "Finished Three Generations of English Women, and began Froudes Life of Carlyle" (*PA* 6-7, 8). These two volumes, then, were an example of the behavior that led Leslie Stephen to exclaim, "Gracious child, how you gobble!" (*L4* 27; 19 Feb. 1929).

Thomas Hughes' *Tom Brown's School Days* and Janet Ross' *Three Generations of English Women* are recorded rather than actual "firsts": the first book Virginia Stephen *remembers* hearing in her father's voice and the first book she mentions in the first diary of hers that we *have*. Leslie Stephen probably read other books to his children before *Tom Brown's School Days*, and we know Virginia was reading widely before her 15th year and her experience with *Three Generations of English Women*. These books are questionable "firsts," then, and even if genuine, the idea that as origins, they might possess some transcendent value, is problematic. Furthermore, they are books mentioned in passing, on the periphery. Woolf never mentions these texts again—indeed, when she meets Janet Ross in 1909, she does not much like her and does not recall, at least in her journal, reading *Three Generations of English Women* (*PA* 397-98)—and she certainly never claims any influence. Nevertheless, I would argue that traces of these texts exist in her work as an essayist and that these traces of Virginia Stephen's reading in Virginia Woolf's essays reflect her uneasy and ambivalent relationship to Leslie Stephen's library in all her work: she both voyages out from his library and never leaves it, both creates a new literary history and uses the old, both transforms her early reading and internalizes it.

Of these two texts, you are probably more familiar with *Tom Brown's School Days* by Thomas Hughes. Its portrayal of a boy's life in public school is still part of our culture; its "villain," Flashman, is still alive in the historical fiction of George MacDonald Fraser, for example. But George J. Worth, writing in 1984, notes that Hughes's work has disappeared from view and that "Even the present status of *Tom Brown's School Days* is questionable" (121). It may be more known about than read. On the other hand, it was re-issued in the Oxford World's Classics series in 1989, and Andrew Sanders notes that it has never been out of print since its first publication in 1857. In its day, it was immensely popular and influential, and Hughes is still credited with creating a new form, "the public-school novel" (Worth 25).

The novel tells the story of a young boy who leaves the Vale of the White Horse in Berkshire to go to first, a private preparatory school, and then to Rugby in the 1830s, when Thomas Arnold was reforming it. As Sanders points out, the "spirit of Arnold pervades the book, but its effect is felt through the experiences of an average boy, not an extraordinary one" (Sanders viii). Tom represents the common English boy, not the intellectual or cultural elite, but Arnold's system, according to Sanders, was geared to exactly that kind of boy, aspiring "to transform the dull boy into the responsive one, and, moreover, to mould that responsive boy into the responsible adult" (ix). However, readers expecting a sappy hymn to "the virtues of respectability" that Lytton Strachey attacked Arnold for in *Eminent Victorians*, will discover a more complex, even surprising, text. The squire, Tom's father, hates the separation of the classes and is delighted his son plays with the village boys; the loving description of the Vale of the White Horse would satisfy a contemporary environmentalist; and the account of the school's system does not ignore the abuses possible within it. The reader *does* get caught up in the tale and *wants* Tom Brown to learn how to give to others, to save his soul, to become a good man; furthermore, the reader learns a great deal about "muscular" Christianity, class relationships, schoolboy games, and the schoolboy code along the way. Although readers are fairly certain Tom will win his struggle against the forces of evil, he could easily go in either direction until the wise school master intervenes: he asks Tom to be the mentor for a younger boy, one with more intellectual gifts and more integrity. Thus, the novel describes an ordinary boy's social and moral education—intellectual growth, though not totally ignored, is not emphasized (in fact, Matthew Arnold was horrified by this portrayal of his father's work [Worth 26]). Tom learns the schoolboy code (do not tell on anyone), courage (life is a struggle, and one must be willing to fight when necessary), honesty (pass tests without cribs), and Christian values (protect the weak).

It's ironic to think of Leslie Stephen, the agnostic who hated his public school days, reading a novel that extols a public school committed to developing the manly Christian virtues; Squire Brown wants Tom's education to turn him into "a brave, helpful, truth-telling Englishman, and a gentleman, and a Christian" (Hughes I, 4: 35). But Thomas Hughes, though ten years older than Leslie Stephen, shared with Stephen a friendship with James Russell Lowell and public support of the North in the Civil War. He was also a Christian Socialist who worked with the working classes all his life and helped found the Society for Promoting Working Men's Associations, the Central Cooperative Agency, the London Emancipation Society, and the London Working Men's College. Hughes was principal of the college from 1872-83, and he represented from 1865-74 the working class London constituency of Lambeth, where Virginia Stephen would teach at Morley College in 1905-07.

In Virginia Stephen's memory, Leslie Stephen quickly moved from reading aloud *Tom Brown's School Days* to "that long line of red backs"—the Waverley Novels, "which provided reading for many years of evenings" (*E1* 127-28). Although *Tom Brown's School Days* would surely have been considered a boy's book—perhaps Leslie read *Tom Brown* to prepare Thoby for school?—his choice of reading material for his children suggests girls and boys can read and appreciate the same texts. Similarly, Sir Walter Scott's novels would not have been considered children's books, so Leslie's choice suggests he also saw no distinction between child and adult when it came to reading. Most important, however,

Virginia Stephen's memory of hearing *Tom Brown's School Days* in her father's voice suggests that this text, not Thoby, first introduced Virginia to boys' education in England.

As I note elsewhere, Woolf's comments about male education contain both resentment and relief at being denied it ("Learning" 12-13; "Educational Inheritance" 9-11). What angered her most was the isolated nature of her "schooling"; she writes that her "education (alone among books) was a very bad one" (*L6* 420), she resents having to "delve from books, painfully and all alone" what Thoby and his friends got in the evenings in front of the fire (*L1* 77), and she agrees with Vita that she lacks "jolly vulgarity. But then think how I was brought up! No school; mooning about alone among my father's books; never any chance to pick up all that goes on in schools—throwing balls; ragging; slang; vulgarity; scenes; jealousies" (*L3* 247). Her list of what "goes on in schools" could have come straight from *Tom Brown's School Days*. Listening to her father read, Virginia Stephen surely noticed the camaraderie of the boys, the joys of late night conversation and food, and the tests of character Tom had to face and pass within the context of support and friendship. I certainly did.

For Woolf, then, *Tom Brown's School Days* may have represented some of the advantages she resented losing because of "Arthur's Education Fund." (Interestingly, the boy Tom Brown mentors is called Arthur.) On the other hand, Hughes's novel may have fed some of her later relief at not having been "stamped and moulded" by the English educational establishment. The novel certainly reveals the nasty side of that "great patriarchal machine" ("Sketch" 153). Though not as brutal as the memories detailed in Woolf's *Roger Fry* or as cruel as those detailed in George Orwell's "Such, such were the joys," the description of Tom Brown's school days includes his introduction to the rigid hierarchy of power. He receives quite an education in bullying, fagging that becomes hazing, and gleeful fighting; indeed, Hughes gives "little sermons in praise of fighting" (Worth 27). Thus, *Tom Brown's School Days* may be one of the texts lying behind *Three Guineas*.

Hughes's novel may also have contributed to Woolf's other nonfiction. Sanders notes that Hughes was following Thackeray in taking "the name Brown as representative of an ordinary Englishman" (381). Is Woolf's choice of Mrs. Brown as a representative English woman a feminist response to Hughes's opening tribute to the Browns, generations of sturdy, typical English men? It's also startling to read Tom's response to learning he will have a study: "was he not about to become the joint owner of a [...] home, the first place he could call his own? One's own," he continues, "what a charm there is in the words!" (Hughes I, 5:41). Does Hughes's description of public school boys routinely using cribs to prepare their Greek and Latin exercises give *her* permission to use anything at her disposal in her own lessons and then to pass on that permission to the working class people who listened to her "Leaning Tower" lecture? Does Hughes's critique of the class system contribute to Woolf's later perception in "Memories of a Working Women's Guild" that being locked in is as bad as being locked out? Finally, does this novel, in which women are almost entirely absent, start Virginia Stephen/Woolf on her voyage toward the British Museum, Professor Trevelyan's *History of England*, and her conclusion that women are "all but absent from history" (*AROO* 43)?

Was *Tom Brown's School Days* also the reason the almost fifteen-year-old Virginia Stephen read the two volumes of *Three Generations of English Women* so avidly? Even more on the margins for us than *Tom Brown's School Days*, this book has long been out of print, and although sometimes mentioned in accounts of Virginia Stephen's education, is not, as far as I can tell, looked at or read. No matter how carefully I turned the pages of the fragile copy I got through Interlibrary Loan, I could not prevent little page corner triangles from breaking off. We know, however, that this book *did* journey from Leslie Stephen's library to Virginia Woolf's and then from house to house (King and Miletic-Vejzovic, eds. 190), and I suspect it's the more influential of these two texts. Partly because Virginia Stephen read it *herself* and read it as an adolescent, but mainly because it reverses the emphasis in *Tom Brown's School Days*—*Three Generations of English Women* focuses on women, including the education of girls, and men are in the background.

The title seems to promise a general history of English women over three generations (DeSalvo 88), but in fact, it traces a *family* history through the lives of three particular women, heightening the reader's awareness of how individual histories become lost to "history." Janet Ross, the fourth generation, writes about her own great-grandmother, grandmother, and mother: Susannah Taylor, Sarah Austin, and Lucie Duff-Gordon. These three women *are* among the chosen few in Leslie Stephen's *DNB*, with Susannah under her husband John's entry, and Sarah and Lucie with entries of their own, so presumably, when the book was published in 1888, readers would have known who they were. The subtitle of the book, *Memoirs and Correspondence of Mrs. John Taylor, Mrs. Sarah Austin, and Lady Duff Gordon*, reveals Ross's sources and method. Providing little narrative, she relies heavily on journals, memoir sketches, and letters to and from the women to construct this biography of her matrilineal heritage, to quite literally "think back through [her] mothers" (*AROO* 76).

What an inspiration this book must have been for the young Virginia who had grown up under the traditional Julia Stephen's tutelage, who had watched her mother play the "Angel in the House," who must have been seeking, even if unconsciously, new role models now that her mother had been dead for over a year-and-a-half. Three women educated mainly at home, teaching their daughters Latin and various other languages, and focused on the life of the mind. Three women with somewhat unconventional lives, strong political views, and families they considered important but not all-consuming. Three generations of independent thinkers and brilliant conversationalists. Three generations of readers and writers. Two generations of *professional* writers, making money from translations, book reviews, travel narratives and letters, and various other kinds of non-fiction. These volumes must have opened Virginia Stephen's eyes to the possibilities—for a woman's life, for a *self-educated* woman's life, for a *professional* woman's life in letters.

Susannah Cook Taylor, 1755-1823, was "not ashamed of being poor," "found time to read and appreciate poetry, and to think for herself," and was "a handsome and gifted woman, whose energetic character and liberal opinions, joined with great kindness of heart made her a centre of the circle of remarkable people who frequented the provincial Athens [Norwich]. She possessed the pen of a ready writer [...]," writes Ross (1: iii, 4). According to the *DNB*, she was a lady of much force of character [who] shared the liberal opinions of her husband, and is said to have danced 'round the tree of liberty at Norwich on the receipt of news of the taking of the Bastille'" (444). Imagine Virginia Stephen reading this excerpt from a letter Susannah Taylor wrote to Henry Reeve, who later marries the Susan mentioned here: "Nothing at present suits my taste so well as Susan's Latin lessons

[. . .] When we get to Cicero's discussions on the nature of the soul, or Virgil's fine descriptions, my mind is filled up. Life is either a dull round of eating, drinking, and sleeping, or a spark of ethereal fire just kindled" (Ross, 1: 12). She writes, in 1807, "The character of girls must depend upon their reading as much as upon the company they keep. Besides the intrinsic pleasure to be derived from solid knowledge, a woman ought to consider it as her best resource against poverty" (Ross, 1: 16). Virginia, still making the rounds with Stella, must have been delighted by this comment, too: "Systematic visiting is a great consumer of time, and in general, it affords but little recompense. The art is, not to estrange oneself from society, and yet not to pay too dear for it" (Ross, 1: 21-22). After Susannah Taylor's death, Basil Montague wrote that in her, "Manly wisdom and feminine gentleness were [. . .] united" (Ross, 1: 27).

Sarah Taylor Austin, 1793-1867, received a "liberal and thorough education" from her mother: Latin, French, Italian, and German, along with the excellent conversations she heard in the house (Ross, 1: 30). Her list of books read between 1815 and 1821 (Ross, 1: 31) reminds me of the reading lists Virginia Stephen kept in *her* diary. According to Janet Ross, many diaries and letters of the time mention the spirited Sarah, including those of Sir James Stephen, Carlyle, and J. S. Mill (1: 37). She observes educational systems in other countries and then writes to Gladstone about creating a national system of education in England, criticizes the "imbecility" of the English mob in regard to the training of women (Ross 2:165), and when in Malta with her husband, breaks with British society by visiting and receiving the Maltese and working to create elementary schools for boys *and* girls. Her marriage to John Austin was difficult; he had a brilliant judicial mind but suffered from depression, so she worked prodigiously, supporting them with her pen, translating many works from the German, editing, and writing *Germany from 1760 to 1814*. According to the *DNB*, she "had a high standard of the duties of a translator" (271), and that rigor comes through in her letters. She is credited with making "the best minds of Germany familiar to Englishmen, and she left a literary reputation due as much to her conversation and wide correspondence with illustrious men of letters as to her works" (*DNB* 271). After her husband's death, she brought out a new edition of John Austin's *The Province of Jurisprudence* with an introductory memoir and then organized, transcribed, and prepared for the press "a large mass of manuscript notes of his lectures" (*DNB* 271), the *Lectures on Jurisprudence, or the Science of Positive Law*. She taught her daughter Latin, took her with them to Bonn, and sent her, for a while, to a small co-ed school. In 1831, when Lucie is 10, Sarah writes that "She seems chiefly to take to Greek, with which her father is very anxious to have her thoroughly imbued. [...] I am quite willing to forego all the feminine parts of her education for the present. The main thing is to secure her independence; both with relation to her own mind and outward circumstances" (Ross 68).

Lucie Austin Duff-Gordon, 1821-1869, is best known for her *Letters from Egypt, 1863-1865*, edited by her mother, and *Last Letters from Egypt*, edited by her daughter, but she, too, began her literary life by translating Neibuhr's *Studies of Ancient Grecian Mythology*. She rescued a boy called Hassan el Bakkeet from a life in the street (he had been turned out because he was going blind) and established him in the Duff-Gordon household at 8 Queen Square, where he became Janet's playmate. Ross writes that she "perfectly recollect[s] Mr. Hilliard, the American author, being much shocked at seeing me in Hassan's arms, and my rage at his asking how Lady Gordon could let a negro touch her child; whereupon she called us to her, and kissed me first and Hassan afterwards" (Ross 2: 196-97). Later, she established and superintended a working-man's library and reading room in East London. She opened her home in England to a circle that included Lord Lansdowne, Dickens, Thackeray, Tennyson, and Henry Taylor. She suffered from consumption, however, so she moved to Egypt for her health while her husband and children remained in London. There, she learns about English bigotry through the Egyptian gratitude for her willingness to eat in the Arab style and her interactions with them (270, 262-63). She comments on the social equality that prevails in Egypt, and notes that "The English would be a little surprised at Arab judgments of them. They admit our veracity and honesty, and like us on the whole, but they [...] are shocked at the way Englishmen talk about [women] among themselves, and think the English hard and unkind to their wives and to women in general" (257). Lucie Duff-Gordon's kindness to the sick and oppressed became legendary, so that when Janet Ross traveled to visit her on a Government steamer, she was proclaimed "the daughter of [...] the great Lady [...] who was just, and had a heart that loved the Arabs," which meant they had difficulty making people take payment for food (273).

These brief summaries cannot do justice to the richness of *Three Generations of English Women*, but in reading it, Virginia Stephen was, at the very least, introduced to three women who had lived lives of struggle against poverty, depression, and illness, but who sustained intellectual vigor, lively salons, and vital work. Their negotiation between talent and family, intellect and duty, ambition and angel, differed from her mother's. Maintaining an intellectually active writing life come hell or high water, they thus offered her an option. They also showed her, in a very practical way, what intelligent, self-educated women could do.

Besides giving her a glimpse into professional writing women's lives, however, *Three Generations of English Women* may have helped spark Woolf's lifelong interest in memoir, letters, and diaries as literary forms ("DeQuincey's Autobiography," "Dorothy Osborne's 'Letters,'" "Rambling Round Evelyn"), her concern with rescuing the lives of the obscure ("Taylors and Edgeworths," "Laetitia Pilkington," "Miss Ormerod"), her interest in acknowledging anonymous but important contributions to literature ("Anon," *A Room of One's Own*), and her critiques of English patriarchy and Empire ("Thunder at Wembley," *Three Guineas*). Could reading about these translators who tried to rid their cultural encounters of English bias have led to her own attempts in "On Not Knowing Greek" and "The Russian Point of View"? Do their struggles to establish professional writing lives begin her journey to "Professional Lives for Women"? Surely more than a thin thread connects this book to *A Room of One's Own*, to Woolf's belief that we think back through our mothers if we are women, that masterpieces grow out of an atmosphere that encourages the work of many toilers, that there's a connection between money and the freedom to write, that discovering and constructing a tradition is necessary and worthwhile.

Finally, *Tom Brown's School Days* and *Three Generations of English Women* encapsulate the tension of Virginia Woolf's educational inheritance, the tension embedded in the

Stephen household and in the debates about female education at the time: should females have access to male education, or self-educate themselves as outsiders ("Educational Inheritance")? After all, *Tom Brown's School Days*, with its assumptions about insider status, and *Three Generations of English Women*, with its hints at outsider status, *both* come from the shelves of the *insider's* library. Is it any wonder that Woolf ultimately embodies for us the simultaneous insider/outsider position? She carried traces of the books from Leslie Stephen's library with her precisely *because* they propelled her out of it.

Works Cited

Daugherty, Beth Rigel. "Learning Virginia Woolf: Of Leslie, Libraries, and Letters." *Virginia Woolf and Communities: Selected Papers from the Eighth Annual Conference on Virginia Woolf*. Eds. Laura Davis and Jeanette McVicker. New York: Pace UP, 1999. 10-17.

———. "Virginia Woolf's Educational Inheritance: The Stephen Household and 19th Century Debates about Education for Girls." *Virginia Woolf Turning the Centuries. The Ninth Annual Conference on Virginia Woolf*. Newark, DE. 13 June 2000.

DeSalvo, Louise. "1897: Virginia Woolf at Fifteen." *Virginia Woolf: A Feminist Slant*. Ed. Jane Marcus. Lincoln: U of Nebraska P, 1983. 78-108.

Hughes, Thomas. *Tom Brown's School Days. By an Old Boy*. 1857. 6th ed. New York: Harper, 1870.

———. *Tom Brown's Schooldays*. Ed. Andrew Sanders. The World's Classics. Oxford and New York: Oxford UP, 1989.

King, Julia and Laila Miletic-Vejzovic, eds. *The Library of Leonard and Virginia Woolf: A Short-title Catalog*. Pullman, WA: Washington State UP, 2003.

Ross, Janet. *Three Generations of English Women: Memoirs and Correspondence of Mrs. John Taylor, Mrs. Sarah Austin, and Lady Duff Gordon*. 2 vols. London: John Murray, 1888.

Sanders, Andrew. "Introduction." *Tom Brown's Schooldays*. By Thomas Hughes. Oxford and New York: Oxford UP, 1989. vii-xxv.

Stephen, Leslie and Sidney Lee, eds. *Dictionary of National Biography*. 63 vols. London: Smith, Elder. 1885-1901.

Woolf, Virginia. "Anon." Ed. Brenda Silver. *Twentieth Century Literature* 25 (1979): 380-424.

———. *Collected Essays*. 4 vols. Ed. Leonard Woolf. New York: Harcourt, 1967.

———. *The Common Reader*. 1925. Ed. Andrew McNeillie. San Diego: Harcourt, 1984.

———. *The Essays of Virginia Woolf*. 4 vols to date. Ed. Andrew McNeillie. San Diego: Harcourt, 1986- .

———. *The Letters of Virginia Woolf*. 6 vols. Ed. Nigel Nicolson and Joanne Trautmann Banks. New York: Harcourt, 1975-80.

———. *A Passionate Apprentice*. Ed. Mitchell Leaska. San Diego: Harcourt, 1990.

———. *A Room of One's Own*. 1929. Foreword Mary Gordon. San Diego: Harcourt, 1989.

———. *The Second Common Reader*. 1932. Ed. Andrew McNeillie. San Diego: Harcourt, 1986.

———. "A Sketch of the Past." *Moments of Being*. Ed. Jeanne Schulkind. 2nd ed. San Diego: Harcourt, 1985.

———. *Three Guineas*. New York: Harcourt, 1938.

Worth, George J. *Thomas Hughes*. English Authors Series. Boston: Twayne, 1984.

"Never See Rachel Again": Virginia Woolf and the End of Domestic Fiction

by Nick Smart

As Virginia Woolf writes and publishes *The Voyage Out* (1915) in the first years of the second decade of the Twentieth Century, she contends with the excitement and difficulty of a paradigmatic shift in the nature of the English novel. Two concurrent projects completed a decade later illustrate the hinge upon which Woolf must have been swinging as she produced *The Voyage Out*.

The Common Reader (1925) essays on Jane Austen, George Eliot and the Brontës show her keen and appreciative reading of nineteenth-century domestic fiction while "How it Strikes a Contemporary" and "Modern Fiction" intensify the conflict with Edwardian novelistic practice so famously launched in "Mr. Bennett and Mrs. Brown" (1923). Meanwhile, *Mrs. Dalloway* (1925) magnificently illustrates the modern novel's intention to privilege spiritual over material truth, an innovation of form and purpose for which she has already praised Joyce's *Portrait of the Artist as a Young Man* (1916). How to tear down the solid fabric of Edwardian fiction and yet preserve the contributions to novelistic form and feminine subjectivity of revered domesticians from Austen to Hardy is a difficulty Woolf addresses in *The Voyage Out*'s meta-narrative.

Perhaps it is not too much to frame Woolf's task in the first novel in the way that Nietzsche's Birth of Tragedy employs "the Apollonian and Dionysian duality" (33) as the dialectic that synthesizes a new form of Greek literature. *The Voyage Out* is well aware that the Apollonian impulse toward clarity and resolution is embodied in the history of the novel by the marriage plot's role in determining hierarchies of discourse (for example, the superiority of Knightley's moral judgment to Emma Woodhouse's), and the outcomes that these hierarchies make inevitable (Emma and Knightley's marriage, subsequent to her seeing the error of her ways). But Woolf's maiden voyage, forerunning the high modern experiments to come, also relies heavily on the rhythms of the Dionysian core, which are forcefully fluid, sometimes to the point of eradication, in pursuit of a truth beyond that which convention allows (so that *Mrs. Dalloway* will be much more an invocation of Clarissa's spirit than an anatomy of her marriage).

Given *The Voyage Out*'s fascination with the interaction of word and music, or image and rhythm, and the way in which this preoccupation superintends the theme of the heroine's coming of age and submission to the marriage plot, it may well be useful to apply this Hellenic interpretive model to the novel in which the protagonist, a vine of her race, is chaperoned so vigorously by a woman named Helen. Dialectic oscillation is the novel's signature movement, always present in the intoxicating or sea-sickening rocking of the waves as Rachel Vinrace, a heroine in the tradition of Emma Woodhouse or Tess Durbeyfield, figures her relation to the novel's traditional structures and thematic concerns. The tumbling to the decks of Rachel's listlessly read copies of Cowper's letters certainly signifies the struggle with literary history (and Gibbon and Milton must be dealt with too, as the novel doggedly anthologizes). To write within the tradition, even as one is taking the tradition out to sea and only slightly veiling a hope for shipwreck, requires a subscription to Apollonian legibility. Woolf is committed in *The Voyage Out* to a faithful rendering of the outlines of a readable historicity which is the novel's responsibility to itself as a form charged with the mission of recapitulating its own stages of development even as it attempts to shed its Apollonian masks in favor of a more universal Dionysian visage. With this effort, Woolf marks her closeness to Thomas Hardy in the line of English novelists.

The coupling of the Dionysian and the Apollonian in the presence of the heroine, of whose indexical relation to the novel's narrative structures Woolf is well aware, would mark a stage beyond the death of the marriage plot novel and its heroine over which Hardy grimly presides in *Tess of the D'Urbervilles* (1891) and *Jude the Obscure* (1895). Hardy's destructive innovations are fully tragic, in Nietzschean terms, and certainly contain the presence of both Apollonian domestic tradition and Dionysian narrative effulgence. Their aim, however, is to leave domestic convention in ruins, to force the novel to reform or perish. But the novel, as even Woolf learns, will not reform.

Under Hardy's watch Tess perishes, Sue Bridehead retreats into conventionality, and as a result of these sacrifices, the formal possibility of feminine narrativity created by Austen and the Brontës is lost. The novel, at the dawn of the century, has no other formula for the calling into being the heroine as the producer of her own text, and so Woolf must travel again the old Roman road of domesticity in order to refine her representations of the nature of consciousness in which women's thoughts and lives are distinct elements. She must overlay her novelistic history and Hardy's, an obligation that makes plain the need to elide the Edwardian example in favor of a less recent but more important precedent. Both ahead and behind its times, Woolf's application of domestic tradition follows the thinking of one member of *The Voyage Out's* chorus of matrons, Mrs. Thornbury, who is "still in the habit of saying Queen instead of King in the National Anthem" (264). It is the moral order of the Victorian literary world, the order that drove Hardy out of the business, with which Woolf contends.

To stage the contest, Woolf worries the familiar trope of location, taking Rachel out of a stable English domesticity and plotting her experiences shipboard and then in the Amazon, but bringing her out, in a conventional social sense, to the discursive conditions of the marriage plot within the confines of a tourist hotel. These settings, Woolf hopes, will allow Rachel to be linked to Emma or Tess, but also unlinked, a new feeling of the heroine looking for the music which might suggest its expression.

The Voyage Out establishes Rachel as a textual element to which the first response must be a pause, rather than a rush to interpretive conclusion, by delivering her to the page, for the first time since the Euphrosyne has set sail, with the blankening: "At that moment Rachel was sitting in her room doing absolutely nothing" (28). Rachel's "nothing" must be given the affirmative sense of the enabling blank of romanticism or the preimagistic field of sensation that is Dionysian art's first stage. Rachel is capable of performing nothingness because she has been raised in (to) a condition of unknowing:

> Her mind was in the state of an intelligent man's in the beginning of the reign of Queen Elizabeth; she would believe practically anything she was told, invent reasons for anything she said. The shape of the earth, the history of the world, how trains worked, or money was invested, what laws were in force, which people

wanted what, and why they wanted it, the most elementary idea of a system in modern life—none of this had been imparted to her by any of her professors or mistresses. (29)

Does this lack of preparation place Rachel beyond the call of the novel's sense of social history and the needs of her cultured suitor? If she were an Austen character we might have to worry about her eligibility for the marriage plot's prize and, therefore, to doubt whether the novel can confirm existing order and restore equilibrium at its closure. Nietzsche's Dionysian artist "has already surrendered his subjectivity in the Dionysian process" (33). Similarly, and unlike heroines with authorial surrogacy like the matchmaker Emma or the narrator Jane Eyre, Rachel's relationship to textuality is unformed. Her books are a "mess" on the floor (28), and her only cultural-textual talent is an overdeveloped knowledge and love of music. Sealed by this musical membrane, Rachel is able to harbor the signs of decadent, generative, subjectivity so that "If this one definite gift was surrounded by dreams and ideas of the most extravagant and foolish description, no one was any the wiser" (30).

Inducing in her readers, then, a reflexive state of unknowing, Rachel is more sensuous and aesthetically magnified than any heroine before her. Her "extravagance" would be in Hardy's heroines a symptom of a criminal lack of social fitness, and even in the Brontës' women suggest a need for either discipline or death. Of course, this will be Rachel's fate as well, but not yet. The heroine Woolf can not quite figure, can not quite render in Apollonian clarity, is the source of Dionysian pleasure for a reader tuned to the presence of a woman as emblem of the novel's form and atmosphere:

> Absorbed by her music she accepted her lot very complacently, blazing into indignation perhaps once a fortnight, and subsiding, as she subsided now. Inextricably mixed in dreamy confusion, her mind seemed to enter into communion, to be delightfully expanded and combined with the spirit of the whitish boards on deck, with the spirit of the sea, with the spirit of Beethoven Op. 112, even with the spirit of poor William Cowper there at Olney. Like a ball of thistledown it kissed the sea, rose, kissed it again. (33)

To begin gauging the reception this kind of heroine might receive, Woolf introduces Rachel to the character that will eventually be the apotheosis of the type, Clarissa Dalloway, who functions in *The Voyage Out* as a contented matron concerned with Rachel's suitability for the marriage plot. While Clarissa tells Rachel she envies her ability to play, she confides in the same breath to Helen Ambrose, "I don't think music's altogether good for people—I'm afraid not…Too emotional, somehow" (45). Solidifying Mrs. Dalloway's dialectic relation to Rachel, the narrator carefully pictorializes, and joins, Clarissa's physicality and her discursivity. When Clarissa writes, (a letter beginning with the fitting "Picture us, my dear…"), she does so prettily, and without threatening the traditional structures of narration or femininity of which she herself *is* the picture:

> Her yawn must have been the image of a yawn. Instead of letting her mouth droop, dropping all her clothes in a bunch as though they depended on one

string, and stretching her limbs to the utmost end of her berth, she merely changed her dress for a dressing gown, with innumerable frills, and wrapping her feet in a rug, sat down with a writing-pad on her knee. Already this cramped little cabin was the dressing room of a lady of quality. There were bottles containing liquids; there were trays, boxes, brushes, pins. Evidently not an inch of her person lacked its proper instrument. The scent which had intoxicated Rachel pervaded the air. Thus established, Mrs. Dalloway began to write. A pen in her hands became a thing one caressed paper with, and she might have been stroking and tickling a kitten as she wrote. (46)

Is this still life, *Woman with Toiletries and Pen*, meant to be only ridiculous, or do we vibrate more sympathetically if we, like Rachel, are seduced a little by the womanly's incorporation of the writerly? Rachel and Clarissa's attraction to each other marks the nature of a true dialectic. In their exchanges, the Dionysian and the Apollonian begin to share valence. As the women confess their desires to question each other, a Paterian dissolution attempts to perform its aestheticizing work. "The shores of Portugal were beginning to lose their substance; but the land was still the land" (57). Woolf can feel the novel she wishes to write close at hand and urges her characters to produce it through their talk.

Imbibing Clarissa's way of living, Rachel suddenly craves intelligibility and is "overcome by an intense desire to tell Mrs. Dalloway things she had never told any one" (59). Clarissa matches Rachel's reach across the boundaries of their forms by seeming to "understand without words" (59). But just as Portugal does and does not cross into the realm of the purely sensual, Mrs. Dalloway and Rachel have do not complete a synthesis that would qualify as a new social or narrative position. The women are poised to call from each other a harmony of narrative and readership that might infuse *The Voyage Out* with a modern receptive circuitry anachronistic to its Victorian field of reference, but, programmatically, the marriage plot and its typical agent, the groom, intrude.

Clarissa and Rachel's communion devolves into a familiar discussion of domesticity, and a miniseries of trash-romantic tone that leaves everyone waiting for the novel to start again when Rachel utters the naive heroine's cliché protest, "I shall never marry," (59). Clarissa counters this Woodhousian nonsense by drawing the young woman's attention to "the robust figure of Richard Dalloway, who was engaged in striking a match on the sole of his boot," (59) and insists that "he gave me all I wanted" (60). Finding Rachel insufficiently impressed by the possible pleasures of a booted Richard, Clarissa prescribes *Persuasion* to cure the experiential deficiency (and to lessen the effects of seasickness by putting the girl to sleep). This is the first of many blows Woolf inflicts with Austen as her cudgel.

Extending the lesson on the history of conduct literature, Richard calls Austen "the greatest female writer we possess" because "she does not attempt to write like a man" (61), and then flirts with Rachel rather shamelessly, inducing her "shivering private visions" (65). Well, what to do with a shivering heroine but to kiss "her passionately, so that she felt the hardness of his body and the roughness of his cheek printed upon hers" (77)? And with that line crossed, the Dalloways, obviously, must disembark, with Clarissa blissfully unaware of her husband's boorishness, Rachel having learned only "so that's why I can't walk alone!"(83), and Richard marking the entire affair only by looking "at her very stiffly for a second before he followed his wife down the ship's side" (79-80). Thus is Rachel left susceptible to the demands of a dislikeable Richard of her own with only the dour tutelage of Helen Ambrose to guide her through the marriage plot's episodes.

Happily married herself, but skeptical of the institution, she would find it salutary for Rachel to be suddenly filled with received notions of sexuality, domesticity, and the role of women of which Woolf has made her unaware:

> "This girl, though, twenty-four, had never heard that men desired women, and, until I explained it, did not know how children were born. Her ignorance upon other matters as important" (here Mrs. Ambrose's letter may not be quoted)... "was complete." (100)

The censoring of Helen's letter marks the question of desire and its role in the process of procreation as the last issue of concern for the novel in relation to Rachel. Woolf, as did Hardy, begins to capitulate to the demands of marriage-plot precedent, abandoning Rachel's formal development in favor of the traditional theme of a heroine's readiness, if not willingness, for marriage, thereby activating our sense of the classic-realist question, is this going to end well or badly?

The abandonment of Rachel's function as a figure of novelistic form coincides with the superimposition on the South American setting of a set piece of English domesticity—the tourist hotel—and the recognition that the jungle will not allow the heroine to remain wild. The taming of Dionysian instinct is, in fact, made more possible by the isolation and scrutiny that go hand in hand in Santa Marina, where Rachel judges that "nothing [is] private" (103).

Given over to public concerns, Rachel's unruly dreams and musical refuge are now denied her. She enters a novel whose intentional field of reference is to be governed by an ideology clearly not its own as Woolf focuses on her account of the literary history she can neither valorize nor overturn. Helen first delivers Rachel to the English and their customs by taking her to the hotel to spy through its windows. The scene is touching, ghostly, reminiscent of Catherine Earnshaw and Heathcliff looking amusedly into the parlor of Thrushcross Grange at a world that will soon swallow Cathy and divide the lovers. Before they flee the grounds, Helen and Rachel see Terence Hewett, who will soon make the novel his.

Before Terence takes over, however, Woolf signals the ascendancy of the marriage plot by repeating the image of a woman writing, sanitizing it of all libidinal call, and still denying the work being done clear discursive value. As Austen always warns, evasion of the marriage plot, especially through discursive detours, dooms a female protagonist to the shame of spinsterhood and curses her speech acts with irrelevance, as the elderly Miss Allan is intended to illustrate:

> Her grey petticoats slipped to the ground, and, stooping, she folded her clothes with neat, if not loving fingers, screwed her hair into a plait, wound her father's great gold watch, and opened the complete works of Wordsworth. She was reading the "Prelude," partly because she always read the "Prelude" abroad, and partly because she was engaged in writing a short *Primer of English Literature*—Beöwulf to Swinburne—which would have a paragraph on Wordsworth.

> She was deep in the fifth book, stopping indeed to pencil a note, when a pair of boots dropped…on the floor above her. She looked up and speculated. Whose boots were they, she wondered. (107)

The boots, of course, are the suitor's, once Richard's now Terence's, who is organizing an outing as if he were Knightley planning a day of strawberry picking. Terence carries *The Voyage Out* forward into courtship and then Rachel's illness, a domestic tableau from which Miss Vinrace could never emerge, and also into the novel's sublimated discourse of resistance. Both Hardyesque as the suitor, and therefore the agent of Rachel's demise and the marriage plot's failure, and a revised Austenian hero, responsible for the values that attend the novel's closure, Terence is the figure around which the text is finally built.

The marriage plot will be foiled by Rachel's death, and the closure of a courtship novel ultimately abjured. In this abnegating stroke, Woolf twines the relation of the novel to the history of literature, and of love to the novel's traditional thematic enterprises. Terence, who will not deny, as Rachel does, having fallen in love, is the custodian of both threads, a role he seems perfectly fitted for as he appears "pressing the poems of Thomas Hardy beneath his arm" (115).

When his Cambridge mate St. John Hirst admonishes Terence that his plan has a fatal flaw ("That's where you'll go wrong…putting virgins among matrons" [114]) the catalog of femininity assumes full breadth. Virgin, Bride, Matron, or else, shudder, spinster: all the options Jane Austen afforded or threatened a heroine with are now arrayed. The echoes grow louder and less satiric as Terence congratulates himself on putting together the party that will inaugurate his courtship of Rachel:

> His invitations had been universally accepted, which was the more encouraging as they had been issued against Hirst's advice to people who were very dull, not all suited to each other, and sure not to come. (133)

A gathering of people who are very dull is just the social circumstance that, on Box Hill, prompts Emma's unkindness to the spinster Miss Bates, producing the censure and mortification that effects her conversion. Woolf must be aware that she is quoting Austen. Universal acceptance is the value underscored within Terence's musing, signifying Woolf's understanding that in a marriage plot novel the heroine must relinquish that which makes her capable of functioning outside of the marriage plot in order to make closure possible.

Accordingly, Rachel, who has long ago been stripped of her relation to the Dionysian possibility, waits for Terence in a room Mrs. Ambrose provides, one in which "music was deserted" and Rachel speaks "partly as herself, and partly as the heroine of the play she had just read" (129). Chidden of music and her subjectivity, Rachel is the heroine of a tragedy here, just not the aesthetically redeeming kind the novel's Nietzschean dreams had promised.

The Voyage Out's tone is increasingly bitter over its final hundred pages, as if Woolf feels sick before Rachel does. The heroine's fatal fever can be read as the only alternative to a stale set piece of moral comedy, a possibility suggested by the deliberate echoes of the wedding of Emma Woodhouse that sound around the deathbed or Rachel Vinrace. Emma and Knightley's wedding is the most definite statement of alliance between matrimony and classic realism's insistence on closure that confirms social stability's preeminent position in the English novel's hierarchy of discourses. In *Emma*'s final passage, the acquiescence of the heroine to the marriage plot produces the signs of harmonic conclusion: fullness, affirmed moral truth, and an ordered society:

> the wishes, the hopes, the confidence, the predictions of the small band of true friends who witnessed the ceremony were fully answered in the perfect happiness of the union. (335)

Appropriating the unmistakable tone of ending with which Austen insists upon happiness, Woolf insists upon the death of Dionysian dreams, of the heroine's will, and of the love story when this is what it costs one to live or write it. As Terence watches Rachel in her last moments, his internal monologue is built of Austen's words:

> she had ceased to breathe. So much the better—this was death. It was nothing; it was to cease to breathe. It was happiness, it was perfect happiness.... It seemed to him that their complete union and happiness filled the room with rings eddying more and more widely. (392-93)

The language that had signified the fullness of matrimony here expresses the absence of the heroine's place in the novel that has never guarded or trusted her existence. This redirection of the signs of stability into the hollow tragedy of her own novel is Woolf's last attempt at revision in *The Voyage Out*, and a signal of what is to come when she configures her heroine in a way that will amplify narrativity. The bride can no longer be the figure of the novel's development, a fact Terence reckons with for us as he stands at his beloved's deathbed surveying a world in which "he would never see Rachel again" (393).

Clearly the reinstatement of domestic fiction's catalog is not an accomplishment Woolf wishes to celebrate. The narrator intones no lines of blessing as famous last words. Instead there is a description of an enigmatic "procession of objects" across St. John's eyes as the surviving characters pass "him one after another on their way to bed," and on their way to extinction (416). These will not be the people of Woolf novels again, nor will Rachel be her heroine. Woolf marries Rachel not to Terence but to the tradition that won't let the heroine develop a subjectivity that defies the preferred alignment of theme and form.

Has the death of Rachel, of the novelistic archetype of bride, been only a hollow modernist repetition of late Victorian tragedy? It might be more than mere apologia for *The Voyage Out*'s surrendering of its own desires, and its transfer of focus from heroine to hero, to argue that Terence functions as forerunner of that very feminine narrativity. As the novel's novelist, Terence is no Richard Dalloway, no mere groom. He understands that *The Voyage Out* has wrought change and that the novel will have to account for its sad lessons. His own work in progress, "The book called Silence," (just the aesthetic category Woolf is credited with introducing to the form by her making of gap and pause into affirmative tropes in the fully modern works to come) "would not now be the same book that it would have been" (323).

What Woolf's female protagonists to come, Clarissa, Mrs. Ramsay, Orlando, even Miss La Trobe, will bring to their novels is an aspect of the heroine's existence never given soulful articulation by Austen, and never viewed by Hardy as sufficient cause for a text's existence. Clarissa Dalloway, the true Clarissa of her own novel, expresses this vibrant, generative narrativity when she makes exuberant note, as she pauses on her domestic errand of shopping for flowers to extol the virtues of "what she loved; life, London, this moment of June" (*MD* 4).

Works Cited

Austen, Jane. *Emma*. 1816. New York: W.W. Norton, 1993.
Nietzsche, Frederick. *The Birth of Tragedy*. 1872. New York: Vintage Books, 1967.
Woolf, Virginia. *Mrs. Dalloway*. 1925. New York: Harcourt, 1990.
---. *The Voyage Out*. 1915. New York: Signet, 1991.

Into the Underworld: Virginia Woolf, the Hogarth Press, and the Detective Novel

by Diane F. Gillespie

But, you may say, we asked you to speak about [voyages]—what has that got to do with [detective novels]? I will try to explain" (*AROO* 3). I certainly am not the first to wonder why so many of us who teach plotless, experimental fiction go home and read, and even write, intricately plotted detective novels.[1] Already in 1929, Marjorie Nicolson published "The Professor and the Detective Novel," an essay in which she disputes the assumption that academics need escape into "vicarious violence" from their narrow, unreal lives of the mind. On the contrary, Nicolson writes, academics need to escape not from their lives, "but from literature," by which she means modernist experimentation (112-14). I, in turn, want to question that assumption. It is not so easy anymore to draw firm lines between subjectivity and objectivity, emotion and intellect, formlessness and form, and purposelessness and cause and effect.

As Beth Daugherty pointed out to me a couple of years ago, even the Hogarth Press published, along with titles by Virginia Woolf, two successful detective novels by a man named C. H. B. Kitchin, *Death of My Aunt* (1929) and *Crime at Christmas* (1934). Although these titles sound more appropriate for another kind of press, we know Leonard enjoyed such reading (Willis 153),[2] and Virginia, as Edward Bishop has noted, liked Hogarth Press novels to make money (51). Leonard accounts for his own attraction to detective stories in 1927 by citing the involvement of the reader in discovering "what happened. We are one of the detectives," he says, and that is "part of the pleasure" ("Detective" 727). Is piecing together clues as we read detective fiction all that different from the thoughtful collaboration required of us when we read Woolf's novels? We might argue that Woolf's experiments anticipate "the metafictional antidetective novel" in which, as Stefano Tani describes it, "the detective is no longer a character but a function assigned to the reader as the criminal is no longer a murderer but the writer himself who 'kills' (distorts and cuts) the text and thus compels the reader to become a 'detective'" (113). Woolf is not so "perverse" a "killer of texts" as Tani describes. She does not engage in complex games with readers, although some of my students would argue that a Woolf novel is, as Marjorie Nicolson says of detective novels, "a battle royal between the author and the reader" (119). Yet, in "Character in Fiction," Woolf does identify with Joyce, Eliot, and Strachey to the extent that, desperate for fresh air, they take axes and shatter traditional literary windows (*E3* 434-35).

But what was the Hogarth Press doing publishing detective novels? I asked again. "If truth is not to be found on the shelves" of a library, "where, I asked myself," in Woolf's ironic tone, "is truth?" (*AROO* 25-26). After all, doing library research is detecting, as Woolf herself demonstrates in *A Room of One's Own* and elsewhere. Indeed, Ellen Hawkes and Peter Manso cast her as a code-cracking sleuth in *The Shadow of the Moth: A Novel of Espionage with Virginia Woolf* (1983). In this spirit, I left my office at Washington State University and walked over to Holland Library. "Have you any notion of how many" detective novels "are written [...] in the course of one year? [...] Are you aware" of the degree to which detective novels are criticized, defended, and discussed? "I should need claws of steel and beak of brass even to penetrate the husk" (*AROO* 26-27). So I left the computer catalogue, went down to Manuscripts, Archives and Special Collections, and put in a request for Kitchin's two detective novels. When they arrived at my table, I examined the dust jackets. The designs indicate that in both cases murder is at the center of the action. A detective novel, according to W. H. Auden, has a basic plot: "a murder occurs; many are suspected; all but one suspect, who is the murderer, are eliminated; the murderer is arrested or dies" (qtd. Charney xx). These two novels likely fit Auden's definition. Richard Kennedy's white jacket for *Death of My Aunt* shows a corked bottle with a red label, a visual allusion to poison. More graphic, the unsigned jacket for *Crime at Christmas* shows, through an irregular hole in the red background, a loosely sketched profile of a woman's head, two hands gripping her throat. The title of the first novel and the jacket design of the second indicate that the crimes in both books are against women. Certainly, I thought, female vulnerability would have caught the attention of potential readers as well as Virginia Woolf's critical eye.

Next, I read the blurbs on the dust-jacket flaps. Attempts in part to justify the Press's decisions to publish such books, the blurbs also help to blur the distinctions between modernist experimental fiction and at least Kitchin's kind of detective novels. Both blurbs balance "detective-work" with "the behaviour of the murdered women's relatives and dependents" or, as the *Crime at Christmas* blurb puts it, with "the behaviour of normal people in abnormal circumstances." When I read the novels, as of course I proceeded to do, I found that the blurb quotes Malcolm Warren, Kitchin's stockbroker turned amateur sleuth, who goes on to say that "by normal people" he means those "whose lives come fairly close to our own, people whose psychology we can follow and sympathize with." He then offers, in one of his many metafictional remarks, a "two-fold" justification "for a detective story [...] First, it presents a problem to be solved and shares, in a humble way, the charm of the acrostic and the crossword puzzle. But secondly—and this," he says, "is its real justification—it provides one with a narrow but intensive view of ordinary life, the steady flow of which is felt more keenly through the very violence of its interruption" (272). Having already written in *Mrs Dalloway* about the violent interruptions in ordinary psychic streams of soldier and civilian alike on an ordinary day in mid-June, and about the interruptions in the psychic lives of the Ramsays and their guests in *To the Lighthouse*, Woolf must have understood, if indeed she did not select, this quotation.

Was she amused, did she even know, that in *Crime at Christmas*, Kitchin's protagonist Malcolm Warren describes another character, Clarence James, as having "become greatly entangled with a coterie in Bloomsbury" (15), a "very highbrow circle" (174)? Warren himself moves on the fringes of the group since "being a stockbroker is not a passport to the world of art and letters—unless," he says, "you are a potential buyer of pictures" (174-75). Clarence James is a Labour party supporter, writes "articles on *art*" (26), is "intolerant…of the things most people tolerate," is probably a proponent of free love, and is "extremely sensitive and highly strung" (174-75). His political views are compromised, however, when he ends up as "editor, at quite a good salary, of a rich magazine" (278).

Intertextual evidence suggests that Kitchin had read Virginia Woolf's novels, at least *Mrs Dalloway*. When Mrs. Harley is thrown to her death in *Crime at Christmas*, she breaks her neck and is partly impaled (like Septimus Smith) on the spikes of the railings below (53). The murderer, moreover, turns out to be a doctor who claims to be a psychologist.

Dr. Green denounces Freud's theories as "pure common sense," their only value being "to knock another nail in the coffin of prudery" (30). Although Malcolm Warren marvels at the obscurities of his own thoughts and motivations and those of human beings in general (136), Dr. Green confidently proclaims that "most people [are] very easy to understand" (109). Kitchin carries Woolf's patent dislike of Dr. Bradshaw further, however, when Dr. Green, the murderer, is himself murdered. Malcolm Warren, who finds the doctor's body, worries in a way worthy of Woolf herself, that "the whole truth may be told in many ways [...] even in the baldest narrative facts must be given some sort of a setting [...] that was liable to infinite misconception" (153-54).

Beyond my preliminary discoveries in the library about the Hogarth Press and the detective novel, "It was [still] disappointing not to have brought back [...] some important statement, some authentic fact" about Virginia Woolf's direct participation (*AROO* 43). I turned, therefore, to Woolf's letters and diaries. Beginning prior to the publication of *Death of My Aunt*,[3] Woolf met Kitchin on a number of social occasions (*D3* 30; *L3* 189), but the record is hardly one of intimacy. Kitchin was just one of the young male writers in her publishing milieu. Nor is there any hard evidence that she read *Death of My Aunt* before or after its publication. As late as August 1927, though, she was rejecting "bloodsucker" novels that would cost a lot to print and would not make a profit (*D3* 150). Two years later, she and Leonard at least might have talked about the commercial value of Kitchin's novel, and when the Woolfs traveled Press books in Devon and Cornwall in May 1930 (*D3* 303), Kitchin's first detective novel must have been among them. Later in 1930, the Woolfs decided to regain their freedom by cutting back their Press operations because, as Virginia asks her diary, "What's the point of publishing these innocuous novels & pamphlets that are neither good nor bad?" (*D3* 327). Was Kitchin's *Death of My Aunt* one of these? She provides no titles.

The Woolfs did not cut back Hogarth Press operations, though, and in 1934 they published Kitchin's *Crime at Christmas*. Virginia sent it to Ethel Sands, along with books by Vita Sackville-West, Constance Butler, and herself (*Walter Sickert: A Conversation*). "I'm afraid the books I'm sending aren't a very bright lot," she writes dismissively. She singles out Kitchin more for himself than for his book: "Crime at Christmas is by a very rich young man who used to work with Philip Ritchie [at the bar], until he took to the Stock Exchange, and discovered a gift for detective stories" (*L5* 339-40). On two occasions in the same year, Kitchin emerges, along with T. S. Eliot, as the Woolfs' guest. Again, Woolf writes about Kitchin, not his books and, confiding this time in her diary, she dismisses him as "fat & white & cunning & not up to the mark" (*D4* 263).

Kitchin's ambivalent attitude towards Bloomsbury and Bloomsbury's ambivalent attitude towards Kitchin may help to explain his eventual falling out with the Hogarth Press. As J. H. Willis notes, Kitchin concluded that the press "was an unsuitable medium for detective novels" and moved to Constable. Leonard grudgingly gave his permission, with the condition that Kitchin make available the sales figures for his next book. Ironically, as it turned out, Kitchin had done better with Hogarth (Willis 173).

Since we think back through her published writings, if we are Woolf scholars, that is where I next searched for clues. Perhaps Woolf was aware of the detective novel and treated it, as she did so much else in her culture, in a revisionary way. Comments in "Modern Fiction" notwithstanding, she does not always object to plot. "Nobody can fail to remember the plot of the *Antigone*," she says, "because what happens is so closely bound up with the emotions of the actors that we remember the people and the plot at one and the same time" ("Notes" *E4* 64). Plot and character are inseparable, as Kitchin suggests, with his focus on the reactions of human beings to events. But what do we mean by "character"? Woolf asks in "Mr. Bennett and Mrs. Brown" (1924). There she admits to having read some of Arthur Conan Doyle. She combines a standard criticism of detective fiction for deficient characterization[4] with a criticism of Arnold Bennett. He may say, she writes, "that Dr Watson in *Sherlock Holmes* is real to him; to me Dr Watson is a sack stuffed with straw, a dummy, a figure of fun" (*E3* 426).

Throughout her career, the characters Woolf herself creates are more likely to use the interrogative style of so much detective fiction to question cosmic and psychological "crimes" than they are to interest themselves in violations of the laws of England. "How could any Lord have made this world?" Mrs. Ramsay asks, thinking of its lack of "reason, order, justice," its "suffering, death, the poor" (*TTL* 98). "Why did she mind what he said?" Lily Briscoe asks herself about Charles Tansley's verbal bludgeoning of her self-confidence, "Women can't write, women can't paint, not so much that he believed it, as that for some odd reason he wished it?" (*TTL* 197). Indeed, interrogations of people's motives, along with conclusions about their essential mystery, are recurrent in Woolf's fiction. "Who and what are these unknown people?" asks Bernard in *The Waves*. "I could make a dozen stories. [...] But what are stories?" (144).

"If all novels revolve around a mystery," as Hanna Charney writes, "They are nevertheless not all detective novels" (xx). Woolf does not use "the familiar English crime conventions," as does Kitchin (Willis 159). She does not write what Carolyn Heilbrun calls the "detective novel of manners," dependent as it is on the upper levels of an "unquestioned social hierarchy" ("The Detective" 276, 283). Heilbrun links Woolf's *A Room of One's Own* (1929), however, with Dorothy Sayers' *Gaudy Night* (1935) in that, as women, "both knew 'by instinct' what the trouble was at Cambridge and Oxford alike" ("The Detective" 287-88). I can find no evidence that Woolf read either Dorothy Sayers' or Agatha Christie's detective writing of the late twenties and thirties, yet roughly during this same time period, when the Hogarth Press was publishing Kitchin's detective novels, a concrete underworld of crime does emerge in Woolf's fiction. In the triad of criminal, victim, and detective, though, Woolf's focus is neither the criminal, however surprising his or her identity and motivation, nor the amateur detective, however reluctant or inept. Instead her focus is the victim. In *The Waves*, *Flush*, *The Years*, and *Between the Acts*, Woolf's victims, or those who identify with them, are women and other outsiders, children, and animals.

Threatening, in other words, civilized society and individual sanity in Woolf's novels of the thirties are not just the patriarchal atrocities of war and empire (ably described by others), but also an underworld of criminal behavior. In *The Waves* (1931), for example, Neville as a little boy reconstructs his reaction "when I heard about the dead man through the swing-door last night when cook was shoving in and out the dampers. He was found with his throat cut. [...] He was found in the gutter. His blood gurgled down the gutter. His jowl was white as a dead codfish. I shall call this [...] 'death among the apple trees' for ever" (24). Neville, in school, surrounds this disturbing image with "the exactitude of the Latin language" (31), his love for Percival, his solitude, and his satire, but the memory ominously returns during the farewell dinner for Percival: "The man lay livid with his throat cut in the gutter. [...] And going upstairs I could not raise my foot against the [...] apple-tree with its silver leaves held stiff!" (124). According to the laws of England, Neville's homosexuality is a crime that also makes him vulnerable.

In *Flush* (1933) Woolf's awareness of a criminal underworld is most overt. The vulnerable parties here are animals who, if not ransomed by their wealthy owners, are killed. In the Whitechapel chapter Elizabeth Barrett Browning's dog Flush, stolen from Wimpole Street, is taken "not a stone's-throw" away into "one of the worst slums in London" (87-88). No detective is required to discover who is responsible; Mr. Taylor and his gang of thieves simply threaten to send "a brown paper parcel [...] containing the head and paws of the dog" if the ransom is not paid (89). Woolf's account, however, interrogates the very notion of criminality. Is the crime to be laid at the door of the well-to-do who ignore the poverty, filth, and disease so dangerous to their own comforts? Are the criminals Barrett's father, brother, Robert Browning, and indeed "all Wimpole Street" who insist that paying the ransom would only be "giving way to tyranny"? (98). From Miss Barrett's and Flush's perspectives, the answer is yes. "But what would Mr. Browning have done if the banditti had stolen her?" Elizabeth Barrett wonders. "Flush was helpless. Her duty was to him" (101). For five miserable days, her hungry and thirsty spaniel waits to be rescued from the thieves and murderers who have confined him to a dark, dirty, and cold room with other hostages like himself. As Susan Squier observes, Flush and Miss Barrett are both imprisoned in a patriarchal system that fosters violence and ignores feelings. Neither is freed until she ransoms Flush and they leave the patriarchal home (127-28). Squier also notes parallels, intentional or unintentional, between the threats against Flush and Jack the Ripper's murder and mutilation of women in 1888 (130).

In *The Years* (1937), as in *The Waves*, a child is vulnerable. In the 1880 section, little Rose Pargiter steals the Nurse's latchkey, concealed every night "in a new place for fear of burglars." The Pargiters' house, like the Barretts', is threatened by the poverty that breeds vice. Appropriately, Rose imagines that she has "her pistol and her shot" and, as "Pargiter of Pargiter's Horse," rides off "to the rescue" of "a besieged garrison" (26-27). What disrupts her confident, tomboyish adventure on her way to Lamley's shop is "the figure of a man" who "suddenly emerged under the gas lamp," "leered at her," and tried to catch her (28). On her way home again, it is Rose who needs rescuing: "As she passed he sucked his lips in and out. He made a mewing noise. But he did not stretch his hands out at her; they were unbuttoning his clothes." In a panic, she runs home. Unable to erase the man's face from her mind, unable to tell her sister Eleanor about it, unable to sleep, and sure the man is pursuing her into her very room, she experiences "a profound feeling of guilt" (41-42). Rose never forgets the experience. "What awful lives children live!" Martin remarks. "Yes," the adult Rose replies, "And they can't tell anybody" (159).

The violent disruption of her self-confidence that turns Rose from a tomboy into a vulnerable, ashamed little girl may well be linked to her suffrage activities later in the novel. In the 1911 section, Rose ends up "in a police-court" and then "in prison" for throwing a brick (204, 231).[5] In the last section of the novel, the elderly Kitty drinks to the elderly Rose, whom she calls "a fine fellow" with "the courage of her convictions" (420). Whatever her methods and their consequences, Rose has managed to regain her confidence and to assert her autonomy in a hierarchical society torn apart by the Great War.

In *Between the Acts* (1941) the crime is rape, and it is Isa Oliver who dwells on it. She reads a newspaper account of a girl taken by troopers to look at an extraordinary horse with a green tail. Instead "they dragged her up to the barrack room where she was thrown upon a bed. Then one of the troopers removed part of her clothing, and she screamed and hit him about the face" (20). Isa's imagination recreates the scene and it is imprinted indelibly upon her mind (22). This rape, as Stuart Clarke has discovered, is based on an actual incident much in the papers of the previous year.[6] In the novel, it joins the allusion to the Procne and Philomela story (109), as well as the violent images of old Bart Oliver abusing his cringing dog, scaring his grandson, and calling him a crybaby (12-13); of the public school violence reported by William Dodge (73), of Giles Oliver releasing his frustrations by stomping on the choking snake (99, 107, 111); of Miss La Trobe gnashing her teeth behind a tree (122); and of the twelve war planes flying over the village pageant (193) in a novel set on the eve of World War II.

"I [have] come at last, in the course of this rambling," (*AROO* 83) to my conclusion. "I have told you in the course of this paper" (*AROO* 117) that Leonard liked detective novels; that Virginia liked the Hogarth Press to make money; that the Woolfs published two successful detective novels by C. H. B. Kitchin and presented them as studies in the "behaviour of normal people in abnormal circumstances"; that those novels also reflect an ambivalent attitude towards Bloomsbury and a knowledge of Virginia Woolf's writing; that she was not impressed by Kitchin as a person, but gave his second detective novel as a gift; that she thought plot inseparable from character and that a successful character did not mean Conan Doyle's Dr. Watson; that, while her own characters often interrogate cosmic and psychological crimes, in the novels of the thirties, an underworld of actual crime underscores her critiques of patriarchal British society and her sympathy with the vulnerable and powerless.

I keep thinking I've missed something important. As Bernard says in *The Waves*, "Let a man get up and say, 'Behold, this is the truth,' and instantly I perceive a sandy cat filching a piece of fish in the background. Look, you have forgotten the cat, I say" (*W* 187). Look, you've been treating *A Room of One's Own* as a piece of detection, and you've forgotten the dead body of Shakespeare's sister, you may well say. I admit, I have no "nugget of pure truth to wrap up between the pages of your notebooks," just "an opinion" (*AROO* 3-4) that Woolf knew enough about the criminal underworld of her society and enough about the detective novel of her day to blur some overly simple writing and publishing binaries and to help those of us whose reading habits seem equally contradictory to do likewise.

Afterword

This paper evolved, without the parody of *A Room of One's Own*, and with additional research, into "Virginia Woolf, the Hogarth Press, and the Detective Novel," *The South Carolina Review* 35.2 (Spring 2003), 36-48. I continue to examine seemingly uncharacteristic Hogarth Press publications, currently books in the category, "Religion."

Notes

1   See Leonardi.
2   The Woolf Library at Washington State University contains some evidence of Leonard's interest: three Agatha Christie detective novels and one by Ngaio Marsh, all published after Virginia's death.
3   The Hogarth Press published Kitchin's *Streamers Waving* (1925) and *Mr. Balcony* (1927) prior to *Death of My Aunt* (1929). When "his big novel *The Sensitive One* (1931)" was not successful, Kitchin returned to the detective genre with *Crime at Christmas* (1934) (Willis 273).

4   See, for instance, chapter three of Roth.
5   So Nicholas could end up in prison for being homosexual (297). Woolf's fiction implicitly questions whom and what the laws in a patriarchy protect.
6   Briggs notes Gillian Beer's use of Clarke's article in the *Virginia Woolf Miscellany* (Spring 1990) to place Woolf's allusion in the context of women's issues of the time, including not only rape, but also abortion ("Editing Woolf," 72).

Works Cited

Bishop, Edward L. "From Typography to *Time*: Producing Virginia Woolf." *Virginia Woolf: Texts and Contexts: Selected Papers from the Fifth Annual Conference on Virginia Woolf.* New York: Pace UP, 1996. 50-63.

Briggs, Julia. "Editing Woolf for the Nineties." *South Carolina Review* 29.1 (1996), 67-77.

Charney, Hanna. *The Detective Novel of Manners: Hedonism, Morality, and the Life Of Reason.* Rutherford, N.J.: Fairleigh Dickinson UP, 1981.

Hawkes, Ellen and Peter Manso. *The Shadow of the Moth: A Novel of Espionage with Virginia Woolf.* New York: St. Martin's/Marek,1983.

Heilbrun, Carolyn G. "The Detective Novel of Manners." *Hamlet's Mother and Other Women.* New York: Ballantine, 1990. 275-89.

Kitchin, C. H. B. [Clifford Henry Benn]. *Crime at Christmas.* London: Hogarth, 1934.

——. *Death of My Aunt.* London: Hogarth, 1929.

Leonardi, Susan J. "Murders Academic: Women Professors and the Crimes of Gender." *Feminism in Women's Detective Fiction.* Ed. Glenwood Irons. Toronto: U of Toronto, 1995. 112-26.

Nicholson, Marjorie. "The Professor and the Detective" (1929). In *The Art of the Mystery Story: A Collection of Critical Essays.* Ed. Howard Haycraft. New York: Grosset & Dunlap, 1947. 110-27.

Roth, Marty. *Foul and Fair Play: Reading Genre in Classic Detective Fiction.* Athens: U of Georgia P, 1995.

Squier, Susan M. *Virginia Woolf and London: The Sexual Politics of the City.* Chapel Hill: The U of North Carolina P, 1985.

Tani, Stefano. *The Doomed Detective: The Contribution of the Detective Novel to Postmodern American and Italian Fiction.* Carbondale: Southern Illinois UP, 1984.

Willis, J. H., Jr. *Leonard and Virginia Woolf as Publishers: The Hogarth Press, 1917-41.* Charlottesville and London: UP of Virginia, 1992.

Woolf, Leonard. "The World of Books: Detective Stories." *Nation & Athenaeum* 40 (26 February 1927): 727.

Woolf, Virginia. *Between the Acts.* San Diego: Harcourt Brace Jovanovich, 1969.

——. *The Diary of Virginia Woolf.* 5 vols. Ed. Anne Olivier Bell. San Diego: Harcourt Brace Jovanovich, 1977-84.

——. *The Essays of Virginia Woolf.* Ed. Andrew McNeillie. Vol. 1. London: Hogarth Press, 1986. Vols. 2-3. San Diego: Harcourt, Brace Jovanovich, 1987, 1988. Vol. 4. London: Hogarth, 1994.

——. *Flush: A Biography.* New York: Harcourt Brace Jovanovich, 1933.

——. *The Letters of Virginia Woolf.* 6 vols. Ed. Nigel Nicolson and Joanne Trautmann. New York: Harcourt Brace Jovanovich, 1975-80.

——. *A Room of One's Own.* New York: Harcourt Brace Jovanovich, 1957.

——. *The Waves.* San Diego: Harcourt Brace, 1959.

——. *The Years.* New York: Harcourt Brace & World, 1965.

REEL PUBLISHING: VIRGINIA WOOLF AND THE HOGARTH PRESS' FILM PUBLICATIONS

by Leslie Kathleen Hankins

Did I lead a life of utter idleness while you were here? Putting off all disagreeable jobs? I suppose so. Masses of manuscripts are now tumbling on my head...
(*L3* 327, letter to Vita 5 February 1927)

How comfortless & uneasy my room is,—a table all choked with papers. &c. I'm now grinding out Waves again, & have perhaps an hour & a half to spend: a short time on Dante; a short time on MSS: a short time here – with another pen.

...Home, & made dinner; & read MSS: But rather casually & unanimously we have decided within the last week to stop the Press. Yes; it is to come to an end. That is we are to go on only with my books & Ls. & Dotty perhaps; & what we print ourselves. In short, we shall revert next October to what we were in the Hogarth House days—an odd reversal, seeing that we are now financially successful. But what's money if you sell freedom? We say. And what's the point of publishing these innocuous novels & pamphlets that are neither good nor bad? (*D3* 326-27, Monday 27 October 1930)

Litineraries or Litter? What is the paper trail of the books and essays of Hogarth Press—especially the more pedestrian or peripheral publications, those we perhaps euphemistically term "ephemeral literature" (as a reviewer called one of the film publications)?[1] I suppose this presentation is a detective story of sorts (to tie in with Diane Gillespie's talk on this panel, "Into the Underworld: Virginia Woolf, the Hogarth Press, and the Detective Novel") to "round up the usual suspects" and some not so usual ones in order to place the film publications of the Hogarth Press within the culture of writing about film in the 1920s. I'd like to begin with a word of thanks to Michael Bott who so generously brought to the conference precious files of materials from the Hogarth Press archives at the University of Reading, materials I will mine in the future.[2]

Hogarth Press in the Midst of Film Culture of the 1920s

Let me begin by placing the Hogarth Press film publications in the context of the film culture of the 1920s. Hogarth Press did not operate in a critical vacuum; its film publications in 1928 and 1931 participated in a boom time for writing about film within a very active and interdependent publishing arena. Though England's film production and intellectual film culture were arguably rather moribund in the early 1920s (much to the chagrin of British *cinéastes*), intellectuals from both literature and film pooled their interests in the mid to late twenties, producing a flurry of pamphlets, a film society, and publishing ventures linking literature and the cinema. International avant-garde film culture was vibrant, cosmopolitan and inspiring. The energy incarnate in Surrealism and the *ciné clubs* of Paris, revolutionary new Soviet cinema, experiments in German Expressionism and trick film, and some American forays into the avant-garde, found its way to England through cinema crusaders, mobile intellectuals, elite little magazines such as *The New Criterion* and *Adelphi*, newspapers such as *The Spectator* and *The Daily Mail*, highbrow fashion magazines such as the London *Vogue* and *Vanity Fair*, and the phenomenal cultural venture of the Film Society. Diverse film forces were represented in innovative international programs by the Film Society and by feisty articles in international journals. As the explosion of film essays indicate, cinema was in vogue in the 1920s; cinema was, in fact, in *Vogue*, in *Vanity Fair*, in *Broom*, in *The Arts*, in *The New Republic*, in *Close Up* and in numerous other publications.[3]

Film Writing in 1920s London: *Close Up*, Richardson and Woolf

What was this arena of film publication like in the twenties? Let me provide a brief overview and some glimpses behind the scenes. A founder of the Film Society, Iris Barry wrote film criticism that was sought after for *The Spectator* beginning in 1924 and later in *The Daily Mail*. Her book of film criticism, *Let's Go to the Pictures*, was published in the Fall of 1926 by Chatto & Windus in London and by Payson & Clarke Ltd in New York. Other Anglo/American ventures publishing essays on the cinema included *Broom*, *Vanity Fair*, *The Arts* and the highly influential London *Vogue* under the short-lived but brilliant editorship of Dorothy Todd. In 1927, *Close Up* and POOL publishing were launched by H. D., Kenneth Macpherson and Bryher, and included Dorothy Richardson for a regular column. I highly recommend that anyone interested in the *Close Up* group read the excerpts published in the volume by James Donald, Anne Friedberg and Laura Marcus, especially the introductions by Laura Marcus.

Dorothy Richardson's private correspondence to Bryher demonstrates how her energetic networking shaped the literary/cinema writing forays. Some of these letters were published in Gloria Fromm's selections, though even more are in the unpublished files in the Beinecke Library. I could not resist gleaning quotes from various letters, indications of her recruiting efforts:

> July-August 1927: ...spent an evening with Edwin Odle who dragged us to the Café Royal. Henry Savage joined up and I told him all about *Close Up*. We were talking Cinema when a man near me asked to join. Mad on films. Developed a good idea on the time element, seemed intelligent if a little donnish. I told him he'd better send in just the *idea* and gave him your address. I'd had only one small whisky and soda, but it occurred to me I'd better go before I began telling the waiters to send in articles. (Fromm 138)

> July 1927: You know Lawrence loathes films? Foams about them. I'm sure he'd foam for you. Villa Mirenda. Scandicci. Florence. And Barbara Low is sound on Educ: the Cinema. Had a first class article a while back in the Contemp. Review. Robert Nichols had years of trying to write scenarios in America & much interesting experience. (*ibid.* 135)

I've written to Lawrence & to Barbara, giving them your present address. [...] Then there's Aldous Huxley. Have you written to him? He might be ready to write about Pickshers in general. I'm sure he must like them —& if you haven't approached him & would like me to do so, I will. [...] Then there's Hugh Walpole. He might write one of his bland & hearty communiques, if you'd like. Anyway, I'll try to make him subscribe. He's on my list for first number. Also Wells—who is at present broken up. Later on he might be approached for a contribution. His son is working at films [...] (ibid. 136-37)

I quote from these letters to give a sense of the flux, serendipity and collegiality behind film essay publication; it is delightful to imagine Dorothy Richardson fortified by a whiskey and soda soliciting for *Close Up* at the Café Royal.

And I must wonder. Did Richardson ply Virginia Woolf with a whiskey and soda? At any rate, there was communication between *Close Up* and Virginia Woolf about their desire to publish her thoughts on cinema, resulting in her postcard of July 10, 1927:

Dear Mr. Macpherson
    I am sorry to say that I cannot let you have my article on the Cinema. I find that the Nation does not want it re-printed in another English Magazine. I was under the impression when I wrote that Close Up was foreign. It is very good of you to say that you would wait for me, but I am so busy during the next few months that I cannot undertake to write anything fresh. With many thanks
    Yrs. Sincerely Virginia Woolf (Beinecke Library, rpt in Donald 345)

Clive Bell's Foray into Cinema and Other Conversations

What emerges from such correspondence behind the scenes—as well as the actual writings about cinema in the twenties—is a reel riot! Some critics slam the movies in one article and praise them in another; and some (such as Woolf) manage to maneuver the about-face within one essay. Clive Bell in a 1922 article notes that he had shifted within the past few months from finding cinema "too low in the scale of human activities to reveal the insufficiency of anything but itself and its admirers" (39) to (mid-essay) finding that it opened up "an invasion of the middle country, of the territory hitherto occupied by those painters and writers who stood between the uncompromising artists and the barbarous horde" (40). By 1929 he had gone even further; in that essay he argues for "the artistic picture-palace," asserting that "If you want an art of the 'cinema' you must make possible the existence of 'cinema' artists; they cannot exist till you who could appreciate their art support studios where it can be created and theatres where it can be shown" (63) One wonders what Bloomsbury conversations were behind their published articles on film? If his shifts in attitude are at all indicative of the cultural climate, it is not surprising that this body of critical literature is volatile and stimulating. Nothing was taken for granted; everything was debated. Critics, very aware of the cosmopolitan debates in Paris and newly Soviet Russia, echoed the theoretical questions of those circles; after experiencing Parisian film culture "and in other 'advanced' picture-palaces," Clive Bell begins the 1929 article with the questions, "Is cinematography an art? Can it be an art?" (39) [4]

The dialogues behind the publications must have been fascinating; in one letter Woolf writes about a vibrant conversation with Eddy Sackville-West (a key member of the Film Society) and Duncan Grant: "We all chatter hard [...] very interesting: we compare movies and operas; I'm writing that for Todd: rather brilliant. All, to me, highly congenial, and even a little exciting, in the spring light; hammers tapping outside; trees shaking green in the Square: suddenly we find its 7 and all jump up." (*L3* 254). From what we witness in the diaries and letters of Virginia and Leonard, the dynamics behind the scenes of Hogarth Press were as amusing and hit or miss as those we see in Dorothy Richardson's letters.

From Conversation to Publication

At any rate, Virginia Woolf and Hogarth Press joined the throng with film contributions. Virginia Woolf published her essay "The Cinema" not for Todd as she proposed in the letter just quoted, but in 1926 in the *Nation & Athenaeum*, *The Arts* and (without her knowledge) in the *New Republic*, and considered reprinting it in *Close Up*. As interesting as we may find her essay, Virginia Woolf's role as a publisher of film theory and criticism also invites study, because Hogarth Press published two pamphlets on film studies by Eric Walter White, one in 1928 and one in 1931. The Press's publication of two offerings of the film criticism of Eric Walter White suggests that Virginia Woolf probably read it, in manuscript or proof. And yet, her attitude toward such peripheral publications of Hogarth Press was mixed. One might argue that pamphlets chosen for publication by Leonard and Virginia must be ones they deemed important, and might shed light on her writing. However, their publishing was also pragmatic; essays chosen might have been chosen for pure market value. Virginia Woolf's private writing certainly indicates that her assessments of the Press selections were not always laudatory ones. In February 1927 she wrote Vita: "did I lead a life of utter idleness while you were here? Putting off all disagreeable jobs? I suppose so. Masses of manuscripts are now tumbling on my head..." and in October 1930 she wrote in her diary that she and Leonard had decided "rather casually & unanimously" to stop the Press, noting: "And what's the point of publishing these innocuous novels & pamphlets that are neither good nor bad?"

I must say those words rather stopped me in my tracks. It rather crushes my potential argument that the pamphlets Hogarth Press published were somehow integral to the evolving aesthetics and/or cinema theory of Virginia Woolf, doesn't it? How shall I now argue that the "disagreeable" tasks of reading these "innocuous pamphlets that are neither good nor bad" played a role in directing Woolf's thoughts on the cinema? Chastised, but persistent, I perused the Hogarth Press publications, to see what I could glean to offer you.

On the Cusp of Cinematic and Literary Cultures

I found myself drawn to one small but intriguing realization about the essays, something that, small and innocuous as it might be, could shed some light on the place of these publishing ventures in film studies. The aspect I found most intriguing was the role literature plays in these film essays. Eric Walter White's first Hogarth pamphlet, *Parnassus to Let*, is an odd artifact on the cusp of film and literary cultures. Its very existence testifies to the highly charged and contradictory moment in cultural history when literature and cinema were poised on a fault line. I was captivated by the way the power struggle between literature and cinema is characterized by White, particularly because that role challenges Woolf's own portrayal of the dynamics.

In 1926, in her essay "The Cinema," Woolf portrayed cinema as the predator and literature as a victim:

> So many arts seemed to stand by ready to offer their help. For example, there was literature. All the famous novels of the world, with their well-known characters, and their famous scenes, only asked, it seemed, to be put on the films. What could be easier and simpler? The cinema fell upon its prey with immense rapacity, and to this moment largely subsists upon the body of its unfortunate victim. (382)

But, in his essay in the Hogarth series, Eric Walter White in 1928 tellingly reverses the roles; for instance, he argues that the muse of the cinema "is certainly Socialist" and he terms film "The Cinderella of the arts," as he asserts:

> how completely the cinema has now succeeded in casting off the shackles of literature [...] For too long literature poisoned the cinema by making her the most tempting offers of plots and titles—tempting, because the plots offered were ready-made and the titles of proved publicity value. Literature is one art, the cinema another: it was impossible that the cinema should continue to take orders from Lady Literature and live below stairs. (*Parnassus* 14-15)

Though the argument in the essay is about cinema as an art and would seem to be on the pro-cinema side of any turf battle between literature and cinema, the essay is heavily dependent upon literature for argument, example, and epigraph. As a reviewer in *Close Up* noted in a scathing review of the essay, the essay gets caught up in discussing literary topics "but Mr. White then remembers that he has proposed to write about the cinema; and his reflections about the cinema are so muddled that I am not surprised that any fourth-rate person should find them unintelligible" (Blakeston 76). And, given the highly contested turf battles between the high arts—particularly film and literature—at the time period, it is interesting that both of White's titles for Hogarth Press refer to connections between literature and cinema. "Parnassus to Let" refers to lines from Walt Whitman's poem, *Song of the Exposition*: "Come, Muse, placard 'Removed' and 'To let' on the rocks of your snowy Parnassus."

Eric Walter White's second publication, *Walking Shadows: An Essay on Lotte Reiniger's Silhouette Films*, evidently was considered important enough by Hogarth Press for it to be fully illustrated; it is a beautiful book with a special cover and frontispiece designed especially for the publication by Reiniger and filled with impressive stills from her film as illustrations. The essay is a thorough and intriguing analysis of the experimental German film-maker, Lotte Reiniger, whose work was a regular highlight of the very popular Film Society screenings, including the 1930 Programme #38, composed of Women Directors. The focus on a woman film-maker, one who experimented with silhouettes and rhythm, is suggestive for Woolf's experimental fictions and her aesthetic essays relating to those projects—though we cannot explore that topic in this short talk.⁵ As with the first pamphlet, White's second essay is framed by literary allusions; *Walking Shadows* has on the title page the quote from *Macbeth* from which the title is taken: "Life's but a walking shadow, a poor player/ That struts and frets his hour upon the stage." Considering the battlefield between the arts, it seems significant to have the title a quote from high literature, from Shakespeare's murderous play about deposing the rightful ruler for an upstart usurper. The title is doubly allusive, however, because it also refers to the title of a highly influential experimental film, *Warning Shadows*, a famous 1922 example of Expressionist cinema directed by Arthur Robinson, an American who lived and worked in Germany during the 1920s. The title of the essay, like the content of White's argument, embodies the tug of war or multi-referentiality of film/literary culture of the day. White mentions the film *Warning Shadows* in the 1928 essay, so he would have been aware of the allusion of his 1931 title. If the title indicates that literature still reigns, the subtitles of White's essays shift the focus to film: "An Essay about Rhythm in the Films" and "[A]n Essay on Lotte Reiniger's Silhouette Films."

As the title pages and epigraphs of these two Hogarth Press film publications begin to demonstrate, the literary/film threshold or intersection is a rich and compelling one to investigate. We cannot here delve into the close reading of the essays that they so richly deserve, but I urge you to make that effort, mining them for more information about Woolf's encounters with film and film studies and witnessing the turf battles—and odd alliances—between literature and film that shape this cultural moment.

Afterword

More scholars have written about Woolf and the cinema since 2001; in additional to my articles and presentations, books by Maggie Humm, David Trotter, and Laura Marcus are now out. But, I kept this paper as it was in 2001, when many of us attended the conference, rather than incorporating later publications. In the Works Cited and the footnotes, I indicate some of my publications that built on my early exploration of film publications of the twenties.

Notes

1. Oswell Blakeston turns Eric Walter White's own phrase against him in a rather snide move, in his review of *Parnassus To Let*: "On page nineteen I find the sentence: 'But although during the last few years the cinema has drawn forth a host of ephemeral literature...' The sentence still stands." (77)
2. These fascinating papers, which included the correspondence between Hogarth Press and Eric Walter White, demonstrate that the press interacted with the Film Society and The Academy Cinema in efforts to promote White's books, including placing an advertisement in the Film Society programme, and making a special slide to be shown during a screening of Reiniger's film at The Academy Cinema. The 1932 programme for the 51ˢᵗ performance of the Film Society thus included in the film notes this advertisement: "Particulars of Lotte Reiniger's methods of working, her theories of montage and illustrations of her silhouette figures, will be found in Eric Walter White's Walking Shadows (Hogarth Press)." (Amberg 208)
3. Editing the cinema section for Bonnie Kime Scott's *Gender in Modernism*, I included materials by Iris Barry, H. D., Bryher, Woolf, and others. My introduction expands the overview given here.
4. I continued and expanded my analysis of Clive Bell's contributions to film criticism in these two rich articles and in his correspondence in a 2006 presentation, "Tracking Clive Bell's Takes on the Cinema in the 1920s," at the 16ᵗʰ Annual International Conference on Virginia Woolf, University of Birmingham, U.K.

June 22-26.
5   I did explore those connections in a paper for the 6th annual Virginia Woolf Conference at Clemson University in 1996: "*Walking Shadows* and 'Statues Against the Sky': Lotte Reiniger's Silhouette Films and Virginia Woolf's *The Waves*."

Works Cited

Amberg, George. *The Film Society Programmes 1925-1939*. New York: Arno Press, 1972.
Bell, Clive. "Cinema Aesthetics: A Critic of the Arts Assesses the Movies." *Theatre Guild Magazine* (October 1929): 39, 62-63.
Bell, Clive. "Art and the Cinema: A Prophecy that the Motion Pictures, in Exploiting Imitation Art, will Leave Real Art to the Artists." *Vanity Fair* (November 1922): 39-40.
Blakeston, Oswell. Review of *Parnassus To Let*. *Close Up* 4:1 (January 1929): 76-77.
Donald, James, Anne Friedberg and Laura Marcus, eds. *Close Up 1927-1933: Cinema and Modernism*. Princeton: Princeton UP, 1998.
Fromm, Gloria, ed. *Windows on Modernism: Selected Letters of Dorothy Richardson*. Athens: U of Georgia P, 1995.
Hankins, Leslie K. "A Splice of Reel Life in Virginia Woolf's 'Time Passes': Censorship, Cinema and 'the usual battlefield of emotions.'" *Criticism* 35:1 (Winter 1993): 91-114.
———. "Across the screen of my brain": Virginia Woolf's "The Cinema" and Film Forums of the Twenties" in *The Multiple Muses of Virginia Woolf*. Ed. Diane Filby Gillespie. Columbia: U of Missouri P, 1993. 148-79.
———. "*Cinéastes* and Modernists: Writing on Film in 1920s London," *Gender in Modernism: New Geographies, Complex Intersections*, ed., Bonnie Kime Scott. Urbana: U of Illinois P, 2007. 809-58.
———. "Iris Barry, Writer and *Cinéaste* in *The Adelphi*, *The Spectator*, the Film Society and the British *Vogue*: Forming Film Culture in London of the 1920s." *Modernism/Modernity* 11:3 (September 2004): 488-515.
———. "Tracking Shots through Film History: Virginia Woolf, Film Archives and Future Technologies." *Virginia Woolf: Turning the Centuries: Selected Papers from the Ninth Annual Virginia Woolf Conference*. Eds. Bonnie Kime Scott and Ann Ardis. New York: Pace UP, 2000. 266-75.
White, Eric Walter. *Parnassus to Let: An Essay about Rhythm in the Films*. Hogarth Essays. Second Series. No. XIV. London: Hogarth Press, 1928.
———. *Walking Shadows: an Essay on Lotte Reiniger's Silhouette Films*. Based on a paper read to the Newport Film Society on December 16th, 1930. London: Hogarth Press, 1931.
Woolf, Virginia. *The Letters of Virginia Woolf*. Eds. Nigel Nicolson and Joanne Trautmann. V. 3: 1923-1928. New York and London: Harcourt Brace Jovanovich, 1977.
———. "The Cinema." *The Nation and Athenaeum* (July 6, 1926): 381-83.
———. The Diary of Virginia Woolf. Ed. Anne Olivier Bell. 5 vols. New York: Harcourt, 1977-84.

VIRGINIA WOOLF AND *TIME AND TIDE*: FORAYS INTO FEMINIST JOURNALISM

by Loretta Stec

In recent years, critics—for example Leila Brosnan in her book-length study *Reading Virginia Woolf's Essays and Journalism*—have begun to analyze with more rigor Woolf's contributions to periodicals and her broadly defined "journalism." As Brosnan points out, "Between 1904 and 1941 only two years passed during which Virginia Woolf published no journalism: 1914 and 1915, years during which she was incapacitated by illness" (84). She produced journalism for multiple periodicals for over 35 years. Woolf began writing reviews in 1904 for the *Guardian, National Review, Academy & Literature*, and what would become a staple of her venues, the *Times Literary Supplement* (44). She gained entrance to these publications through the connections of family and class, and was famously delighted at receiving her first check for money earned as a reviewer as she describes in "Professions for Women," taking her first step toward becoming a potentially self-supporting, independent woman. Later in her career she branched out to publish in, among other venues, the *New Statesman and Nation, The Yale Review, The Atlantic Monthly, The Listener,* and *The New Republic,* as well as *Vogue, Good Housekeeping* and *Cosmopolitan*. In statements about the profession of journalism and its meanings to her, Woolf generally expressed ambivalent sentiments, and seemed to keep at the work for financial reasons, and perhaps for wider publicity, for reasons of "money and fame" as Brosnan puts it (53), despite what Woolf felt were its negative effects on her fiction writing.

In considering this journalistic production, I kept being struck by the conspicuous infrequency of *Time and Tide* in the list of periodicals for which Woolf wrote. After all, *Time and Tide* was a premier political-cultural weekly during the 1920s and 1930s and beyond; it was published by a feminist and included analysis largely from a feminist perspective, especially in its early years. It seems that it would have been a potentially excellent site for Woolf's feminist sensibilities while being oriented enough toward the arts not to be too narrow or dogmatic in its selection of articles and points of view, a problem Woolf expressed about other periodicals. Why did Woolf publish only three pieces in *Time and Tide* during all her years of journalistic life? My speculative answer is that, first, Woolf seems not to have thought about her journalism in light of contributions to a political public sphere, to ongoing debates about political issues that affected the citizenry at large, or even women in particular. This seems to be so despite the importance of *A Room of One's Own* and *Three Guineas*, and arguably much of her other work, to that public sphere of debate. Secondly, Woolf resisted writing for journals with what she called a "declared character" (*L6* 252, July 1938), preferring to remain intellectually and creatively free, an outsider. Thirdly, ideological differences between Woolf and the editor of *Time and Tide*, Lady Rhondda, about the emphases of feminism may have kept Woolf at a distance from what appears likely to have been an amenable space for her journalistic production. Finally, given Woolf's ambivalence about writing journalism, she desired to be paid well for her efforts, and her income from other publications became increasingly substantial, making them much more desirable venues for Woolf than *Time and Tide*.

Begun in 1920 by the wealthy Margaret Haig Thomas, the Viscountess Rhondda, *Time and Tide* became, in the words of one historian, "one of the most outstanding and influential journals of the twentieth century" (Mellown 441). According to Kingsley Martin, editor of the *New Statesman and Nation*, "it made a strong run at becoming the leading weekly review in Great Britain in the 1930s" (qtd. in Eoff 128). Circulation ranged from 12,000 to 15,000 in the early 1920s, reaching a high point of 40,000 during World War II (Eoff 121; 144). A political and cultural weekly, "modeled after the prestigious *New Statesman* but directed and staffed by women only [until the mid-1930s] and owing no allegiance to any particular party," *Time and Tide* became a periodical appealing to its readers, particularly women, not as consumers, but as citizens (Eoff 119). The editorial in the first edition of the new journal explains that Lady Rhondda and her colleagues began *Time and Tide* to provide analysis of the "new and unknown world" of the post-World War I era from an independent point of view, "not dictated by any party or personal bias." The editorial discusses the gender of the periodical's board, explaining: "That the group behind this paper is composed entirely of women has already been frequently commented upon. It would be possible to lay too much stress upon the fact…On the other hand, this fact is not without its significance," for this new postwar political world includes women and they deserve attention they have not received before. The goals of the weekly were in line with those of liberal feminism, to "treat men and women as equally part of the great human family" (7). Given how little attention mainstream media gave to women at all, *Time and Tide* was progressive in putting a focus on both genders, and on many and varied issues, often from a feminist angle.

The periodical was not, however, limited to political analysis. Many of the most prominent writers of the era published their views, and sometimes their fiction or poetry, in *Time and Tide*, from G.B. Shaw, H.G. Wells, Wyndham Lewis, and T.S. Eliot, to Rebecca West, Katherine Mansfield, Sylvia Townsend Warner, Naomi Mitchison, Rose Macaulay, and Vera Brittain. One critic reveals that Ezra Pound "contacted the review first" to seek publication, having written "petulantly" in a letter, "T and T appears to have printed nearly everyone ELSE" (Eoff 126). The journal also regularly ran book and theatre reviews, and covered special cultural events. Woolf was among the important writers who published in *Time and Tide*, but I think it interesting that she published more articles in Dorothy Todd's *Vogue* than in this cultural-political forum aiming to provide feminist points of view to the culture at large. Throughout Woolf's career, *Time and Tide* published favorable reviews of her work, and quickly printed a eulogy upon her death. Her references to the journal and to its founder and eventual editor, Lady Rhondda, in her diaries and letters indicate Woolf was very familiar with its existence and its content. Nevertheless, Woolf's contributions to *Time and Tide* were limited; in it she published: a reflective essay titled "The Sun and the Fish" in 1928; excerpts from *A Room of One's Own* in 1929; and a review of the autobiography of Marie, the Queen of Roumania in 1934. That's all.

I believe we can see *Time and Tide* as an important contributor to the diminished public sphere of the interwar era. As Nancy Fraser puts it in a valuation of Habermas's theory, the "indispensible" concept of the public sphere designates a theatre in modern societies in which political participation is enacted through the medium of talk. It is the space in which citizens deliberate about their common affairs... This arena is conceptually distinct from the state... [and] from the official economy; it is not an arena of market relations but rather one of discursive relations, a theatre for debating and deliberating rather than for buying or selling. (57)

While there is no denying that by the early twentieth century, the press was quite thoroughly commodified, and periodicals were hardly the free spaces of debate that might exist in an ideal democracy, I would like to suggest that some periodicals, primarily weeklies, attempted to keep cleared a space for "rational-critical debate" (Habermas 161) without excessive influence by commercial interests. My concern is with feminist journals, as distinct from "women's magazines" or parts of newspapers designated as "women's pages" (except perhaps the *Manchester Guardian*'s). Some of these feminist journals are open to charges of commercialism; others were allied with political parties and therefore were not "independent." Habermas admits that even in the midst of "rational-critical debate... be[ing] replaced by consumption, and the web of public communication unravel[ing] into acts of individuated reception" (161), some "residual functions" of the "liberal public sphere" remain within democracies, and I would like to claim *Time and Tide* as serving that function, if in a circumscribed manner. I see this journal as a kind of culmination of the many women's periodicals that sprang up in the late nineteenth and early twentieth centuries, and that helped to constitute a kind of feminist counter-public sphere in journalism, a space of multiple debates about the nature of society and the future of humanity.

Some of Woolf's comments about journalism in general might shed light on her choice not to publish much in this periodical despite its function as part of a feminist counter-public sphere. Woolf wrote in 1923 to Roger Fry: "Journalism is altogether such a beastly business" (*L3* 38, 18 May 1923). In a letter to Vita Sackville-West in 1936 she wrote: "Only when I read other people's articles I can't see any cause to write more. Lord, how I hate the weekly papers! Then why write articles? Because I must make 500 pounds" (*L6* 98, 17 Dec 1936). (The editor explains that Woolf earned £721 from royalties on her past books in 1936, and in 1937 she earned £2466, making the £500 pound sum metaphorical.) In 1925, the period when she had written for *Vogue*, she queried: "And whats the objection to whoring after Todd [editor of *Vogue*]? Better whore, I think than honestly and timidly and coolly and respectably copulate with the Times Lit. Supp." (*L3* 200). In 1939 she wrote: "I've been slipping into the frying pan of journalism—letting myself in for a monthly article, making, or attempting to make, £15.15 terms. All this is very frittering, exciting, degrading" (*D5* 240, 6 October 1939). According to Alex Zwerdling, "Woolf was determined to avoid steady journalism not only because it took her away from her most serious work but because it was an aspect of the mass culture she and other modern artists had come to despise. Bloomsbury elitism has important links with the fear of democratic institutions that flourished in the early twentieth century" (109-11). Woolf seemed to find it personally trying to write under a deadline and for an editor, but also seemed to hold quite a bit of high culture disdain for journalistic forms of writing. She does not comment on or discuss journalism as having a vital function in political debate; her statements about journalism do not position her as an author eager to enter the fray of the public sphere to influence opinion or use periodicals as an integral part of democracy. In addition, even when commenting on the publication of *Three Guineas*, Woolf claimed: "I'm uneasy at taking this role in the public eye" (*D5* 141, 20 May 1938). Unlike many of her contemporaries who wrote both journalism and fiction—e.g. Rebecca West, Winifred Holtby, Naomi Mitchison—Woolf did not actively participate in *Time and Tide's* cultural and political project as part of a feminist counter-public sphere.

Woolf often complains also of the constraints of writing for a particular periodical. For example, in a letter explaining to John Lehmann why she does not wish to write anything for his journal *New Writing*, she says:

> I loathe having to keep to dates and so many thousand words...The other reason is that I find the foreword to *New Writing* distinctly inhibiting...my instinct is to fight shy of magazines which have a declared character. Why lay down laws about imaginative writing? Probably I'm an incorrigible outsider. (*L6* 252, July 1938)

She also complains of being censored by the *Times Literary Supplement*, and defends her writing for *Vogue* by saying, "Todd lets you write what you like, and its your own fault if you conform to the stays and the petticoats" (*L3* 158). In an essay published in 1934 in a "short-lived Oxford magazine," provocatively titled *Lysistrata*, Woolf mocks the masculine bias of the world of journalism and critical reviewing by suggesting, "the editor forbids feminism" (qtd. in Sandbach-Dahlstrom 280-81). And as one critic remarks, "Woolf was right to think of the British literary world of the 1910s and 1920s [and I would add the 1930s and beyond] as a male-dominated culture. Almost all the literary editors, magazine owners, publishers, and reviewers were men" (Lee "Crimes" 121). So Woolf found it constraining and inhibiting in general to write for periodicals, and perhaps *Time and Tide*, even though it proclaimed itself "independent" had too much of a "declared character" for Woolf's taste. On the other hand, if she found anti-feminist editors, many of whom were men, particularly "inhibiting," she would presumably have received more generous and woman-friendly treatment at *Time and Tide*.

So perhaps Woolf did not write for this journal because she did not think about her journalism as contributing to the public sphere of political debate; because she resisted writing for an editor and under a deadline; and because she disliked magazines with a "declared character." Perhaps also, Woolf did not find the "declared character" of *Time and Tide*, or more particularly its founder, to be sympathetic.

Woolf was quite familiar with Lady Rhondda, publisher, and from 1926, editor of *Time and Tide*. Multiple references to Lady Rhondda exist in Woolf's diaries and letters, and they socialized occasionally, particularly in the 1930s. As early as 1922, Woolf records a conversation with Molly Hamilton, who

> had been the guest of Lady Rhondda in the South of France; & Lady R. who is a good able superficial woman...is a feminist & Molly is not. But the Lady Rs. ought to be feminists I said; & you must encourage them, for if the rich women will do it, we neednt & its the feminists who will drain off this black blood of bitterness which is poisoning us all. (*D2* 167, 17 February 1922)

The highly suggestive phrase "this black blood of bitterness" refers in my view to what other writers of the era called the "sex war," that struggle for gender equality that concerned both Woolf and Lady Rhondda in different ways. This passage suggests that Woolf wished herself an outsider to feminism as well as to journalism. Woolf's thinking also seems to have taken a different trajectory than Lady Rhondda's, and as "Lady Rhondda shaped *Time and Tide* to her wishes, and controlled it absolutely, turning it into a liberal and reformist, rather than a strictly feminist periodical" (Eoff 131-32), her differences with the editor may have kept her at a distance from *Time and Tide*.

These differences are best illustrated in the brief correspondence Woolf engaged in with Lady Rhondda about *Three Guineas*. Rhondda wrote to Woolf immediately upon beginning to read *Three Guineas* to express how "profoundly it moved" her, and she declares herself a "very grateful Outsider" (Snaith 17). Woolf recorded her delight in her diary at Lady Rhondda's letter, and continues, "Of course Ly R. is already partly on my side; but again as she's highly patriotic & citizenlike she might have been roused to object" (*D5* 142, 24 May 1938). Woolf responded to Lady Rhondda's letter as follows:

> Your letter has given me great pleasure all day. I admit I am nervous about 3 Guineas...for the subject is a risky one...the fact that you liked what you read relieves me of some of my fears. So thank you very much for writing to say so... I'm very glad you called yourself an outsider—the first to take that name! (*L6* 229, 24 May 1938)

Lady Rhondda then wrote again explaining further her understanding of the issues raised by *Three Guineas*:

> I do hope it may be true that there is really an inherent difference between men and women on that matter of combativeness. If there really is, & <u>if</u> we could get the power we might really help. But in my own heart I find, it seems to me, such echoes of all the pride, vanity and combativeness I ever see in men that I don't need to have it explained, I *know*. Still it is true that we don't do the actual killing—& don't want to—so perhaps...if there may only be time. (Snaith 21-22)

Then in a postscript, she continues:

> Yes I do believe something...could be done with that outsiders idea...No woman who tried to run a Weekly Review could remain unaware of how much she was an Outsider. Its not only that to run that kind of paper one *must* know something of the inside gossip that is going on & almost all the Official Gossip Centers are closed to women...It is also that the presumption amongst the average general public is that that kind of paper can't be run by women & all advertisers belong to the general public...I go through the paper every week taking out women's names & references to matters especially concerning women because if I left them in it would soon kill the paper. But its maddening. (Snaith 22)

Woolf replies:

If we emphasize our position as outsiders and come to think of it as a natural distinction it should be easier for us than for those unfortunate young men.... What you say about the difficulty of running Time and Tide is very interesting. But isnt that proof of what I say—I mean as a woman shut out from so many of the newspaper sanctuaries you have to fight to enter; and thus don't think, as those within naturally do, how to shut others out. (*L6* 236, 10 June 1938)

So what we witness in this exchange of letters is a general agreement between these two feminists, but a definite difference of emphasis.

During the 1920s especially, *Time and Tide* stressed the differences in conditions, if not in essences, between men and women. The journal toned down its demands for social change once full suffrage had been reached and other forms of "equality" were visible; it also increasingly attempted to appeal to male as well as female readers. Woolf's correspondence with Lady Rhondda reveals that beneath the rhetoric of liberal feminism, Lady Rhondda had hoped for if not assumed basic differences between men and women, in agreement with the Woolf of *Three Guineas*, but had come to doubt those differences when she witnessed women, including herself, every bit as vain, combative, and competitive as men. At the end of the 1930s, Lady Rhondda then, was herself moving, and thus moving her journal *Time and Tide*, from a position emphasizing the sex war to a position that emphasized greater sameness, the common humanity of men and women, throughout her editorship of *Time and Tide*. Woolf is generally read as moving ideologically from an emphasis on equality and androgyny in *A Room of One's Own* to a "recognition of the power of difference" in *Three Guineas* and other works at the end of the 1930s, while complicating and contradicting each of these positions (Barrett 350-51). The intersecting but divergent ideological trajectories of these two public figures illustrate some of the tensions of feminist thought in the interwar period, and suggest some of the potential reasons Woolf did not contribute many articles to *Time and Tide*.

The final possibility in this list of speculative reasons for a conspicuous absence is, of course, money. While *Time and Tide*'s standard remuneration for contributions is difficult to unearth, the history of financial problems of this publication suggests it would not have been comparable to a mass market or highly profitable journalistic venue. Hermione Lee reports that *Vogue* paid £10 for 1000 words in 1924; that Woolf bragged to Vita Sackville-West in 1927 that she would receive "£120 to write four reviews for the *Herald Tribune*"; and that by the late 1920s, Woolf was often "making double income from the same piece, published once in America and once, or more than once, in England" (*Virginia* 551). Given these lucrative possibilities, and the distanced and ambivalent attitudes toward journalism Woolf reveals in the passages quoted above, *Time and Tide* simply was not an attractive enough space for Woolf's literary production, even as the journal bolstered her career in numerous ways.

Afterword

Since the Woolf conference in 2001, scholars of the modernist period have continued to analyze journalistic production as a key component of the era. While a number of scholarly texts could be cited, two in particular are relevant to this paper. The first is Patrick Collier's *Modernism on Fleet Street* which includes a chapter focused specifically on Woolf's ideas about book reviewing. In this chapter, Collier provides more evidence of Woolf's disdain for journalism. He also emphasizes her conflicting attitudes toward readers, and elucidates her preference for a private, domestic space of criticism rather than a public, "professional" world of reviewers beholden to the literary marketplace (94). Collier's argument is about different issues than those in this talk; his fine chapter, however, substantiates my claim that Woolf had few hopes for an active public sphere (in the sense Nancy Fraser defines it above) in journalism. Collier claims that Woolf's answer to the commodification of the press and its collusion with capitalist militarism was "the abandonment of the public sphere" during her work of the 1930s (103). He concludes that "Woolf felt the failures of journalism and the corruption of the wider public sphere [which] had rendered a constructive symbiosis between audience and writer impossible" (79). Even a unique publication like *Time and Tide* could not offer Woolf enough latitude, freedom, and power to make writing for its pages worthwhile.

Michelle Tusan's *Women Making News: Gender and Journalism in Modern Britain* attests to the unique quality of *Time and Tide*, but also places the journal within the broader context of postwar feminist periodicals. Tusan carefully outlines how various periodicals attempted to reach a feminist readership, and how Lady Rhondda's *Time and Tide* of the 1920s "invented its own idealized egalitarian feminist platform" in order to do so (225). *Time and Tide* published "radical opinion pieces" in the 1920s even while aiming itself at both male and female readers (226). By the 1930s, however, the weekly "cultivated a new sensibility. Feminism took a back seat to a broad-based cultural critique of society that was devoid of much of the fiery polemics of the 1920s" (230). Tusan corroborates that as Woolf was becoming more radical, most explicitly in *Three Guineas*, *Time and Tide* was moderating its feminist goals in favor of a broader liberal humanism. Both of these recent pieces of scholarship give additional evidence for my speculations about why Woolf was unwilling to make *Time and Tide* a significant site for her journalistic production.

Works Cited

Barrett, Michele. "Introduction." *A Room of One's Own* and *Three Guineas*. Reprinted in *Virginia Woolf: Introductions to the Major Works*. Ed. Julia Briggs. London: Virago Press, 1994. 349-94.

Brosnan, Leila. *Reading Virginia Woolf's Essays and Journalism*. Edinburgh: Edinburgh University Press, 1997.

Collier, Patrick. *Modernism on Fleet Street*. Aldershot, England: Ashgate, 2006.

Eoff, Shirley M. *Viscountess Rhondda, Equalitarian Feminist*. Columbus: Ohio University Press, 1993.

Fraser, Nancy. "Rethinking the Public Sphere: A Contribution to the Critique of Actually Existing Democracy." *Social Text*, No. 25/26 (1990): 56-80.

Habermas, Jürgen. *The Structural Transformation of the Public Sphere*. Trans. Thomas Burger. Cambridge, MA: MIT Press, 1998.

Lee, Hermione. "'Crimes of Criticism': Virginia Woolf and Literary Journalism." *Grub Street and the Ivory Tower: Literary Journalism and Literary Scholarship from Fielding to the Internet*. Ed. Jeremy Treglown and Bridget Bennett. Oxford, England: Clarendon, 1998. 112-34.

———. *Virginia Woolf*. New York: Alfred A. Knopf, 1997.

Mellown, Muriel. "Time and Tide." *British Literary Magazines: The Modern Age, 1914-1984*. NY: Greenwood Press, 1986. 441-52.

Sandbach-Dahlstrom, Catherine. "'Que scais-je?': Virginia Woolf and the Essay as Feminist Critique." *Virginia*

Woolf and the Essay. Beth Carol Rosenberg and Jeanne Dubino, eds. New York, NY: St. Martin's, 1998. 275-93.

Snaith, Anna. "Wide Circles: The *Three Guineas* Letters." *Woolf Studies Annual*. Vol 6. New York: Pace University Press, 2000.

Spender, Dale, ed. "Time and Tide." 14 May 1920. Reprinted in *Time and Tide Wait for No Man*. London: Pandora Press, 1984. 6-8.

Tusan, Michelle. *Women Making News: Gender and Journalism in Modern Britain*. Urbana and Chicago: University of Illinois Press, 2005.

Woolf, Virginia. *The Diary of Virginia Woolf*. Ed. Anne Olivier Bell. 5 vols. New York and London: Harcourt Brace Jovanovich, 1982.

——. Excerpt From *A Room of One's Own*. *Time and Tide* (22 November 1929): 1403-04 and (29 November 1929): 1434-36.

——. *The Letters of Virginia Woolf*. Ed. Nigel Nicolson and Joanne Trautmann. 6 vols. New York and London: Harcourt Brace Jovanovich, 1980.

——. "Royalty." Rev. of *The Story of My Life* by Marie, Queen of Roumania. *Time and Tide* (1 December 1934): 1533-34.

——. "The Sun and the Fish." *Time and Tide* (3 February 1928): 99-100.

Zwerdling, Alex. *Virginia Woolf and the Real World*. Berkeley: University of California Press, 1986.

WOOLF AND THE UNSAYABLE:
THE ROAR ON THE OTHER SIDE OF SILENCE

by Diana L. Swanson

In *Middlemarch*, George Eliot writes that "if we had a keen vision and feeling of all ordinary human life, it would be like hearing the grass grow and the squirrel's heart beat, and we should die of that roar which lies on the other side of silence"(135). In much of her fiction, Woolf is intent on capturing "the other side of silence." Readers have always responded to Woolf's probings and evocations of the ebb and flow of "ordinary human life," of the internal life of individuals alone and in relationship, during the course of a day (as in *Mrs. Dalloway* or "The Window" in *To the Lighthouse*) or years (as in *The Waves* or *The Years*). We have paid less attention to Woolf's attempts to represent the non-human world. In this paper, I try to listen to Woolf's evocation of the "roar" of non-human reality; I argue she turned to this roar in her years of formal experimentation in the late nineteen-teens and early twenties and it ever after helped to create the worldview of her longer works.

Much current theory argues that there is no such thing as "nature" outside of human constructions or conceptions of it. But is this not a profoundly solipsistic view of the world? Most of the world is made up of animate and inanimate beings and things which exist without a language of words and which go on whether we notice them or not. Is this silent (to our ears) world then unimportant? Do we not depend every moment on that world, whether we recognize it or not? Laurence Coupe suggests that "in seeking to avoid naivety, [theory] has committed what might be called 'the semiotic fallacy.' In other words, it has assumed that because mountains and waters are human at the point of delivery, they exist only as signified within human culture. Thus they have no intrinsic merit, no value and no rights" (2). This position, he says, is an error belonging to "the arrogance of humanism" (2). And by denying the real existence of the non-human world, do we not condemn ourselves to a thin and lonely world? As Bill McKibben says in *The End of Nature*, "nature's independence *is* its meaning; without it there is nothing but us" (58).

So part of the question of how to recognize and to write the nonhuman has to do with recognizing its otherness, its difference and independence from us, while not objectifying it, that is, not making the nonhuman world simply a reflection of ourselves or a tool for our use. Woolf writes about this in her essay on Dorothy Wordsworth in which she compares the way Dorothy wrote about nature to the way Mary Wollstonecraft did. "Dorothy never confused her own soul with the sky," Woolf says (*CR2* 149). In my opening quotation from George Eliot, "hearing the grass grow and the squirrel's heart beat" is a simile for being keenly attuned to people's feelings, for being fully compassionate. Eliot is using the grass and the squirrel to represent an aspect of human life. I am interested here in exploring how literature can represent the grass and the squirrel as themselves; how literature can represent nature in itself rather than as a function of human endeavor or a metaphor for human striving. Woolf's conception of literary form as architectural is of help here. Creative literature (as opposed to expository literature) gestures towards what is unsayable. It creates a space, an emotional and mental space, in which that which is wordless can be made perceivable. Like sculpture or architecture, it can work with empty space; a building is not the space within it in which we live and move but it creates that space. So literature can create meaning which it does not say, which it cannot say.

Today I want to focus on "The Mark on the Wall," "Kew Gardens," and "Monday or Tuesday," written from 1917 to 1921: studies for a new way of writing. These experimental stories and sketches, which prepared Woolf for *Jacob's Room* (1922) and the rest of her modernist novels, attempt, in part, to represent the non-human world, particularly the natural world, in itself. About ten years later, in 1930, Woolf described "Monday or Tuesday" and another short sketch, "Blue and Green," to Ethel Smyth as "the wild outbursts of freedom, inarticulate, ridiculous, unprintable, mere outcries" (*L4* 231). For Woolf, these sketches pushed the boundaries of the unsayable but were the products of moments of freedom and vitality, of seeing past the old rules and realities.

"The Mark on the Wall" dramatizes this shifting from an old reality to a new one through the musings of the first person narrator. Meditating on the mysterious dark mark on her wall, the narrator considers the nature of reality:

> how shocking and yet how wonderful to discover that these real things, Sunday luncheons, Sunday walks, country houses, and tablecloths were not entirely real, were indeed half phantoms, and the damnation which visited the disbeliever in them was only a sense of illegitimate freedom. What now takes the place of those things I wonder, those real standard things? Men perhaps, should you be a woman; the masculine point of view which governs our lives, which sets the standard, which establishes Whitaker's Table of Precedency, which has become I suppose, since the war half a phantom to many men and women, which soon, one may hope, will be laughed into the dustbin where the phantoms go, the mahogany sideboards and Landseer prints, Gods and Devils, Hell and so forth, leaving us all with an intoxicating sense of illegitimate freedom—if freedom exists. (*CSF* 80)

Looking at the mark on the wall gives the narrator "a satisfying sense of reality" which makes Whitaker's precedencies turn shadowy, a satisfying sense of "the impersonal world which is proof of some existence other than ours" (*CSF* 82). Her meditations lead the narrator to imagine the life experiences of a tree:

> the close dry sensation of being wood; then the grinding of the storm; then the slow, delicious ooze of sap.... The song of birds must sound very loud and strange in June; and how cold the feet of insects must feel upon it, as they make laborious progresses up the creases of the bark, or sun themselves upon the thin green awning of the leaves, and look straight in front of them with diamond-cut red eyes. (*CSF* 82-83)

This narrator is starting to shift the human from the center.

The point of view of "Kew Gardens" is centered in the flower bed with the snail. The story begins in "the oval-shaped flower-bed" with its green stalks and red, blue, and yellow petals with the light filtering through them. "The light fell either upon the smooth grey back of a pebble, or the shell of a snail with its brown circular veins" (np). We see and hear the people walking past only to the extent that they are within ear and eye shot of the flower bed. We hear parts of their ongoing conversations and as they walk on into the distance, they "soon [diminish] in size among the trees and [look] half transparent as the sunlight and shade [swim] over their backs in large trembling irregular patches" (np). The patches of sunlight and shade play over the backs of the human beings as they do over the pebbles and the snail in the flower bed beneath the red, blue, and yellow blooms; the human beings are in the same relations to the sun and Kew and its trees as the snail is to the sun and the flower bed and its flowers. In this story, Woolf gets the rest of the world into the picture—bugs, plants, snail, thrush, earth, pebbles, sunlight, shade—and has shifted the center of focus away from the human. More than that, she creates a snail's eye view of the world:

> brown cliffs with deep green lakes in the hollows, flat blade-like trees that waved from root to tip, round boulders of grey stone, vast crumpled surfaces of a thin crackling texture—all these objects lay across the snail's progress between one stalk and another to his goal. Before he had decided whether to circumvent the arched tent of a dead leaf or to breast it there came past the bed the feet of other human beings. (np)

And again we hear bits and pieces of conversation, see a few moments of these people's walk through Kew, but we do not follow any of the human characters to any sense of resolution. The story asks us to give up our focus on people and their desires and goals which are implicitly compared to the snail's goal, and the thrush's and the butterflies', and asks us to experience rhythm, shape, color, light, texture from the snail's perspective as much or more than from the perspective of the human beings. Vanessa Bell's decorations for the 1927 edition assist in this emphasis on rhythm, shape, texture, light and dark, helping to make reading this story a sensuous and contemplative experience rather than the pursuit of a linear narrative or the fate of a character. Woolf asks us to *be in* Kew Gardens rather than to go through Kew Gardens.

"Kew Gardens" pans out in a wide-angle shot, so to speak, just at the end, placing the gardens in the context of the city, where "the motor omnibuses were turning their wheels and changing their gear; like a vast nest of Chinese boxes all of wrought steel turning ceaselessly one within another the city murmured; on the top of which the voices cried aloud and the petals of myriads of flowers flashed their colours into the air" (np). In "Monday or Tuesday," the hectic human city and the human pursuit of "truth" is framed at beginning and end by the sky and a heron. The body of this short sketch is composed of choppy sentences in which prosaic snippets of everyday human life weave in and out of a questioning search for truth:

> Desiring truth, awaiting it, laboriously distilling a few words, for ever desiring— (a cry starts to the left, another to the right. Wheels strike divergently. Omnibuses conglomerate in conflict)—for ever desiring—(the clock asseverates with twelve distinct strokes that it is midday; light sheds gold scales; children swarm)—for

ever desiring truth. Red is the dome; coins hang on the trees; smoke trails from the chimneys; bark, shout, cry "Iron for sale"—and truth? (131)

This hectic rush of the business of human life and this anxious and unsatisfied search for truth contrast with the peace and presence of the heron and the sky. The sketch begins thus: "Lazy and indifferent, shaking space easily from his wings, knowing his way, the heron passes over the church beneath the sky. White and distant, absorbed in itself, endlessly the sky covers and uncovers, moves and remains" (131). And it ends: "Lazy and indifferent the heron returns; the sky veils her stars; then bares them" (131). Once again, though through a different device than in "Kew Gardens," Woolf questions the centrality of the "human condition," the human point of view.

Although each of these three short stories works somewhat differently, the techniques they share for suggesting the reality, the existence, of the natural world which goes on around and in spite of us are reporting and juxtaposition. By reporting I mean description that refrains from comparing the nonhuman to the human and from making the nonhuman serve as symbols for or projections of the human. Reporting in this sense is the technique Woolf describes Dorothy Wordsworth using:

> This "I so much alive" was ruthlessly subordinated to the trees and the grass. For if she let "I" and its rights and its wrongs and its passions and its suffering get between her and the object, she would be calling the moon "the Queen of the Night"; she would be talking of dawn's "orient beams"; she would be soaring into reveries and rhapsodies and forgetting to find the exact phrase for the ripple of moonlight upon the lake. (*CR2* 149)

Woolf argues that Dorothy's "plain statement[s]" and "brief notes unfurl in the mind and open a whole landscape before us" (151). Similarly, for example, Woolf's plain reporting of "brown cliffs," "blade-like trees," "vast crumpled surfaces" opens a snail's whole landscape before us without imposing human perspectives. By juxtaposition, I mean the placing of human and nonhuman side by side without comment, as Woolf does in "Kew Gardens" and "Monday or Tuesday," which allows new views of reality, of existences and relationships, to unfurl for us. In these ways, Woolf's stories make a space, a vessel or container, for something which they are not, something which they cannot *express*, but which they allow to be seen and felt.

These writing strategies suggest a reading strategy of restraint, suggest that we refrain from interpretation of the natural world in these texts, refrain from making symbols of it. For example, a recurring motif in *The Years* which I've often wondered about is the pigeons' cooing: "Take two coos, Taffy. Take two coos." In the past, I've tried to think about what the symbolism of these recurring pigeons and their cooing could be. Now I think that's not the point; the point is their presence. Thinking about the natural world in Woolf's fiction has suggested to me that I slow down, be with the text, *experience* it.

The writing of her experimental stories and sketches of 1917-1921 effected a Copernican shift for Woolf; she came to see the human world as no longer the center of the universe. This new way of seeing and writing the non-human world enabled Woolf's reframing and defamiliarizing of the human world in her later novels and in *A Room of*

One's Own and *Three Guineas*. Whitaker's precedencies, the hierarchies of a masculinist, classist society, lose their aura of solid, inevitable reality placed in this new cosmology. Following trajectories first sketched in the earlier stories, the sky, birds, the moon, the sea, the wind, make ways of their own through these later texts. In this way, Woolf uses rhythm and reporting to create experiences of presence and creates telling juxtapositions between human feelings and events and the world which goes on, as the narrator of "The Mark on the Wall" puts it, "without paying any attention to us" (82).

Works Cited

Coupe, Laurence. General Introduction. *The Green Studies Reader: From Romanticism to Ecocriticism*. Ed. Coupe. London and New York: Routledge, 2000. 1-8.
Eliot, George. *Middlemarch*. Ed. Bert G. Hornback. New York and London: W. W. Norton, 1977.
McKibben, Bill. *The End of Nature*. New York: Anchor/Doubleday, [1989], 1999.
Woolf, Virginia. "Dorothy Wordsworth." (1929) *The Second Common Reader*. (1932) New York: Harcourt Brace Jovanovich, 1960. 148-55.
—. *Kew Gardens*. (1919) A facsimile edition of the 1927 Hogarth Press edition with decorations by Vanessa Bell. London: Hogarth (Chatto & Windus), 1999.
—. *The Letters of Virginia Woolf*. Vol. 4. Ed. Nigel Nicolson and Joanne Trautman. New York: Harcourt Brace Jovanovich, 1978.
—. "The Mark on the Wall." (1917) *The Complete Shorter Fiction of Virginia Woolf*. Ed. Susan Dick. New York: Harcourt Brace Jovanovich, 1985. 77-83.
—. "Monday or Tuesday." (1921) *The Complete Shorter Fiction of Virginia Woolf*. Ed. Susan Dick. New York: Harcourt Brace Jovanovich, 1985. 131.

The Politics of the Borderline:
the Private, the Public and *Between*...

by Urszula Terentowicz-Fotyga

In Woolf scholarship, the border between the private and public realms has always been a line of conflict. The debate between modernists and feminists, between those who portray Woolf as a sensitive, ethereal poetess and those who see her as an angry and committed "political creature" resurfaces again and again in different shapes and contexts. The tradition of reading Woolf in exclusive terms, as either pathologically private or militantly public, is very much alive. While researching into Woolf's reception in Poland, I was surprised at how, in a different social, political and cultural environment, the concepts of private and public continue to occupy the centre of critical attention. In fact, in a more limited range of responses, the trends and paradoxes of Woolf's reception appear more marked and salient. Undoubtedly, for Woolf's detractors in particular, the two terms offer a convenient tool to whip the writer for staking out the territory on one side of the borderline. Thus, in the Polish reception, the proponents of social realism find Woolf guilty of excessive poetizing. Her interest in the human psyche is considered as a dangerous and harmful form of escapism. In contrast, those critical of her feminist agenda, praise her poetic detachment and regard the openly political works as marginal and ultimately failed experiments.[1]

While the two groups disagree as to whether Woolf's faults lie in being too poetic or too political, they do have one thing in common. Both arguments depend on accepting a clear-cut opposition between private and public spheres, both read Woolf's prose in terms of "either/or." While this tendency may be particularly prominent in a more limited context of national reception, it reflects a broader spectrum of Woolf studies. Though most of us agree that the writer's continuing attraction lies precisely in her refusal to be pinned down, our approach, nonetheless, tends to gravitate either towards her private or public persona. Somehow, we like *The Waves* or *Three Guineas* more; we warm either to Rhoda or to Rose; favour either the fragile Woolf in Beresford's portrait or the sharp intellectual in Man Ray's photographs.

Certainly, the tendency to lock the writer into private or public realms is fuelled by her writing. The dichotomy, structured through the poetics of space, lies at the core of her fiction. The terms private and public recur throughout her works and encapsulate other important dichotomies of masculine and feminine, language and silence, verbal and visual.[2] Yet, saying that these oppositions are the paradigm of Woolf's construction of reality is telling only part of the truth. The binary structure, which informs the early novels, clearly falters in her later works. The reconceptualization of these notions was a complex and gradual process and involved, among other things, recognizing the private as deeply political. What interests me today, however, is Woolf's redefinition of private and public in her last novel in the context of her poetics of identity. *Between the Acts*, I will argue, negotiates the boundaries which in the early novels were carefully demarcated. By playing with the notions of inner and outer, private and public, individual and communal, Woolf offers a new conceptualization of identity, one that questions the notion of the self as bounded and singular. While critics tend to read the theme of subjectivity in *Between the Acts* in the context of language and narrative (Ames, Vandivere, Hussey 130-55), I am going to focus on the semiotics of space in two mirror scenes, in which Woolf's deconstruction of binary oppositions is most evident.[3] At the centre of the two scenes are two women artists: Isa Oliver and Miss La Trobe.

Isa Oliver is one of Woolf's most baffling characters. Aloof, focused on the inner world, dissatisfied with her body, she might appear as another incarnation of Rhoda, the most private of Woolf's women protagonists. Isa and Rhoda are linked by the symbol of a rider as well as by water imagery: both speak of their desire to be covered and dissolved by waters. Rhoda's iconic image of the swallow dipping her wings in midnight pools is echoed in Isa's imagining a "thrush...dipping and diving as if he skimmed waves in the air" (*BTA* 64). The microcosm of petals rocked in a basin reverberates in Isa's picture of leaves falling onto the water (ibid.). Yet, Isa is also markedly different from Rhoda and from other "private" women protagonists. Unlike Rhoda, she is married and despite the pronounced hatred for "the domestic, the possessive; the maternal" (*BTA* 14), there are many instances of her deep, maternal love. More importantly, in contrast with Rhoda's imaginary worlds, Isa's sphere of creation is verbal. Her poetic ramblings are immersed in different, often contradictory, codes and registers: artistic and everyday, intimate and banal, lofty and commonplace, poignant and trite. Though not addressed to anyone in particular, they are actually spoken out, often overheard and commented on by other characters. The effect of this mixture is often rather comic: "'There to lose what binds us here,' she murmured. 'Soles. Filleted. In time for lunch please,' she said aloud. 'With a feather, a blue feather...flying mounting through the air ... there to lose what binds us here...'" (12). Thus, unlike Rhoda's poignant, highly private and idiosyncratic vision, Isa's poetic creations balance in between different realms. They are neither fully private nor public, neither inner nor outer, but remain suspended in the space of "betweenness."

This symbolic hovering between different realms is best encapsulated in the scene at the beginning of the novel, in which Isa explores her feelings while standing in front of the mirror. It is worth quoting in detail, as it illustrates brilliantly how Woolf toys with the dichotomic nature of inside and outside.

> She...stood in front of the three-folded mirror, so that she could see three separate versions of her rather heavy, yet handsome, face; and also, outside the glass, a slip of terrace, lawn and tree tops.
>
> Inside the glass, in her eyes, she saw what she had felt overnight for the ravaged, the silent, the romantic gentleman farmer. "In love," was in her eyes. But outside, on the washstand, on the dressing-table, among the silver boxes and tooth-brushes, was the other love; love for her husband, the stockbroker—"The father of my children," she added, slipping into the cliché conveniently provided by fiction. Inner love was in the eyes; outer love on the dressing table. But what feeling was it that stirred in her now when above the looking-glass, out of doors, she saw coming across the lawn the perambulator; two nurses; and her little boy George, lagging behind?
>
> She tapped on the window with her embossed hairbrush. They were too

far off to hear. The drone of the trees was in their ears; the chirp of birds; other incidents of garden life, inaudible, invisible to her in the bedroom, absorbed them. Isolated on a green island, hedged about with snowdrops, laid with a counterpane of puckered silk, the innocent island floated under her window. Only George lagged behind.

 She returned to her eyes in the looking glass. "In love," she must be; since the presence of his body in the room last night could so affect her; since the words he said, handing her a teacup, handing her a tennis racquet, could so attach themselves to a certain spot in her; and thus lie between them like a wire, tingling, tangling, vibrating – she groped, in the depths of the looking glass, for a word to fit the infinitely quick vibrations of the aeroplane propeller that she had seen once at dawn at Croydon. (11-12)

The space, as described in this fragment, is taken into several frames: the outside of the window and the inside of the room, the outside and the inside of the mirror, the external, material world and Isa's inner world. Yet, the different spaces, rather than being mutually exclusive, undulate and interpenetrate. The window, one of the most potent symbols in Woolf's fiction, both connects and separates. The little scene in the garden, which appears as an extension of the reality framed by the mirror, is enclosed in the bedroom and yet remains separate—Isa can see only bits and fragments of the garden, while the little party on the "innocent island" remains altogether oblivious of her presence. The mirror reflects and merges the different spaces and, at the same time, breaks them into pieces in its three separate parts, in the same way that it breaks Isa's body. The different spaces merge so that it is difficult to say which is inside, which is outside and while the description is constructed around the oppositions of internal and external, the two notions are practically asemantic.

 The confusion affects Isa, who goes about exploring her memories by groping "in the depths of the looking glass." And while the outer love, the love for her husband is most internalized; the inner one is metaphorically connected with outer space. Isa's emotional confusion is accompanied by the fragmentation of the body—the three parts of her face in the mirror reflect her three social roles—the mother, the wife and the lover. The different selves are neither completely separate nor do they merge readily into one identity. Hovering between these scraps and particles, Isa tries to reassemble and reimagine her self as a site of "betweenness." Her self constitutes in the process of hovering not only between these different roles but also in the space between the inner self and its material representations. Her self is in her eyes and her memories but it is also somewhere there "among the silver-boxes and tooth-brushes" and all the bric-a-brac she uses to impress chambermaids in hotels. The mirror, the central artefact of the room, becomes a perfect symbol of Woolf's remapping of the notion of identity, which questions the oppositions between inside and outside, private and public, material and spiritual. But the mirror scene can also be read as an early indication of the thematic focus on the question of identity and representation, which Woolf explores further in the scenes of the pageant.

 While the whole novel reflects on the notion of plural, unbounded self, the pageant actually enacts, to borrow Hall's phrase, the "endlessly performative self" (1). The text of the play constructs a palimpsestic reality, in which different historical, literary and cultural worlds are juxtaposed and contrasted and the actual performance makes this reality even more complex. The boundaries, which in a real theatre separate the artistic from the everyday, in the outdoor setting and amateur interpretation, are purely symbolic. As a result, the separation of art and life becomes problematic. Without the curtain to shut out the scenery, the action of the play is constantly disrupted by the interferences from the natural world: the flying sparrows, the rain, the mooing cows. As different realities interpenetrate, the rules of the space become manifestly difficult to define—neither those of a real theatre nor those of the everyday seem in effect:

> Could they talk? Could they move? No, for the play was going on. Yet the stage was empty; only the cows moved in the meadows; only the tick of the gramophone needle was heard. The tick, tick, tick seemed to hold them together, tranced. Nothing whatsoever appeared on the stage. (*BTA* 51)

The effaced boundaries between art and life are particularly problematic for those participating in the pageant.[4] The amateur stars take on their parts without necessarily shedding their private selves. Albert Perry as the young Prince is still Albert Perry. Eliza Clark, dressed up as Queen Elizabeth, remains the shopkeeper from the local grocery. As evidenced by her rendering of the Queen's "greatness," the metaphors, in this palimpsestic reality, become painfully literal:

> And when she mounted the soap box in the centre, representing perhaps a rock in the ocean, her size made her appear gigantic. She could reach a flitch of bacon or haul a tub of oil with one sweep of her arm in the shop. (*BTA* 52)

A perfect embodiment of the materialized metaphor is the village idiot, playing himself. His irrational behaviour proves a very real, not just a metaphorical threat.

The confusion about the different roles concerns not only the actors but also those on the other side of the stage. Their part, "a very important part," Oliver says, "is to be the audience" (37), which involves, among other things, bearing "the intolerable burden of sitting silent, doing nothing, in company" (41). If experiencing the awkwardness of being "too close; but not close enough" (41) is hard, the vagaries of the performance make it even harder. The unclear rules of the amateur theatre put the spectators in a position where the most basic principles become ambiguous and questionable; right from the very start, when it is not clear whether the play has begun and, in effect, whether they are supposed to adopt the role of the audience: "Was it, or was it not, the play? Chuff, chuff, chuff sounded from the bushes. It was the noise a machine makes when something has gone wrong. Some sat down hastily; others stopped talking guiltily. All looked at the bushes. For the stage was empty" (47-48). The kaleidoscopic reality of the pageant defamiliarizes not only the signifying practices but also the social roles inscribed in it. With the semiotic space offering conflicting codes and representations, the process of identification becomes increasingly problematic. Without familiar boundaries and clearly defined roles, the audience loses the sense of self as the centre of semiosis: "Yet somehow they felt—how could one put it—a little not quite here or there. As if the play had jerked the ball out of the cup; as if what I call myself was still floating unattached, and didn't settle. Not quite themselves they felt." (90) Around this crisis of identity, Woolf builds the sense of community. The language of the play takes over during the intervals as different characters discover the similarities between their lives and those portrayed on stage.

While one of the main tasks facing the audience is interpreting the playwright's artistic vision, to those assembled at the terrace it proves extremely difficult. Equipped only with an enigmatic programme, they are at a loss even as to what epochs, realities and characters are actually presented on stage. With the blurred boundaries of the open-air theatre, characters forgetting their lines, words blown away and constant interruptions from the surrounding nature, most remain puzzled about the meaning of the play. Successful completion of the task, in this case, depends on determining what is part of the artistic vision and what belongs to the world without, or, as one character puts it, what is intentional and what accidental (*BTA* 102). Thus, while the interpretative process hinges on setting the boundary between the semiotic and non-semiotic elements of the performance, telling the two apart proves extremely tricky, as Miss La Trobe herself is deliberately and consciously equivocal about it. Though in turn despairing and exulting at the external interruptions, she clearly takes full advantage of the blurred boundaries offered by the open-air theatre.

As the action moves forward in time, the boundaries separating the reality of the pageant and the world of the audience become more and more effaced and in the last scene they disappear completely. The culmination of the spectacle is the part entitled "The Present Time. Ourselves" (106), in which the audience are first left to themselves in silence and then faced with mirrors reflecting their confused faces. The scene, as many critics noted, focuses on the question of representation (Lee 211, Bishop 123-24, Ames 402), but, more importantly for the present considerations, it undermines the boundaries between the different roles inscribed in the pageant. For once, the audience become the actors, the authors and the theme of the play; they become the signs, the scriptwriters and the readers, all at the same time. Their confusion, bafflement and outrage become the semiotic content of the play. Miss La Trobe's gimmickry exposes not only them as the audience and contemporaries but also as individuals. The aim of the finale is to "show us up, as we are, here and now" (*BTA* 110). The boundary between the private and the public selves, fragile throughout the performance, is erased entirely and leaves the spectators upset and vulnerable, as one of them admits: "Ourselves? But that's cruel. To snap us as we are, before we've had time to assume.... And only, too, in parts.... That's what's so distorting and upsetting and utterly unfair" (109). In the last act of the pageant, the spectators are locked in a semiotic circle, forced to interpret themselves as signs. If throughout the play they have a sense of self as "suspended, without being, in limbo" (106), the finale forces them to face and recognize the impossibility of identification. Hence, the Reverend's seemingly unproblematic slipping into his role of "a clergyman in the livery of his servitude" is perceived as a violation, "an intolerable constriction, contraction, and reduction to simplified absurdity" (112-13).

Yet, *Between the Acts* is a novel that defies closure and conclusion. The impossibility of uniting the complex and fragmented self is counterbalanced by the urge and the need to do so. The characters' experience of the self as multiple and unbounded is accompanied by their desire for identification and representation, which, once again, is illustrated by a mirror scene. Woolf subtly subverts the symbolic meaning of the mirror as she counterpoints Miss La Trobe's and Isa's mirror encounters with those of Mrs Manresa.[5] In the scenes discussed above, the mirrors function as means of effacing the boundaries between the different selves and dislocating the self-sustaining subject. But Mrs Manresa, unlike other spectators, consistently refuses to succumb to the uniting, expository strategies adopted by Miss La Trobe. Throughout the pageant, she uses the mirror to consolidate her public self. The gesture of taking out a little mirror to powder her nose and redden her lips functions as a symbolic refusal to be dispersed or displaced. The gesture gains particular significance in the finale, when, as Bartholomew enthusiastically notes, she appears as the only one that "preserved unashamed her identity, and faced without blinking herself" (110). As DiBattista aptly sums it up:

> Her bold gesture substantiates and upholds the metaphoric connection between identity and role, the self and its masks.... She, of all the characters in the novel, defies the expository and mind-divided glance that seeks to separate the soul from its social mask, the self from its social disguises, the painted from the hidden faces. (222) [6]

The Reverend's tentative and well-meaning interpretation of the play fulfils a similar role as it counterbalances the openness of the spectacle. His attempt at capturing the elusive meanings and providing the pageant with closure, though seen as "the most grotesque" (*BTA* 113), is nevertheless acknowledged and embraced. In effect, the audience too take on their roles and, folding "their hands in the traditional manner as if they were seated in church" (ibid.), allow him to name and define. Yet, before we hasten to conclude that *Between the Acts* speaks for the necessity of consolidating one's complex experience into a singular role, Woolf makes another volte-face, subverting once again the wish for closure and clarity. As the Reverend's summary and Miss La Trobe's epilogue call on the audience to reassemble and consolidate, Mrs Manresa abandons her mirror and lets the tears ravage her make up.

Woolf's construction of subjectivity in her last novel lives up to the spirit of "betweenness." The deconstruction of oppositions of inner and outer, private and public, individual and communal is only a starting point for the subject formation. As the pageant complicates the spectators' effort to construct identity, it makes the need to define and represent both absurd and unavoidable. The characters' acceptance of the self as infinitely hovering between different selves and spaces is counterbalanced, as the last act of the novel suggests most poignantly, by their tentative acceptance of the necessity to take on their parts in the eternal spectacle that stretches back into the pre-historic past. Woolf's poetics of identity in *Between the* Acts does not offer neat conclusions but neither does it end in a void.[7] In her construction of subjectivity one can detect both the postmodern acceptance of the self as a process and the modernist dream of finding the essential self, one that transcends different masks and performances.[8] Behind the poetics of "betweenness" lie Woolf's politics of evasions and *Between the Acts* can be read as her last, and possibly most vigorous, refusal to be pinned down and consolidated into a figure, be it private or public.

Notes

1 The most contrasting examples of the two approaches are reviews by Promiński and Sadkowski. For a more detailed discussion of the reviews, see Terentowicz-Fotyga "From Silence" 130-31, 143-44.
2 For a thorough analysis of Woolf's engagement with the public/private division and how the two concepts relate to other aspects of her writing, see Snaith and Terentowicz-Fotyga *Semiotyka Przestrzeni*.
3 For a feminist interpretation of some of the mirror scenes in *Between the Acts*, see Barrett. 29-30. Barrett claims that the mirror gradually loses its mimetic power, but I will argue that Mrs Manresa's mirror encounter at the end of the novel substantiates rather than diminishes its ability to reflect.
4 Ames (401) and Ferrer (100) note that the lack of separation between the audience and actors is a generic feature of the pageant and testifies to its inscription in the carnivalesque tradition. Ruotolo discusses the blurred boundaries in the context of theatrical illusion (219-21).
5 Ames too notes the difference between Isa's and Mrs Manresa's mirror encounters. The first, he argues, speaks of the protagonist's solitude, the other remains "true to the carnival spirit, the spirit Bakhtin associates with crooked and distorting mirrors" (402).
6 See also, Ferrer 136.
7 Analysing the subject formation in linguistic terms, Vandivere draws different conclusions. She argues that in *Between the Acts* there is "no hope for coherence or coherent subjectivity, for the illusion of meaning becomes not only a hole but also a hole within a hole" (230). Vandivere does not seem to allow, however, for the role of unifying strategies, which counterbalance the dissolution and fragmentation of the self and language.
8 Similar conclusions have been drawn by critics analyzing Woolf's notion of subject formation in Orlando. For example, Burns argues that the breakdown of inner and outer spaces reflects the novel's central tension between notions of essential personal identity and contextually re-defined subjectivity" (344).

Works Cited

Ames, Christopher. "Carnivalesque Comedy in *Between the Acts*." *Twentieth Century Literature* 44.4 (1998): 394-408.
Barrett, Eileen. "Matriarchal Myth on a Patriarchal Stage: Virginia Woolf's *Between the Acts*." *Twentieth Century Literature* 33.1 (1987): 18-37.
Bishop, Edward. *Virginia Woolf*. Houndmills, Basingstoke: Macmillan, 1991.
Burns, Christy L. "Re-Dressing Feminist Identities: Tensions between Essential and Constructed Selves in Virginia Woolf's *Orlando*." *Twentieth Century Literature* 40.3 (1994): 342-64.
DiBattista, Maria. *Virginia Woolf's Major Novels: The Fables of Anon*. New Haven, London: Yale UP, 1980.
Ferrer, Daniel. *Virginia Woolf and the Madness of Language*. Trans. Geoffrey Bemington and Rachel Bowlby. New York: Routledge, 1990.
Fleishman, Avrom. *Virginia Woolf: A Critical Reading*. Baltimore, London: Johns Hopkins UP, 1975.
Hall, Stuart. "Who Needs Identity?" *Questions of Cultural Identity*. Ed. Stuart Hall and Paul du Gay. London: Sage, 1996. 1-17.
Lee, Hermione. *The Novels of Virginia Woolf*. London: Methuen, 1977.
Hussey, Mark. *The Singing of the Real World: The Philosophy of Virginia Woolf's Fiction*. Columbus: Ohio UP, 1986.
Promiński, Marian. "W stronę Virginii Woolf." *Życie Literackie* 22.4 (1957): 4-5.
Ruotolo, L.P. *The Interrupted Moment: A View of Virginia Woolf Novels*. Stanford: Stanford UP, 1986.
Sadkowski, Wacław. "Lęki i wdzięki Virginii Woolf." *Wiadomości Kulturalne* 33 (1997): 10.
Snaith, Anna. *Virginia Woolf: Public and Private Negotiations*. Houndmills, Basingstoke: Palgrave, 2000.
Terentowicz-Fotyga, Urszula. "From Silence to a Polyphony of Voices: Virginia Woolf's Reception in Poland." *The Reception of Virginia Woolf in Europe*. Ed. Mary Ann Caws and Nicola Luckhurst. London, New York: Continuum, 2002.
———. *Semiotyka Przestrzeni Kobiecych w Powieściach Virginii Woolf*. Lublin: UMCS, 2006.
Vandivere, Julie. "Waves and Fragments: Linguistic Construction as Subject Formation in Virginia Woolf." *Twentieth Century Literature* 42.2 (1996): 221-33.
Woolf, Virginia. *Between the Acts*. London, New York: Penguin, 1992.

Rachel Vinrace's and Anna Morgan's Parallel Voyages: Exploring the Relationship Between Illness and Modernism

by Joyce Kelley

In her still illuminating 1981 essay "The Blank Page and the Issues of Female Creativity," Susan Gubar argues that, in texts from Scott Fitzgerald to T. S. Eliot, "the female literary body has been feared for its power to articulate itself" (246). Indeed, using Isak Dinesen's short fable "The Blank Page," in which women's bridal bloodstains are exhibited publicly like artwork in a gallery, she asserts that many women "experience their own bodies as the only available medium for their art, with the result that the distance between the woman artist and her art is often radically diminished" (248). I would like to build upon Gubar's theory by suggesting that the woman writer's "art" may be inscribed on the bodies of her own female characters. Specifically, I would like to examine two works in which women writers use the female body as a text on which to move beyond the conventions of realism. In both *The Voyage Out* by Virginia Woolf (1915) and *Voyage in the Dark* (1934) by Jean Rhys, the young female protagonists succumb to illnesses which allow for the release of a new kind of art, a new modernist language. In both works, the illnesses of the young women follow transgressions of acceptable boundaries, one geographical and one sexual, and both authors adapt and subvert the stereotype of illness as retribution. Though both characters are identified with silence, both achieve voice through their illnesses. Each author creates modernist language by drawing upon the instability of the mind and body and the simultaneous heightening and unbalance of the senses during illness to redefine the bounds of consciousness and thus reshape language. Through their illnesses, the bodies of both young women are thus recreated as sites for modernist literary production.

Virginia Woolf's own essay "On Being Ill" perhaps best examines her views on the relationship between illness and inspiration. Here Woolf expresses surprise that illness has not become "one of the prime themes of literature":

> Considering how common illness is, how tremendous the spiritual change that it brings, how astonishing, when the lights of health go down, the undiscovered countries that are disclosed, what wastes and deserts of the soul a slight attack of influenza brings to view, what precipices and lawns sprinkled with bright flowers a little rise of temperature reveals. (193)

Woolf speaks of illness as if it were a destination apart from the everyday world, "undiscovered countries" filled with bright images opening to the mind. I mention this attention to geographic space because both Woolf and Rhys significantly explore illness in novels founded upon the metaphor of a voyage, The *Voyage* Out, and a *Voyage* in the Dark. Both voyages may be read not only as Rachel and Anna's awakenings in a foreign country but also as metaphors for the illnesses themselves which carry both the young women and their authors into new linguistic terrain.

There is a historical connection between women's bodies and illness which Woolf and Rhys first reinscribe and then revise in their effort to break women's silence. As Susan Sontag explores in her work *Illness as Metaphor*, various illnesses such as tuberculosis and hysteria have customarily been linked with feminine sexuality. In the Victorian novel as in Victorian society, women were frequently ill. Feminist scholars have often seen these illnesses as resulting from the pressures of a male-dominated social structure. Some physicians saw illness as the consequence of women stepping out of moral or sexual codes. Sontag quotes Karl Menniger's "dangerous" assertion that "illness is in part what the world has done to a victim, but in a larger part it is what the victim has done with his world" (Sontag 46-47). Thus was illness seen both as punishment and as expected response to woman's transgressive activity. As Diane Price Herndl explains in *Invalid Women*, "Illness became the condition that could best accommodate the contradictory cultural and medical expectations of womanhood" (39). Herndl asserts that there were merely three avenues open to an ill woman: she could "die, go mad, or get well" (15). On a broad structural level, Woolf and Rhys do not move their heroines beyond these established paths; both Rachel and Anna seem to become ill as a consequence of going where a young woman is not supposed to go.

While spending time in South America, Rachel in *The Voyage Out* yields to a strange and serious illness shortly after returning from an expedition upriver into "the great darkness" (265) of the forest to inspect native life up close. Rachel's illness and death are seen ultimately as no random misfortune; Evelyn comments near the novel's end, "There must be a reason" and continues, "It can't only be an accident" (357). Helen argues on the expedition that the party members have "ventured too far and exposed themselves" (286), her words implying an improper transgression done with the body. Although other men and women have gone on such expeditions and "returned again without damage done to mind or body" (264), the suggestion remains that "damage" from such an encounter would be expected, and Rachel ultimately dies from the fever she contracts. In Rhys's original ending of *Voyage in the Dark*, Anna Morgan also dies; her transgression has been a sexual one, and she suffers from an improper abortion.[1] Nonetheless, Woolf and Rhys radically move beyond former literary applications of illness on a linguistic level. These authors invert tradition by using the ill body as a medium for female voice and, particularly, for a parlance which enables artistic exploration.

Susan Gubar specifically writes in her essay that "in terms of the production of culture" woman consistently has been "an art object" but not "the sculptor" (244). Heretofore, the female body, a receptacle for illness, also has been coupled with notions of silence. Women's characteristically fluid bodies have always been placed under careful surveillance, lest they should move beyond appropriate boundaries. Victorian restrictions of women's bodies like the Contagious Diseases Acts suggested that the transmission of sexual disease was fostered by the bodies of impure women, and made the body of any woman violating social norms subject to sexual search by authorities. Josephine Butler and other public women orators spoke out against these acts, standing up and forwardly articulating sexual issues and employing vocabulary that had formerly gone unspoken, thus turning their bodies into vehicles of transgressive language. In a similar manner, the young women in Woolf's and Rhys's novels transgress accepted boundaries with their bodies. "To hinder the description of illness in literature, there is the poverty of language," Woolf writes in "On Being Ill" (194). She specifically calls attention to the social and linguistic boundaries broken by illness; "there is...a childish outspokenness in illness," she writes. "Things are said, truths blurted out, which the cautious respectability of health conceals" (196). Thus does illness provide a way for a woman to break through social restrictions of language and, more specifically, provide a manner for an author to explore and articulate new linguistic forms.

Rachel in *The Voyage Out* is a naive twenty-four year old experiencing an exotic world away from her secluded English life, a world of men, love, passion, and finally, illness. First awakened to this new sexual realm by Richard Dalloway's kiss and then propelled forward by Terence's love, Rachel's pathway to marriage is cut short by her fatal illness. Critics of Woolf's novel interested in Rachel as a character have tended to focus on her lack of voice in the text. June Cummins, for example, in her essay "Death and the Maiden Voyage" notes Rachel's "lack of access to language," silenced "by others and by her own self-censorship" (206). Indeed, Woolf's novel in this regard approximates Terence's own inspiration, "a novel about Silence...the things people don't say" (*VO* 216). Throughout the novel Rachel is identified with such silences. Evelyn accuses Rachel of "always thinking of something you don't say" (251) and Rachel, when writing, laments "the gulf" between her world and "the sheet of paper" before her (296). What critics are less likely to note, however, is that Rachel, in all her silence, is calling for a new kind of language. A talented pianist, the young woman expresses herself more through her music than through speech, for, as Susan says of music, "It just seems to say all the things one can't say oneself" (167). In an argument with Terence over the importance of her music, Rachel exclaims, "Think of words compared with sounds!" (292). Rachel, like Woolf herself, is demanding a new language; "Why don't people write about the things they do feel?" she asks (297). It seems highly appropriate that Woolf should choose such a person as the vehicle for her own art.

Other critics have noted the sequences of modernist language invading Woolf's more traditional novel form. For instance, in his work *Between Language and Silence* Howard Harper speaks of Woolf's "emphasis on the necessities and ambiguities of perception" which make *The Voyage Out* seem "startlingly modern at times, despite its obvious debts to Victorian tradition" (13). Lytton Strachey too perceived something unusual in the linguistic departures of *The Voyage Out* when he remarked in a 1916 letter to Woolf that there was something "very unvictorian," even "Tolstoyan" in her treatment of Rachel's illness (quoted in Richter, 93). Passages occurring even before Rachel's fever point to shifts in perception and language; perhaps most significant are the sections occurring during the expedition upriver when, lost in their love for each other, Rachel and Hewet become entranced in a series of underwater fantasies. The tropical forest seems to provide a place where language can be transformed; when Rachel and Hewet finally confess their love, "The silence was then broken by their voices which joined in tones of strange unfamiliar sound which formed no words" (271). Here Rachel and Hewet are learning and participating in a new language, but Rachel alone seems to take these fundamentals and transform them into a whole new rendering of reality. In what perhaps could be seen as a pre-illness delusion, Rachel suddenly imagines the towering heads of Helen and Hewet over her:

> Both were flushed, both laughing, and the lips were moving. ... Broken fragments of speech came down to her on the ground. She thought she heard them

speak of love and then of marriage. ... When this fell away, and the grasses once more lay low, and the sky became horizontal, and the earth rolled out flat on each side, and the trees stood upright, she was the first to perceive a little row of human figures standing patiently in the distance. For the moment she could not remember who they were. (284)

Rachel's fractured vision presages her later shifts in visual perspective during her illness, what Woolf refers to in her essay "On Being Ill" as "the great experience" of "how the world has changed its shape" (195). Although Rachel then moves back into what we might call the "real" world, she carries a germ of this experience back with her to her life at the hotel.

E. L. Bishop writes that "In *The Voyage Out* Woolf was already reaching toward the novel of silence; and in the account of Rachel's death, a scene paradigmatic of the work as a whole, the author succeeds in rendering experience beyond the usual reach of language" (355). I would like to make a similar reading, not, as Bishop does, of Terence's reaction to Rachel's death, but of the scenes of Rachel's illness preceding her death. Here Rachel begins to detect the onset of illness when her mind begins to play with written language. On a hot afternoon, Rachel and Terence have been seeking a book which can "withstand the power of the sun" (326). As Rachel listens to him reading Milton, she begins to feel as if she can "almost handle" his words, and that they are "laden with meaning" (326). Christine Froula argues that Milton's verse about the mythical Sabrina is "the cause of Rachel's illness" for it reflects "female destiny" and a constrictive marriage plot in which Rachel is herself trapped (84). While the poem's interpretive resonances are significant, also crucial is the way Rachel's mind is reacting to the pure linguistic quality of the poem's words. Rachel finds in these words something similar to what Woolf describes when she writes in her essay:

> In illness words seem to possess a mythic quality. We grasp what is beyond their surface quality...—a sound, a colour, here a stress, there a pause. ... In health, meaning has encroached upon sound. ... But in illness...we creep beneath some obscure poem...and the words give out their scent and distill their flavour. ("On Being Ill" 200)

This passage stresses layers of depth, color, and sound resonating beyond surface appearance which are perceptible only through illness. Significantly, this new linguistic discovery approximates what Woolf herself would like to achieve in her own modernist work where "the accent" should "fall[ ] differently from of old," where "the moment of importance" might come "not here but there" ("Modern Fiction" 212). What Rachel is experiencing is distinctly modernist, for the poetry itself fractures so that the words "meant different things from what they usually meant" (326). Just as modernist poets may use words more for sound than for meaning, using language as springboards to suggest an array of different images, Rachel "went off upon curious trains of thought suggested by words such as 'curb' and 'Locrine' and 'Brute,' which brought unpleasant sights before her eyes, independently of their meaning" (327). Later, lying in bed, she tries to remember the poem but "the adjectives persisted in getting into the wrong places" (329). This rearrangement and reordering of language for Rachel is crucial to Woolf's own project.

As well, Rachel's illness has abolished chronological time, another experiment of Woolf's modernist fiction: "Hours and hours would pass thus, without getting any further through the morning, or again a few minutes would lead from broad daylight to the depths of the night" (330). Space and proportion change for Rachel as her eyes distort reality; recalling the earlier passage during the expedition, Helen's stooping form "appeared of gigantic size, and came down upon her like the ceiling falling" (347). Rachel's body itself even becomes fragmented; when the nurse speaks of a toe sticking out of the bedclothes "Rachel did not realize that the toe was hers" (331). As her vision distorts, things become "semi-transparent" (346), the very word Woolf uses in her essay "Modern Fiction" to describe the "envelope" of life which the writer should try to grasp. Rachel tries in vain to move from "her world" back into the "ordinary world," but speaks of a "gulf" which she "could not bridge" (329), a "gulf" approximating the earlier one separating her visual reality from her sheet of paper (296). Rachel herself has now become the paper on which Woolf is creating her work of art.

Jean Rhys similarly uses the illness of her heroine, Anna Morgan, to experiment with language and form. Originally drafted in the years between 1911 and 1913, two years before the first printing of *The Voyage Out*, *Voyage in the Dark* shares some remarkable similarities with Woolf's text that have previously gone unacknowledged. Anna, like Rachel, has been removed from her homeland. Born in the West Indies, eighteen-year-old Anna comes abroad only to find a cold, lusterless England where she exists in a sort of waking dream. In the novel's oft-quoted opening sentence, Anna describes her arrival in England "as if a curtain had fallen, hiding everything I had ever known" (7). Her voyage away from her homeland leaves her with a disjuncture of self, and she can never quite fit her past and present experiences together. During the course of the novel, Anna vividly recalls images of her West Indian childhood, images which interrupt and exist alongside her bleak London experiences. Paid little as a chorus girl in London, a position giving her the status of "public woman," lonely and naive Anna soon finds herself in a relationship with a wealthy married man, Walter Jeffries. Chilled by the cold climate of England in comparison to her warm Caribbean homeland, Anna enjoys the way her lover's money makes her forget "about feeling ill" (27). When that relationship ends, however, when he is, in turn, "sick of [her]" (141), Anna is left with little choice of vocation. Eventually, she turns to prostitution and subsequently becomes pregnant, suffers a badly performed abortion, and quickly becomes seriously ill. Although Rhys explores the boundaries between memory and present consciousness throughout her work, Rhys's most radical experimentation with language comes at the end of her novel with the onset of Anna's illness. Indeed, Anna's final experience closely resembles Susan Sontag's description of illness as "the night-side of life, a more onerous citizenship. Everyone who was born holds dual citizenship, in the kingdom of the well and in the kingdom of the sick" (3). Anna's illness, her own "voyage in the dark," fits in directly with her split sense of self. Here in Part Four of the novel, scenes of West Indian Masquerade are juxtaposed with present events to create a dizzying whole. The original ending, which Rhys herself called "the only possible ending" (Brown 41), that which ends in Anna's death, is even more strikingly modernist in nature, and demands a closer reading.

Like Rachel, Anna is crucially tied to silence, she too "always thinking of something [she doesn't] say" (*VO* 251). Externally a somewhat quiet figure, most of Anna's thoughts are never articulated through language, and Anna's spoken words rarely reflect her interior thoughts. Rather than choosing to have a conversation with a current companion, Anna more frequently is having a private, perhaps even unrelated thought. "Don't you ever talk at all?" Carl asks Anna, reminding the reader of her external quietness (119). Anna lives mostly in this internal world of her own mind, making her seem talkative to us but quiet and reserved to others. It is through Anna's inner thoughts that she achieves voice and, specifically, it is through her final illness that this voice takes on new significance.

Anna and Rachel's experiences of illness are notably similar. Early in the novel Anna gives the contradictory assertion that "when you have fever you are heavy and light" (33) and, like Rachel, notes a change in perspective: "The room looked different, as if it had grown bigger" (34). Similarly, on the way home from the abortion she feels as if it is her world and not she herself which is falling apart; she holds a fear that "the slanting houses might fall on me or the pavement rise up and hit me" (178). However, it is Anna's own body which is transgressing socially appropriate boundaries, ultimately moving out beyond even her control.

In "The Blank Page" Gubar suggests that "one of the primary metaphors provided by the female body is blood, and cultural forms of creativity are often experienced as a painful wounding" (248). In the ending of Rhys's novel, Anna is bleeding onto her sheets as a result of the abortion, and streams of language flow out along with that bodily secretion. Of this scene, critic Sylvie Maurel concludes, "On the borderline between life and death, consciousness and unconsciousness, she seems to be able to articulate an aesthetic of continuity akin to the semiotic economy of her Arcadian childhood, regardless of the script onto which she has been forced" (97-98). Although Maurel seems to be reinscribing colonialist models by suggesting that Anna's childhood was a pastoral paradise, she is correct in articulating that Anna is, while dying, producing a new language. As Maurel writes, "while Anna has just had an abortion, she gives birth to a regenerated discourse" (100). Just as Anna is writing on her blank sheets with her body, Rhys is writing onto Anna's body. Attempting to capture Anna's quickly shifting hallucinations, Rhys begins by revealing Anna's fractured memories in both small snippets and longer lines which run on, unhindered by punctuation:

> Smile please the man said not quite so serious
>   He dodged out from behind the black cloth
>   You tell her to madam
>   He had a long black-yellow face with pimples on his chin   he
> dodged in again under the black cloth
>   I looked down at my legs and the white socks coming half-way up
> my legs and the black shoes with a strap over the instep and the doll in
> my lap   it could say Maman Papa and shut its eyes for Dodo.
>   (45, original ending)[2]

Like the blood itself, the words begin slowly, coming in surges, and then begin to flow more freely.

The most abstract sections of Rhys's original ending concern Anna's memories of West Indian masquerade. In the revised ending, it is perhaps clearest that Anna has specifically connected the masquerade with her abortion because of a linguistic tie; Mrs.

Polo's reference to the bleeding, "It ought to be stopped" (185), recalls word for word a comment Hester once made about the carnival, "*it ought to be stopped*" (184). In addition, Anna likely has connected Hester's statement that "this isn't a decent or respectable way to go on and ought to be stopped" with her own actions (original ending, 51). Carnival, whose root means "flesh" and suggests a sexual association with the body, is a public display paralleling Anna's status of "public woman" or prostitute. Anna, too, has stepped over appropriate boundaries set for young ladies, taking her body into improper spaces, and now her body, dizzy with loss of blood, "went on whirling round and round" in dance (original ending, 53). The masks that she sees which "are more like their faces than their own faces were" (original ending, 50) recall the accusatory gaze of the people she passes on the streets, people who "watch you, their faces like masks" (164). Thus does Rhys explicitly connect Anna's illness with her breach of social custom, the "fall" she experiences at the end of her delirium consciously aligned with her sexual "fall." Throughout this final section, color and music create a collage of images, creating a new form of art which, like Rachel's music, transcends ordinary expression. In the original version, the novel ends with the doctor asking for the gramophone, which has, complying with Anna's wishes, been playing all along.

When the gramophone is turned off and the "concertina-music" in Anna's mind dwindles, the blood also "stops" and, appropriately, so does Anna's voice (original ending, 56).

Anna's "voyage" thus ends, like Rachel's, with death. Perhaps Anna and Rachel do not die in vain, however, for in their illnesses their voices have moved far beyond their former capabilities of expression. Early in *The Voyage Out*, Rachel sees her life as "the only chance she had—the short season between two silences" (82). This "season," however, coming before the "silence" of death, has proved incredibly fruitful. Using the female characters' illnesses as an artistic medium, both Woolf and Rhys have achieved a new sort of modernist expression by writing on the bodies of their heroines, allowing their characters to speak in ways that they previously could not. The voyages of Rachel and Anna may end, but for Woolf and Rhys they are just beginning as both writers move forward into new, yet unexplored linguistic terrain.

Afterword

Years later, this short conference paper became the first building block for my dissertation, *Excursions into Modernism: Women Writers, Travel, and the Body* (2007).

Notes

1 In the revised ending, Anna lives but awakes to a life filled with the horror of "starting all over again, all over again. . ." (188). With their published endings Woolf and Rhys violate a Victorian reader's expectations; according to convention, the pure, love-stricken girl should move on to matrimony while the fallen woman should pass on to another world.

2 All references to the original ending come from Nancy Hemond Brown's transcription of the original manuscript in her essay "Jean Rhys and *Voyage in the Dark*." *London Magazine* 25.1-2 (April-May 1985): 40-59. I have tried to keep the unusual spacing Brown preserves in her reprint. Quotes not marked "original ending" are from the 1982 Norton version of the text.

A very similar revision of this passage begins Rhys's autobiography, *Smile Please*. Here, quotation marks and other marks of punctuation distinguish it from the stream-of-consciousness version of the original ending.

Works Cited

Bishop, E. L. "Toward the Far Side of Language: Virginia Woolf's *The Voyage Out.*" *Twentieth Century Literature* 27 (Winter 1981): 343-61.
Brown, Nancy Hemond. "Jean Rhys and *Voyage in the Dark.*" *London Magazine* 25.1-2 (April-May 1985): 40-59.
Cummins, June. "Death and the Maiden Voyage: Mapping the Junction of Feminism and Postcolonial Theory in *The Voyage Out."* *Virginia Woolf: Texts and Contexts.* Ed. Beth Rigel Daugherty and Eileen Barrett. New York: Pace University Press, 1996.
Froula, Christine. "Out of the Chrysalis: Female Initiation and Female Authority in Virginia Woolf's *The Voyage Out."* *Tulsa Studies in Women's Literature* 5.1 (Spring 1986): 63-90.
Gubar, Susan. "The Blank Page and Female Creativity." *Critical Inquiry* 8.2 (Winter 1981): 243-63.
Harper, Howard. *Between Language and Silence: The Novels of Virginia Woolf.* Baton Rouge: Louisiana State University Press, 1982.
Herndl, Diane Price. *Invalid Women.* Chapel Hill and London: University of North Carolina Press, 1993.
Maurel, Sylvie. "*Voyage in the Dark*: 'Two Tunes.'" *Jean Rhys.* New York: St. Martin's Press, 1998: 81-101.
Richter, Harvena. *Virginia Woolf: The Inward Voyage.* Princeton: Princeton University Press, 1970.
Rhys, Jean. *Voyage in the Dark.* New York and London: W. W. Norton & Company, 1982.
Rhys, Jean. *Voyage in the Dark, Original Ending* in Nancy Hemond Brown's essay, "Jean Rhys and *Voyage in the Dark.*" *London Magazine* 25.1-2 (April-May 1985): 40-59.
Sontag, Susan. *Illness as Metaphor.* New York: Farrar, Straus and Giroux, 1978.
Woolf, Virginia. "Modern Fiction." *The Common Reader.* New York: Harcourt Brace and Company, 1925.
Woolf, Virginia. "On Being Ill." *Collected Essays.* Vol. 4. London: The Hogarth Press, 1967: 193-203.
Woolf, Virginia. *The Voyage Out.* New York: Harcourt Brace & Company, 1920.

Tradition and Individual Talents:
Rebecca West's and Virginia Woolf's Reviews and Essays

by Kathryn Harvey

"Tradition," wrote T. S. Eliot in *The Egoist* in 1919, "cannot be inherited, and if you want it you must obtain it by great labour. It involves, in the first place, the historical sense…[which] compels a man to write not merely with his own generation in his bones, but with a feeling that the whole of the literature of Europe from Homer and within it the whole of the literature of his own country has a simultaneous existence and composes a simultaneous order" (506). Eliot's essay has been viewed as a defining moment of literary modernism. Removing the personality of the author as a factor in both literary creation and criticism and emphasizing an almost exclusively male literary tradition were legacies of Eliot's treatise. That these legacies could be effected with such force from the pages of a low-circulation literary periodical is remarkable, certainly out of proportion to the essay's initial readership. Rebecca West and Virginia Woolf, on the other hand, put forward their own formulations of modernist aesthetics largely within mainstream newspapers and magazines, but these have gone largely unexamined by critics of modernism.

This paper is divided into two main sections. The first provides a brief overview of West's and Woolf's journalism. The second section examines their responses to T. S. Eliot's opinions about personality and emotion in literature and about the composition of literary tradition. The brief conclusion invites further consideration of West's and Woolf's reviews and essays as testing grounds for literary theorizing and of the implications their publishing venues may have had on the relative lack of influence their views had on early conceptualizations of modernism.

I. West's and Woolf's Reviews and Essays

Rebecca West began her career in professional journalism in November 1911 with a review for the small feminist periodical *The Freewoman*. Over the years, West wrote more than 700 reviews and essays on a very broad range of topics—literature, politics, history, and travel, to name a few—in venues such as *The Freewoman*, *Clarion*, *New Republic*, *Time and Tide*, *New Statesman*, *The Bookman*, *New York American*, *New York Herald Tribune*, and London's *Daily News* and *Daily Telegraph* (Pykett 175-76). She also edited for a short period in 1912 the women's page in the *Daily Herald* (Pykett 173-74; West, *Young Rebecca* 351).

As Lyn Pykett points out, from the very beginning West adopted "the role of *enfant terrible*" (173). For instance, she proclaimed in her first review: "There are two kinds of imperialists—imperialists and bloody imperialists" (*Young Rebecca*, 12). West's acerbic witticisms had not let up four months and six articles later, when in a review of *Woman Adrift*, she proclaimed: "Mr Harold Owen is a natural slave, having no conception of liberty nor any use for it. So, as a Freewoman, I review his anti-feminist thesis, *Woman Adrift*, with chivalrous reluctance, feeling that a steam-engine ought not to crush a butterfly" (*Young Rebecca*, 28). These two examples are typical of her style. According to Jane Marcus in "A Voice of Authority," West "polished the weapons of invective and denunciation into the tools of a fine art. She was never afraid of her own anger; it was justified" (244).

In all venues, whatever else she might have had to say about a book, West drew attention to political issues. For instance, West wrote a perceptive and glowing review of Woolf's *Orlando* which commented that Woolf's "left lobe (which is critical) is obviously without cease letting her right lobe (which is creative) know what it doeth" ("High Fountain" 592). West praised Woolf's ability to "[enquire] deeply into fundamentals and never more deeply than when she is most frivolous in form. People who like literalism will be most irritated, no doubt, by the passages in which Orlando changes her sex. But it is here that Mrs. Woolf shows exactly the magnificence of her power of transacting complex thought and perception on a plane of artistic creation" (ibid 595).[1] With an equally passionate anger, West offered the following denunciation of Sir Almroth Wright's *Unexpurgated Case against Woman Suffrage*:

> It is the worst book ever written and distressing. I have horrible nightmares of Sir Almroth Wright's limp sentences wandering through the arid desert of his mind looking for dropped punctuation marks.... Sir Almroth Wright imagines that woman does not deserve a vote because she is the "insolvent citizen." She does not earn her keep. Apparently motherhood is an extravagant hobby of hers which she carries on simply to give trouble. It would be brutal to remind him that she was the joint producer in the home of all England's wealth till that doubtful blessing, the industrial system, came along; and that since then the greatest fortunes have been piled out of the work of sweated women. (*Young Rebecca*, 210-11)

We can say many things about West's wonderful reviews and essays, but one fact for certain is that an author always knew where s/he stood with West.

Virginia Woolf began her reviewing career in December 1904 with a less brash start, publishing a competent review of *The Son of Royal Langbrith* by William Dean Howells in the *Guardian*, a weekly for members of the clergy. Between 1904 and 1918, a stage Jeanne Dubino has called Woolf's "apprenticeship period" (26), Woolf published more than 200 reviews and essays. By 1941, Woolf had published more than 550 journalistic pieces in such periodicals as the *Atlantic Monthly*, *Athenaeum*, *Nation and Athenaeum*, *New Statesman*, *The Bookman*, *Daily Herald*, *Daily Worker*, *Good Housekeeping*, *Harper's Bazaar*, *New York Herald Tribune*, *New Republic*, *Times Literary Supplement*, and *Vogue*.

Heavy on plot summary, her first review mitigated negative criticism with an ample smattering of praise. Unlike West, Woolf did not initially flaunt a confident, frankly authoritative tone. Her confidence remained understated, but is apparent in all of her journalism, even when she calls her own authority into question. West seemed to demand that readers take her side as she meted out praise or scorn; Woolf, as Michael Kaufmann points out, "addressed her audience as her familiars and as her equals" (140). We side with West because we agree that Sir Almroth Wright's attitude is distressing; we feel comfortable with

Woolf because she presents herself humbly, affably, and knowledgeably.

Despite the understatement in so much of Woolf's journalism, she could be every bit as bitingly witty as West. Take, for example, her review of W. L. George's *A Novelist on Novels* in the June 13th 1918 issue of the *TLS*. Woolf begins: "Mr George is one of those writers for whom we could wish, in all kindness of heart, some slight accident to the fingers of the right hand, some twinge or ache warning him that it is time to stop, some check making brevity more desirable than expansion" (*E2* 255). Then with reference to the wartime paper shortage, she adds, "He…altogether uses more paper than the country can well afford" (*E2* 255).

Whereas West's journalism was bolstered from the beginning by her commitment to feminism, Woolf's was inspired by her own literary heritage and the prospect of making money from reading and writing.[2] As the daughter of a prominent man of letters, Woolf herself initiated the move from under her father's shadow.[3] Through the friend of a friend, she obtained her first series of journalistic commissions. In response to a letter of congratulations on the review, Woolf responded in a humble (and I sense not an entirely dissembling) tone: "Not that a review deserves praise, it is necessarily dull work reviewing I think, and I hate the critical attitude of mind because all the time I know what a humbug I am, and ask myself what right have I to dictate whats [sic] good and bad, when I couldn't, probably, do as well myself!" (*L1* 167, December 22nd 1904).

For the next ten years, as Hermione Lee reminds us, Woolf "made money entirely from her journalism," predominantly as a successful reviewer for the *Times Literary Supplement* (92), and although she often dismissed her own journalistic endeavours, she continued with them right up to March 1941 (see Kirkpatrick 177). Clearly she delighted in the income, but reviewing also prompted her to read books she might not otherwise have given a moment's thought. Reviewing novels, books of literary criticism, biographies, collections of letters, and histories compelled her to evaluate the techniques and opinions of others and to justify her own opinions regarding aesthetic value, modernity, and literary tradition.

According to Dubino, during her apprenticeship period, "Woolf began to articulate critical principles that she would continue to develop over the rest of her life" (26). Hermione Lee echoes this assessment, noting that Woolf's "development into the kind of novelist she wanted to be, in the 1910s and 1920s, was worked out in large part through the essays of that period—reviews of individual writers, and more discursive, synthesising considerations of 'modern' writing" (Lee 92).[4]

II. Personality, Emotion, and Literary Traditions

In "Tradition and the Individual Talent," Eliot insisted that "the poet has, not a 'personality' to express, but a particular medium, which is only a medium and not a personality, in which impressions and experiences combine in peculiar and unexpected ways" and this effect "give[s] us a new art emotion" (510). He furthermore claimed that "Honest criticism and sensitive appreciation are directed not upon the poet but upon the poetry" (508). West and Woolf both took exception to his scientific approach to literature as much as they objected to what they saw as the contemporary lack of character in fiction.

In May 1924, Woolf read a paper called "Mr Bennett and Mrs Brown" to the Heretics Society at Cambridge. She accused the Edwardians (Wells, Galsworthy, and Bennett) of losing sight of human character: "They have looked," she said, "very powerfully, searchingly, and sympathetically out of the window; at factories, at Utopias, even at the decoration and upholstery of the [railway] carriage; but never at [Mrs Brown], never at life, never at human nature" (19). And the Georgians (including Forster, Lawrence, Strachey, Joyce, and Eliot), she complained, "had to begin by throwing away the method that was in use at the moment. He was left alone there facing Mrs. Brown without any method of conveying her to the reader" ("Mr Bennett and Mrs Brown" 22). She continued, "At the present moment we are suffering, not from decay, but from having no code of manners which writers and readers accept as a prelude to the more exciting intercourse of friendship" (25). For writing—whether experimental, realistic, naturalistic, or impressionistic—to be successful, readers had to be helped along by the author whose responsibility it was to teach a new way of reading.

Woolf revised and re-titled the lecture "Character in Fiction" for publication in Eliot's *Criterion* (July 1924), a magazine known to champion a predominantly male coterie's concept of the modernist canon (see Levenson 219). But Woolf's readership did not end in a magazine for the "literary elite"; the *New York Herald Tribune* published the article one year later in two instalments. So Woolf's dispute with Bennett eventually found its way into the American mainstream press.

In 1926, this debate continued in the pages of the *New York Herald Tribune*—not with a response from Bennett but with a column by Rebecca West. In "Uncle Bennett," West supported Woolf's position and even employed tactics that would have been familiar to readers of Woolf's article: she took a situation from one of Bennett's novels and imagined how Wells, Shaw, and Galsworthy would have handled it. Not brilliantly, she concluded: "But at any rate, they would have got something out of it, whereas Uncle Bennett gets nothing at all" (206). Still, she admits, the Edwardian uncles were not without their gifts. The mistake was in believing that writers such as Wells, Bennett, Galsworthy, and Shaw had spoken to the human condition.

The elusive "truth" about human nature constituted a fundamental area of contestation in modernist literature. For West and Woolf, fictional representations of human nature manifested themselves most prominently in the representation of human consciousness. For instance, West observed that *Orlando* "is a work which illuminates an important part of human experience by using words to do more than describe the logical behavior of matter, by letting language by its music and its power to evoke images[,] convey meanings too subtle and too profound to be formulated in intellectual statements" ("High Fountain of Genius," 592). Or, as Woolf approvingly noted about Dorothy Richardson's *The Tunnel*, "[T]he reader is not provided with a story; he is invited to embed himself in Miriam Henderson's consciousness, to register one after another...impressions as they flicker through Miriam's mind, waking incongruously other thoughts, and plaiting incessantly the many-coloured and innumerable threads of life" (*E3* 11).

Both West and Woolf believed to be important precisely those qualities that Eliot with his call for impersonality in literature deplored. According to Michael Kaufmann, "Woolf believed feeling must somehow comprise the form; Eliot insisted feeling must be strictly subordinated to form, associating too overt a display of emotion in literature with adolescent and feminine excess" (143). In the essay "Personalities," Woolf takes issue with "the critics [who] tell us that we should be impersonal when we write, and therefore impersonal when we read. Perhaps this is true," she says, but quickly suggests we investigate the question further with her (273-74). In "All About Books," she lamented the fact that young literary scholars emerged from their university training knowing the "whole course of English literature from one end to another; how...one influence cancels another; and one style is derived from another" and that "such methods...produce an erudite and eugenic offspring. But, one asks, turning over the honest, the admirable, the entirely sensible and unsentimental pages, where is love?" (125). Where is personality, emotion—in essence—the magic of literature?

Similarly, in "What is Mr T. S. Eliot's Authority as a Critic?" West accuses Eliot of being unable to appreciate "the attempts to find new and valid classifications [of emotion] in place of old ones which have proved invalid, and the pressing of the analysis of emotion to a further stage" (*Gender of Modernism* 589). As Margaret Stetz has argued, West was less interested in the purely formal technique of a work than in writers' relations to their environments and to literary tradition (50). West's "model of the relationship between tradition and the individual talent emphasized how the former could help the latter—indeed, how tradition might put itself at the service of liberating the personality" (ibid. 53).

But one must, as Eliot said, work hard at acquiring a sense of tradition. For both West and Woolf, this meant not just learning about past male writers but of discovering and analyzing the female writers. Theirs was a doubly difficult task. Furthermore, this enterprise required an understanding of the conditions of women's lives, as Woolf argued in *A Room of One's Own*. West greatly appreciated this book, calling it "an uncompromising book of feminist propaganda...the ablest yet written" ("Autumn and Virginia Woolf" 211). She drew specific attention to Woolf's thesis that "the belittlement of women's work must have snuffed out many a fiery particle in the way of female genius" (211-12).

Unlike Eliot, both West and Woolf recognized the importance of historical context, and we can see this similarity in their writing on Charlotte Brontë. According to West, Brontë was not a sentimental writer because of an "innate ineptitude for the artistic process, but [because of] the pressure of external circumstance" (431). We can better appreciate her artistic gifts if we know the difficult life she and her sisters led and if we learn about the environment in which they tried to forge their literary careers.

Woolf is of much the same opinion: "I do not know," she wrote, "whether pilgrimages to the shrines of famous men ought not to be condemned as sentimental journeys... The curiosity is only legitimate when the house of a great writer or the country in which it is set adds something to our understanding of his books. This justification you have for a pilgrimage to the home and country of Charlotte Brontë and her sisters" ("Haworth," *E1* 5). Twelve years later, Woolf reaffirmed the importance of personality in literature: "At the conclusion of *Jane Eyre* we do not feel so much that we have read a book, as that we have parted from a most singular and eloquent woman, met by chance upon a Yorkshire hillside" ("Charlotte Brontë," *E2* 28).

Conclusion

All the above passages reporting West's and Woolf's thoughts on literature appeared in their journalism—much of it in the popular press. This being the case, I believe that we need to look more closely at their reviews and essays not simply to highlight their own development as writers but in order to re-examine the ways in which modernism has hitherto been understood. And I will end with a question: might the emphasis on the role of little magazines and the exclusion of "popular" journalism have been a significant factor in the absence of West and Woolf from early constructions of modernism?

Notes

1   It is interesting to note that Woolf thought West showed a better understanding of the book than any other reviewer.
2   Consider these feelings also in light of her later comment in *A Room of One's Own*: "Money dignifies what is frivolous if unpaid for" (65).
3   When she made her first serious inquiries into journalism, Woolf was in the process of writing a piece on her father for F. W. Maitland to quote from in his biography of Leslie Stephen.
4   Given the obvious importance of Woolf's journalism to her fiction-writing, I find it interesting that *A Writer's Diary*, consisting of selections made by Leonard Woolf from his wife's journals, entirely omits these apprenticeship years. The effect of this is clearly to perpetuate the notion that such writing played no formative function to her work as a novelist.

Works Cited

Dubino, Jeanne. "Virginia Woolf: From Book Reviewer to Literary Critic, 1904-1918." *Virginia Woolf and the Essay*. Eds. Beth Carole Rosenberg and Jeanne Dubino. New York: St. Martin's, 1997. 25-40.
Eliot, T. S. "Tradition and the Individual Talent." *Modern British Literature*. Eds. Frank Kermode and John Hollander. Toronto: Oxford UP, 1973. 505-11.
Kaufmann, Michael. "A Modernism of One's Own: Virginia Woolf's *TLS* Reviews and Eliotic Modernism." *Virginia Woolf and the Essay*. Eds. Beth Carole Rosenberg and Jeanne Dubino. New York: St. Martin's, 1997. 137-155.
Kirkpatrick, B. J. *A Bibliography of Virginia Woolf* 3rd ed. Oxford: Clarendon P, 1980.
Lee, Hermione. "Virginia Woolf's Essays." *The Cambridge Companion to Virginia Woolf*. Eds. Sue Roe and Susan Sellars Cambridge: Cambridge UP, 2000. 91-108.
Levenson, Michael H. *A Genealogy of Modernism*. Cambridge: Cambridge UP, 1984.
Marcus, Jane. "A Voice of Authority." *Faith of a (Woman) Writer*. Eds. Alice Kessler-Harris and William McBrien. Contributions in Women's Studies 86. New York: Greenwood Press, 1988. 237-46.
Pykett, Lyn. "The Making of a Modern Writer: Rebecca West's Journalism, 1911-1930." *Journalism, Literature, and Modernity: From Hazlitt to Modernism*. Ed. Kate Campbell. Edinburgh: Edinburgh UP, 2000. 170-90.
Seeley, Tracy. "Woolf and Rebecca West's Fiction-Essays." *Virginia Woolf Miscellany* 39 (Fall 1992): 6-7.
Stetz, Margaret D. "Rebecca West's Criticism: Alliance, Tradition, and Modernism." *Rereading Modernism: New Directions in Feminist Criticism*. Ed. Lisa Rado. New York: Garland, 1994. 41-66.
West, Rebecca. "Autumn and Virginia Woolf." *Ending in Earnest: A Literary Log*. 1931. Freeport, NY: Books for Libraries P, 1967. 208-13.
———. "Charlotte Brontë" 1932. *Rebecca West: A Celebration*. Ed. Samuel Hynes. New York: Viking P, 1977. 429-38. [Originally published in *The Great Victorians*. Eds. H. J. and Hugh Massingham, London, 1932.]
———. "High Fountain of Genius." *The Gender of Modernism*. Ed. Bonnie Kime Scott. Bloomington: Indiana UP, 1990 592-96.
———. "Notes on Novels." [on Virginia Woolf's *Jacob's Room* and Joseph Hergesheimer's *Cytherea*] *The New Statesman* November 4, 1922. 142, 144.
———. "Uncle Bennett." 1926. *The Strange Necessity*. London: Jonathan Cape, 1928. 199-213. [originally in *New*

York Herald Tribune October 10, 1926.]

———. "What is T. S. Eliot's Authority as a Critic?" *The Gender of Modernism*. Ed. Bonnie Kime Scott. Bloomington: Indiana UP, 1990. 587-92.

———. *The Young Rebecca: Writings of Rebecca West 1911-1917*. Ed. Jane Marcus. London: Virago, 1983.

Woolf, Virginia. "All About Books." *The Captain's Death Bed and Other Essays*. New York: Harcourt, Brace and Company Inc., 1950. *[Major Authors on CD-ROM: Virginia Woolf.]*

———. *The Essays of Virginia Woolf*. 6 vols. Ed. Andrew McNeillie. London: Harcourt Brace Jovanovich, 1986-.

———. *The Letters of Virginia Woolf*. 6 vols. Eds. Nigel Nicolson and Joanne Trautmann. London: Harcourt Brace Jovanovich, 1975-82.

———. "Mr Bennett and Mrs Brown." 1928. *The Hogarth Essays*. Comps. Leonard S. Woolf and Virginia Woolf. Freeport, NY: Books for Libraries P, 1970. 3-29.

———. "Personalities." *Collected Essays*. New York: Harcourt, Brace and Company Inc., 1950. *[Major Authors on CD-ROM: Virginia Woolf.]*

———. *A Room of One's Own*. 1928. London: Penguin, 1945.

Voyaging through "Contested Cultural Territories" in Virginia Woolf's *Mrs. Dalloway* and Anita Desai's *Clear Light of Day*

by Christine W. Sizemore

Anita Desai, who has been called "the foremost contemporary Indian woman novelist in English" (Dharwadker 103), has often acknowledged the influence of Virginia Woolf. When Desai first started to write, not only did she write in English, "the flexible...elastic...and...nuance[d]" (Desai, "Against the Current" 533) language of her schooling rather than her mother's German or her father's Bengali, she also said that one of the strongest early influences on her was Virginia Woolf (Libert 48). When Feroza Jussawalla asked her in 1992: "Would you get angry if someone said you were the Virginia Woolf of India and you 'mothered' the psychological novel in India?" Desai responded: "No, I would be denying something which is fairly obvious...the influence of Virginia Woolf upon my own work" (173).

In 1989 Asha Kanwar did a comparative study of Virginia Woolf and Anita Desai in which she paired novels by each writer to analyze the lyrical styles and theme of time in both. Kanwar compares Desai's 1980 novel *Clear Light of Day*, which she notes was nominated for the Booker Prize (34-35), to Woolf's *To the Lighthouse* (34). Here, however, I want to juxtapose *Clear Light of Day* with *Mrs. Dalloway* and look not just at the lyrical style and theme of time, which *Mrs. Dalloway* also shares with *Clear Light of Day*, but also examine some of the similar narrative structures and the way both novels critique the British Empire and colonialism. Both novelists portray a deep skepticism about their respective countries' nationalism and both critique men's absorption of imperialistic views, whether Woolf's critique of the colonizer or Desai's of the colonized. Both writers connect imperial domination in the public sphere with gender ideologies in the private sphere of marriage and the family. At the center of these conflicts in both novels are female protagonists whose struggle to escape the "stasis" caused by these hierarchies is aided by other women. Both protagonists find answers to their yearnings in the liminal space of gardens and in a mystical empathy for others.

The protagonists of both these novels are women who are caught, to use Chandra Mohanty's phrase, in "multiple, fluid structures of domination which intersect to locate women differently at particular historical conjunctures" (13). For Clarissa Dalloway those structures of domination center around a patriarchy intertwined with imperialism and class. For Bimila Das, Desai's protagonist, they include the Hindu and British colonial ideologies of womanhood and their political manipulation. Both novels link marriage and colonialism. The immediate threat of domination, however, does not come only from the expected hyper-masculine colonial British military leader but also from the weaker men like Peter Walsh in *Mrs. Dalloway* or Dr. Biswas in *Clear Light of Day*. Both these men want to absorb a woman in a romantic marriage which would both erase a woman's personal identity and both men, although one is British and one Indian, are closely linked to the forces of colonialism and orientalism. Clarissa and Bim reject marriage proposals with these men, but both still inhabit what Homi Bhabha calls "contested cultural territories" (297) that manifest themselves in the novels' atmosphere of "stasis" (Zwerdling 122, Karamcheti 142). Zwerdling connects this atmosphere of stasis in *Mrs. Dalloway* to the "rigidity" of the governing class and the "petrifaction" which is the price they pay for the stoicism with which they have responded to the sufferings of World War I (122). This stasis is exhibited not just in the Hugh Whitbreads and Lady Bexboroughs, however, but also with the power imposed over women in marriage and imposed by Britain in the colonies. Clarissa's home is in many ways not her own. She has been moved upstairs to an attic room after her bout with the flu. When Peter Walsh comes to call, he rushes in even though Clarissa is mending her dress and thinks it's "outrageous to be interrupted …on…the day she was giving a party" (*MD* 59). Woolf's most vehement critique in the novel, however, is her portrait of Septimus's domineering doctor, Sir William Bradshaw. Bradshaw's doctrine of "Conversion," the sister of the stoic "Proportion," which he prescribes for Septimus, not only causes Lady Bradshaw's "slow sinking…of her will into" that of her husband but it is also the same force that operates effectively in "the heat and sands of India, the mud and swamp of Africa" (100). This image of the powerful virile controlling man prefigures Woolf's argument in *Three Guineas* where the political control of the "Fuhrer or Duce…Tyrant or Dictator" is clearly linked to the private world of the patriarchal family: "the tyrannies and servilities of the one are the tyrannies and servilities of the other" (142). The ideologies behind fascism in *Three Guineas* and behind colonialism in *Mrs. Dalloway* are intertwined with the desire of powerful men to control their own wives, daughters and anyone in a class below them or a country colonized by them.

It is not just the powerful figures like Dr. Bradshaw, however, who possess an ideology of control that works both on women at home and in the colonies, it is also the much weaker, even ineffectual, and romantic figure of Peter Walsh, who is linked to this subjecting of others. Although Clarissa is fond of Peter, she realizes as soon as she sees him again, how right she was not to marry him. His romantic idea of marriage would have left her no space at all. Peter is furthermore linked both by his career in India and his attitudes toward women with British imperialism. When he sees a young woman in the street passing Gordon's statue, in his mind she sheds "veil after veil, until she became the very woman he had always had in mind; young, but stately; merry, but discreet; black, but enchanting" (52). By calling attention to the statue of General Charles Gordon, who fought successfully in China and then was killed by the Mahdi in Khartoum in 1865, Woolf evokes the history of British imperialism and then links it to an orientalist sexuality as Peter first imagines the young woman "shedding veil after veil" and then wraps her in a vaguely Shakespearean diction, "merry, but discreet; black, but enchanting." Peter follows her down the street thinking of himself as "an adventurer, reckless…swift, daring…a romantic buccaneer" (53). Kathy Phillips, in *Virginia Woolf Against Empire*, also sees this passage as describing a "colonization [that] yields a vicarious sexual thrill as power over weaker countries" (17). Furthermore Phillips notes that it is Peter's calling of the ambulance "[o]ne of the triumphs of civilisation" (151) that sets up the ironic commentary on English civilization which, like an ambulance, "carries death" not only for the shell-shocked victims of World War I but also for those in the colonies caught by the colonizers' "deadly drives for power and money" (Phillips 1).

Desai also links ideologies of marriage, women and nationhood in her critique of patriarchy both under British colonialism and under Hindu nationalism. There are some clear differences, however, between the ways that representations of women and national ideologies are intertwined in India in the 1940s from the way Woolf saw them as operating in England in 1925 (*Mrs. Dalloway*) and 1938 (*Three Guineas*). Indian psychologist Ashis Nandy and historian Partha Chatterjee explain the complex intertwinings of ideas of "femininity" and "nation" in India. Nandy says that India's concept of femininity is different from the West's: in India "the concept of *naritva*, so repeatedly stressed by Gandhi...included some traditional meanings of womanhood in India, such as the belief in a close...conjunction between power, activism and femininity" (*The Intimate Enemy* 53). In his article "Woman versus Womanliness in India" Nandy traces the association of women and power back to pre-Aryan times and explains how the "dominance of woman [in this matrifocal agrarian culture] was retained...in the symbolic system" of the Brahmanic tradition (305). Thus, Nandy explains, "the ultimate authority in the Indian mind has always been feminine" ("Woman vs. Womanliness" 305). Gandhi, Nandy says in *The Intimate Enemy*, used both the sense of activism and power associated with femininity and the ideal of self-sacrifice to undermine some of the hyper-masculine ideals of British colonialism (48-55). Nandy sees many of these nationalist strategies as effective in combating colonialism but at a cost to Indian women. Partha Chatterjee also analyzes how nationalists used these associations politically against colonialism, but at the expense of women's achievement. The nationalist movement emphasized that India and the East were superior to the West in the spiritual domain. Social space was then divided into inner and outer realms: "the home and the world. ...The home...must remain unaffected by the profane activities of the material world—and woman is its representation" (238-39). Chatterjee explains that a "respectable woman" could "acquire the cultural refinements afforded by modern education without jeopardizing her place at home" (246); thus, Chatterjee continues, the "'new' woman defined in this way was subjected to a *new* patriarchy" (244). Indian women could still be seen as possessing power, but it was a spiritual power that was associated with the home and with traditional Hindu ideas of women as self-sacrificing. Rajeswari Mohan argues that it is precisely this intersection of colonial education and "indigenous constructions of femininity" which locates the female characters in *Clear Light of Day* "at the nexus of contradictory gender ideologies" (48). Mohan says that

> Under the pressure of territorial displacement, class formation and religious identification during the independence movement, these ideologies assume complicated and indeed hardened forms that, despite their apparently liberatory potential, more often than not circumscribe options available to women. (50)

At the opening of *Clear Light of Day,* Bim is caught within these conflicting traditions in her family house in old Delhi in a space that Indira Karamcheti says feels like "constriction and stasis"(142). Bim seemingly has all the trappings of a westernized, independent existence. She is a teacher at a girls' college and has turned down an offer of marriage, but she is bound by a Hindu sense of duty which makes her feel that she is the one who must look after her father's business, her retarded younger brother and the poor relative, Aunt Mira, who raised them and who is now sunk into alcoholism. Bim's older brother, Raja, although also raised as a Hindu, feels no such obligation. He feels free to leave home during the partition of India in 1947 and move south to Hyderabad, where there is a large population of Muslims, to join the family's former Muslim neighbor and marry his daughter.

The continuing effects of colonization are illustrated in the novel not only in the violence associated with partition and the breaking up of families, but also in the character of Dr. Biswas, a romantic figure like Peter Walsh. Dr. Biswas is mocked because he has internalized an idealized image of European culture and rejected his own. He says to Bim "'when I first heard Mozart, Miss Das, I closed my eyes, and it was as if my whole past vanished, just rolled away from me—the country of my birth, my ancestors, my family, everything—and I arrived in a new world'" (83). When Bim turns down his offer of marriage, Dr. Biswas misreads her rejection and romanticizes her into a stereotype of the self-sacrificing Indian woman: "Now I understand why you do not wish to marry. You have dedicated your life to others.... You have sacrificed your own life for them" (97). Because of class and gender restrictions, Bim's Aunt Mira *was* forced to act out this role; her alcoholism is a sign of the damage it has done to her. Bim, however, is not making that choice. She and Raja laugh at Dr. Biswas' words. Bim, two generations younger than Clarissa and well-educated, is free to turn marriage down, but she still needs to be healed of her resentment toward Raja and her feelings of stasis.

Both Clarissa Dalloway and Bim Das must find a different space in which to escape the stasis of their surroundings. In both novels it is the space of a garden, a liminal space that is both home and not-home in which both women can access memory and open up to relationships with other women. Lisa Williams notes that for Woolf the garden is an image of "a refuge from isolation" (79). It is in her memories of the garden of Bourton that Clarissa reconnects with her feelings about Sally Seton and it is in the rose garden of the house in Old Delhi that Bim begins to talk to and share childhood memories with her sister, Tara. Both Clarissa and Bim must use the space of a garden to go back in time and use these memories to face their respective histories of violence and exclusion. For Clarissa this violence is the violence of World War I and its aftermath; for Bim it is the violence associated with the partition of India in 1947. After facing and mourning these histories, Clarissa and Bim are able to reconstruct earlier relationships with women which help them recuperate their identity, Clarissa in her memories of Sally Seton and Bim in her shared memories with her younger sister Tara.

Interestingly, both authors use the same kind of imagery to describe this use of memory in narrative. Woolf writes about what she calls her "tunneling process" (*D2* 272) in which she digs "out beautiful caves behind my characters. ...The idea is that the caves shall connect, & each comes to daylight at the present moment" (*D2* 263). As Williams notes, this process allows Woolf to create "a fictional form [in which]...the past becomes contained in the present moment, and all that has been lost is accessible through memory" (81). Desai uses very similar language to describe her narrative technique in which succeeding chapters go back first to 1947 and then to Bim, Tara and Raja's childhood and finally return to the present. Desai says: "My technique has been to pick out just a few episodes and images...and repeat them over and over, seen from different angles at different times of their lives so that each twist of the prism casts a new light" (Srivastava 225). Woolf's phrase "come to daylight at the present moment" and Desai's idea that "each twist of the prism casts a new light" illustrate through the imagery of light that their characters can come to healing by the intertwining of memory, forgiveness and empathy.

For Clarissa the garden which gives her access to both memory and empathy is Bourton, the garden of her youth where she was kissed by Sally Seton. Even in her fifties, the fresh morning air of London recalls Bourton:

> What a lark! What a plunge! For so it had always seemed to her, when, with a little squeak of the hinges, which she could hear now, she had burst open the French windows and plunged at Bourton into the open air. How fresh, how calm...the air was in the early morning; like the flap of a wave...chill and sharp. (3)

Even in later years Clarissa can recreate this exhilarating feeling of freedom. Bourton is a place of freedom and also a place of desire. In the garden, which contains both openness and also at dusk, seclusion, Clarissa experiences a moment of intimacy and desire when she is kissed by Sally Seton. Neither young girl is allowed to live out her desire; the patriarchal world interrupts quickly in the form of Peter Walsh who comes up to them and breaks their intimacy and later that world asserts control in the traditional marriages each girl is steered into, but the memory, "a diamond, something infinitely precious" (35) is available to Clarissa. It is a moment like the ones Woolf describes in "A Sketch of the Past," a "moment of being" in which the "nondescript cotton wool" (70) of ordinary life gives way to rapture. After thinking back to this healing memory, Clarissa is able by the end of the novel to feel sympathy for Septimus when she hears of his suicide and to experience a mystical identification with the old woman who lives across the street whom Clarissa sees through a lighted window.

The Clear Light of Day opens with a description of the garden outside the Das family house. Bim's sister Tara, who has just returned home to visit, wakes up at early dawn and looks out at the rose garden:

> She saw her sister's figure in white, slowly meandering along what as children they had called 'the rose walk'...a strip of grass, still streaked green and grey, between two long beds of roses at the far end of the lawn where a line of trees fringed the garden. (1)

Before Tara and Bim can fully reconcile the conflicting traditions that have molded them, they must go back in memory and reverie to confront the past history of nation and family. The intertwining of national and family history has left Bim in a state of bitterness. It is Tara who helps Bim find a way out of the constricted space of her resentment. It is in community with each other as they walk in the old neglected rose garden that they are able to resolve their memories and accept the choices that they made. After talking to Bim, Tara is able to let go of her guilt at leaving Bim with the responsibilities of the house, their retarded younger brother, and Aunt Mira. Likewise Tara helps Bim to give up her resentment and anger at their older brother Raja. Bim looks out into the garden at daybreak and

> her eyes opened...she saw how she...loved Raja and Tara and all of them who had lived in this house with her.... Although it was shadowy and dark, Bim could see as well as by the clear light of day that she felt only love and yearning for them all. (165)

In Clarissa's memory of Sally Seton, her sympathy for Septimus and her momentary identification with the old woman she sees at the window and in Bim's forgiveness of her siblings, both characters find a new space of healing, a "Moment of Being" in "the clear light of day" which transcends the rigid political and gender spaces of their history and time.

Afterword

I incorporated some of my ideas in this paper about Anita Desai's novel *Clear Light of Day* in a chapter on national identities and women's search for place in my book on postcolonial womenwriters, *Negotiating Identities in Women's Lives: English Postcolonial and Contemporary British Novels* (Westport, CN: Greenwood Press, 2002). I have an article on *Mrs. Dalloway* that will be coming out in the forthcoming MLA Approaches to Teaching *Mrs. Dalloway* volume.

Works Cited

Bhabha, Homi K. "DissemiNation: Time, Narrative and the Margins of the Modern Nation." *Nation and Narrative*. Ed. Homi Bhabha. London: Routledge, 1990. 291-322.

Chatterjee, Partha. "The Nationalist Resolution of the Women's Question." *Recasting Women: Essays in Colonial History*. Eds. Kumkum Sangari and Sudesh Vaid. New Delhi: Kali for Women, 1989. 233-53.

Desai, Anita. "Against the Current: A Conversation with Anita Desai." Ed. Corinne Demas Bliss *Massachusetts Review* 29.3 (Fall 1988): 521-37.

———. *Clear Light of Day*. New York: Penguin, 1980.

Dharwadker, Aparna and Vinay. "Language, Identity and Nation in Postcolonial Indian Literature." *English Postcoloniality: Literatures from Around the World*. Eds. Radhika Mohanram and Gita Rajan. Westport, Conn.: Greenwood Press, 1996. 89-106.

Jussawalla, Feroza and Reed Way Dasenbrock. "Anita Desai." *Interviews with Writers of the Post-Colonial World*. Jackson, Miss.: Univ. of Mississippi Press, 1992. 157-79.

Kanwar, Asha. *Virginia Woolf and Anita Desai: A Comparative Study*. New Delhi: Prestige Books, 1989.

Karamcheti, Indira. "The Geographies of Marginality: Place and Textuality in Simone Schwarz-Bart and Anita Desai." *Feminist Explorations of Literary Space*. Eds. Margaret Higonnet and Joan Templeton. Amherst; U of Mass. P, 1994. 125-46.

Libert, Florence. "An Interview with Anita Desai 1 August 1989. Cambridge. England." *World Literature Written in English*. 30.1 (1990): 47-55.

Mohan, Rajeswari. "The Forked Tongue of Lyric in Anita Desai's *Clear Light of Day*." *Journal of Commonwealth Literature* 32.1 (1997): 47-66.

Mohanty, Chandra Talpade. "Introduction: Cartographies of Struggle." *Third World Women and the Politics of Feminism*. Eds. Chandra Talpade Mohanty, Anne Russo and Lourdes Torres. Bloomington, Ind.: Indiana UP, 1987. 1-47.

Nandy, Ashis. *The Intimate Enemy; Loss and Recovery of Self Under Colonialism*. New Delhi: Oxford UP, 1983.

———. "Woman Versus Womanliness in India: An Essay in Social and Political Psychology." *The Psychoanalytic Review* 63.2 (1976): 301-15.

Phillips, Kathy J. *Virginia Woolf Against Empire*. Knoxville, Tenn.: U of Tennessee P, 1994.

Srivastava, Ramesh K. "Anita Desai at Work: An Interview." *Perspectives on Anita Desai*. Ed. Ramesh K. Srivastava. Delhi: Vimal Prakashan, 1984. 208-26.

Williams, Lisa. *The Artist as Outsider in the Novels of Toni Morrison and Virginia Woolf*. Westport: Greenwood Press, 2000.

Woolf, Virginia. *The Diary of Virginia Woolf*. Ed. Anne Olivier Bell. Vol. 2. New York: Harcourt Brace Jovanovich, 1978.

———. *Mrs. Dalloway*. New York: Harcourt Brace Jovanovich, 1925.

———. "A Sketch of the Past." *Moments of Being*. Ed. Jeanne Schulkind. 2nd ed. New York: Harcourt Brace Jovanovich, 1985.

———. *Three Guineas*. New York: Harcourt Brace Jovanovich, 1938.

Zwerdling, Alex. *Virginia Woolf and the Real World*. Berkeley: Univ. of Calif. Press, 1986.

Consumption Asunder: Woolf, Dunmore, and the Mind/Body Split

by Andrea Adolph

Imagine a novel in which childhood is spent in a tranquil St. Ives, or one in which an airplane flies overhead, a whimsical advertisement in its wake. Now imagine that the novel in question is *not* the product of Virginia Woolf, but instead is a novel published in 1996 by Orange Prize-winner Helen Dunmore. Set in the Sussex countryside not far from Lewes and Brighton, Dunmore's novel *Talking to the Dead* contains many Woolfian echoes. In 2001 correspondence, Dunmore herself confirmed Woolf's presence in the novel, stating, "the garden in TALKING TO THE DEAD is based upon the Charleston garden—I expect that you have noticed that I've drawn on the relationship between Vanessa Bell and Virginia Woolf, to some extent, in my depiction of the relationship between Nina and Isabel." The always shaky authorial intent aside, Dunmore's text is textured with both the geography and the iconography of Woolf's fiction, and *Talking to the Dead* on some level is indebted to Woolf's life and to her writing.

In this paper, however, I'd like to discuss specific parallels between Dunmore's novel and Woolf's last endeavor, *Between the Acts*. Though the references just mentioned are taken from various of Woolf's texts and life experiences, *Between the Acts* provides a backdrop for Dunmore's narrative and for her cast of characters, and *Talking to the Dead* exhibits both revision of and response to Woolf's final novel. Woolf presents to us Giles and Isa, the married couple; Mrs. Manresa, the sexual transgressor; and William Dodge, the simpatico homosexual. Dunmore redraws Woolf's characters archetypally as Richard and Isabel; Nina, Isabel's sister who dallies with Richard in his own wife's garden; and Edward, Isabel's gay confidante. The predominant characterizations are uncannily similar in both texts, as are the relationships between the various characters in each. Importantly, the pairs of dominant women in both novels—Isabel and Nina; Isa and "the Manresa"—not only mirror each other, but also work together in similar ways as representatives of the realms of mind and of body. In order to underscore each character's position vis-à-vis the body, Woolf and Dunmore both rely upon food imagery and on representations of eating. Both pairs of women are characterized, in part, through their oppositional relationships to food and to eating, and their respective states of "embodiedness" (or lack thereof) result from the connections that can be made between the act of eating and the material body.

Though one can assume with relative certainty that characters in fictional texts have bodies, those bodies are not always significantly present within the text. For a variety of reasons, the physical body does not appear readily in many texts; the female body certainly does not appear readily in Woolf's fiction, but is frequently masked in metaphor. Textured and evocative methods of foregrounding the material body within a text call for the crafting of a character from the actions of his or her body, often from its most manual, rote activities. The use of food imagery, especially when connected to representations of food consumption, is one way such a foregrounding of the body can occur. Because images of eating and consumption easily signify the human body, fictional characters whose representations revolve around food consistently invoke the idea of the physical body.

When eating and food are central to the make-up of a fictional character, issues of embodiment, power, and subjectivity emerge as essential to characterization. As a biological necessity, the act of eating cannot be reduced simply to one component of a Foucauldian "useful" body (136). Certain eating habits do complement certain cultural prescriptions, but eating as a basic practice transcends (or, rather, rescinds) the trappings of culture. Though de Certeau sees cooking, rather than eating, as an "everyday" and therefore resistant activity (xix), eating is even less a product of cultural mandate than is food preparation. Eating is primal action; it is central to the creation and sustenance of life. Eating is one of the few processes that all bodies have in common and, as a process that defines the body as active, and therefore as a site of other potential activities, eating signifies the body's potential for conscious agency beyond a social network. The body's agency is not simply a result of or a response to external influences of society or culture. There is an internal, psychic will to movement, toward agency, and eating-as-action contains within it the body's propensity for resistance and for unique, subjective experience.

In both Woolf's and Dunmore's texts, one side of the mind/body duality emerges as material and physical in part due to the relationship between eating, the body, and the agency attributed to the active body. Nina and Mrs. Manresa are both drawn as voracious consumers, and in turn their bodies and the other actions of those bodies become the major components of their characterizations. Mrs. Manresa, who wears too many rings and whose husband is "a Jew...got up to look the very spit and image of the landed gentry" (40), not only consumes to excess with regard to material goods, but is also the predominant consumer of food throughout Woolf's text. The initial luncheon at Pointz Hall allows Woolf to showcase Manresa's appetite for champagne and for cream, which she "let...curl luxuriously into her coffee" and "to which she added a shovelful of brown sugar" (55). For Mrs. Manresa, food is also an extension of her ability to communicate: she "[pinches] a bit of bread" for emphasis during lunchtime chatter, and, once she has consumed their fruit, makes the pits of cherries into oracular items as she uses them to chant the child's rhyme "Tinker, tailor, soldier, sailor," in that way confirming her position as the "wild child of nature" (50). Her freedom with food is paralleled by her freedom with her own body: she racily recounts to mixed company of how she removes her stays and rolls in the grass upon arriving in the country (42).

Like Mrs. Manresa, Dunmore's Nina Close is a creature of the flesh, and Nina revels in the freedoms that her body affords her. As with Manresa, only more so, Nina's relationship to food is emphasized. She eats alongside the men of the text, and admits to greed where food is concerned (39). Nina, too, is the chef of the novel, and spends a good deal of her time in the kitchen of her sister's home, a room that "calls out in [her] that small almost sexual shiver [she] can't fake" (17). "'People who like eating make the best cooks,'" she tells Richard (47), connecting her consumption of food with her ability to act and with her own aesthetic, her own method of communication. As she rhapsodizes over a dinner she plans, the material of her ingredients blend with the movements of her own body and invite readers to participate along with her:

The salmon is in the oven, the potatoes ready to boil, the tomatoes in a warm heap on the table, to be cut as late as possible and sprinkled with brown sugar. The beans are waiting in a colander. The tomatoes are intensely red against the damaged surface of the table. Their skins are tough. I'll score them with the point of a knife, dip them in boiling water, and slip them out of their skins. (70)

Nina's confidence in the kitchen goes beyond traditional domesticity. The kitchen and its edible contents provide Nina with a venue in which to create and to control. Food allows Nina freedom, just as it does Mrs. Manresa.

Of course, the freedom of physical, embodied agency includes sexual agency, which carries more stigma than do other of its forms, and neither Nina nor Mrs. Manresa is able to rise above the social stereotypes associated with the woman of appetite. In *The Flesh Made Word*, Helena Michie does an excellent job of explaining the cultural connections that have historically been made between gustatory and sexual appetites, pointing out how excessive eating traditionally signifies this rather vilified aspect of women's bodies, and how "[d]elicate appetites are linked not only with femininity, but with virginity" (16). Though both Nina and Mrs. Manresa on many levels seem to illustrate positive examples of female embodiment and female agency, both are also subject to reader assessment influenced by cultural codes that call into question the sexual, embodied female. There is great potential in each of these female characters for change in the way women who are firmly established as "of the flesh" might be viewed, but neither Woolf nor Dunmore moves beyond the linking of voracious eating with certain other hungers. Giles Oliver causes Mrs. Manresa "to furbish up her ancient batteries" (47), and does something pass between them later in the novel that necessitates a reapplication of "the Manresa's" lipstick (133)? Nina, her late twentieth-century counterpart, has an affair with her brother-in-law Richard that is not cloaked in innuendo, but is conducted out in the open of her sister's garden. Both women exhibit elements of chutzpah and agency that might mark them as unique creatures otherwise, but their transgression, their sexuality, instead marks them as doubtful figures, as questionable models for a new female archetype based upon the body's freedoms rather than upon its limitations.

When I first began this area of research, I wanted to explore the ways in which women might have used food and eating in their writing in order to invest in the female body as a site empowerment and, perhaps, as one way to reclaim the female body from the limited representations cast by other, mostly male authors. Even such a common practice as eating, though, carries with it related stigma, and, more interesting for me, these consuming women also seem always to appear in texts alongside an opposing, disembodied and traditionally feminine figure, such as Woolf's Isa and Dunmore's Isabel. As I began to examine these pairs of women in literature and how they reflect the mind/body duality inherent in Western culture, I became less interested in the physical side of the binary, and have had to take into account the life of the mind present in these other characterizations. Woolf's Isa is a striking example of how the mental arena of language and of the intellect can be used as a method not only to create a character, but also to juxtapose the mind with the corporeal realm. Isa's body *size* is not the issue here, for she is "[t]hick of waist, [and] large of limb" (16); rather, her relationship to language and her ephemeral, almost completely discursive existence is what sets her apart from the Manresas of the world and from the physical half of the mind/body split. While she does not necessarily suffer from an eating disorder, she is never depicted while eating, and her characterization lacks a consuming component. When contrasted with the mechanisms used by Woolf to create Mrs. Manresa's character, those used to construct Isa place her in direct opposition to the consuming character. Isa's constant poetic monologues take the place of any direct action, and often instead describe potential action metonymically: language *is* Isa's primary form of activity, and because of this, her psyche, and not her physicality, signifies her whole being. Her connection to William Dodge furthers the effacement of her body. While Mrs. Manresa is caught up in her flirtation and/or infidelity with Giles, Isa is in the greenhouse with Dodge and has "nothing to fear, nothing to hope" (113) due to his sexual orientation. Isa's extramarital relationship is intellectual rather than sexual. The traditional cultural tendency to ignore and efface the male homosexual body makes Dodge a natural counterpart of the disembodied Isa.

Like Isa, Dunmore's Isabel makes her strongest interpersonal connection on a non-sexual, intellectual level. Her friendship with Edward is "a serious distraction from the business of the baby" Isabel has just given birth to, and, from Nina's vantage point, seems to consist of "Edward, moody on a footstool, his chin on his hands, explaining to Isabel the enigma that is himself" (33). In turn, Isabel "[pours] out the oil of her understanding and advice on him" (84); language for Isabel is therapeutic rather than poetic, but it serves, still, as the basis for her primary function in the real-time narrative of *Talking to the Dead*. She is unlike her embodied, consuming, sexual sister and, as a mother and wife, can appear to be a corrective prescription for Nina's transgressive behavior. A representative of the mental sphere, as a traditionally feminine woman she also represents the constructs of gender rather than the enigma of biology. Unlike Woolf's female pairing, in which the two women are physically alike and only characterized differently, Dunmore's women are created as opposites with respect to both physical traits and consumption practices. Isabel is physically weak and has a history of eating difficulties, and though she is a new and nursing mother, refuses most of the food prepared by Nina, instead existing on the oatcakes and dried apricots stashed away in her bedside table. Though lacking in the physical stuff of agency and of empowerment, Isabel transcends the body through an adherence to socially sanctioned roles for women, while Nina, though a rational and decisive sexual and social agent, falters when placed alongside her elder sibling. Only toward the novel's end, when her role in the death of an infant brother years before comes to light, is Isabel's moral high ground destabilized. In childhood, Nina might have wished her younger brother dead in order to maintain the affections of her mother and of Isabel herself, but Isabel, we discover, is the sister who committed the fratricide in order to please her beloved sibling. Because the sisters are together responsible for the novel's ultimate sin, neither the psychical nor the physical can ultimately be perceived as *the* transcendent human quality. Dunmore plays upon social conventions related to the female body and to eating and appetite in order to conceal until the final moment of closure a set of less easily deciphered codes of ethics and of morality than a mind/body duality can allow, and shows the way beyond the mutual exclusion so embedded in Western thought.

Though both Woolf and Dunmore use the trope of consumption and the binary of mind and body in order to characterize their respective pairs of female characters, each text exhibits a desire for synthesis of these two realms, for a move beyond the fragmentation of human experience. Long before the essentialist/constructivist debate within contemporary theoretical discourse, Woolf understood the need for a combination, rather than a polarization, of the intellectual and the corporeal. More than half a century later, Helen Dunmore echoes Woolf's understanding and revises the gesture toward synthesis further than Woolf herself was able to. Neither writer is content with the limited model of representing women through a separation of the mind from the flesh and, though both Woolf and Dunmore extend the role of the embodied female in their texts, both also acknowledge the need for her counterpart, for the psychic dimension without which the body would be no more than inert matter. The pairs of women in each text are, to some degree, complicit in the progressions and outcomes of the narratives that deliver them, together providing a more complete idea of female experience than either character might offer individually. Mrs. Manresa is a leap beyond the interiority that readers associate with Woolfian fiction, but without Isa, Woolf would have been left with only a caricature of female embodiment and of the desire implicit in the figure of the consuming woman. The final pages of the novel, though, render the binary more intact than the novel promises, and when Mrs. Manresa motors away from Pointz Hall, Woolf seems to sacrifice the power of the body to some superior concept of intellect. I think, however, that the Isa we are left with in the novel's final passage, the woman who morphs into Everywoman and becomes caught up in the persistent drama of a world that "chuff chuff chuff"s along, is a different woman from the one we are introduced to at the novel's onset. Isa has settled into a body that will "fight," "embrace," and likely reproduce itself (219); her mind makes room for the physical and the external. Like the individuals and the community who struggle with "*Unity—Dispersity*" (210), the mind and the body are drawn together at the end of Woolf's novel in a final alchemy of granite and rainbow.

Afterword

Since the time of the Bangor conference, I have continued to work on the nexus of food and sexuality in women's texts, and I have published articles on related issues in both Dunmore's and Woolf's novels. I have not revisited the connections between these texts, though, and revisiting this paper has rekindled an interest in doing so.

Works Cited

de Certeau, Michel. *The Practice of Everyday Life*. 1974. Trans. Steven Rendall. Berkeley: U of California P, 1984.
Dunmore, Helen. E-mail to the author. Spring 2001.
———. *Talking to the Dead*. 1996. Boston: Back Bay, 1998.
Foucault, Michel. *Discipline and Punish: The Birth of the Prison*. Trans. Robert Hurley. 1975. New York: Vintage, 1995.
Grosz, Elizabeth. *Volatile Bodies: Toward a Corporeal Feminism*. Bloomington and Indianapolis: Indiana UP, 1994.
Michie, Helena. *The Flesh Made Word: Female Figures and Women's Bodies*. New York: Oxford UP, 1987.
Woolf, Virginia. *Between the Acts*. 1941. New York: Harcourt Brace Jovanovich, 1985.

Notes on Contributors

Genevieve Abravanel is an Assistant Professor of English at Franklin and Marshall College. Her recent and forthcoming publications include articles on Thomas Hardy, H.D., and F.R. Leavis. She is currently finishing a book tentatively entitled *Americanizing Britain: The Rise of Modernism in the Age of the Entertainment Empire*.

Andrea Adolph is Associate Professor of English and coordinator of service-learning at Kent State University Stark Campus, where she teaches courses on British literature and women writers. Her book, *Food and Femininity in Twentieth-Century British Women's Fiction*, is forthcoming from Ashgate.

Beth Rigel Daugherty, Professor of English at Otterbein College in Westerville, OH, co-edited the MLA volume on teaching *To the Lighthouse*, has published work in *Woolf Studies Annual*, edited collections, and other *Selected Papers* volumes, and is currently working on a manuscript titled *The Education of a Woman Writer: Virginia Woolf's Apprenticeship*.

Jane de Gay is Associate Principal Lecturer in English at Leeds Trinity University College. Her many publications on Woolf include *Virginia Woolf's Novels and the Literary Past* (Edinburgh: Edinburgh University Press, 2006).

Marion Dell is co-author of *Virginia Woolf and Vanessa Bell: Remembering St. Ives*, with Marion Whybrow (Padstow: Tabb House, 2004). She has recently retired as Associate Lecturer with the Open University and is now a freelance writer and lecturer.

Jeanne Dubino is Chair and Professor of English at Appalachian State University in Boone, North Carolina. She has published on Woolf's essays and travel writing, nineteenth-century British travelers to Turkey and Kenya, Kenyan fiction, and popular film and culture. Her most recent project is an edited volume entitled *Virginia Woolf and the Literary Marketplace*.

Diane F. Gillespie, Professor Emerita of English, Washington State University, is author of *The Sisters' Arts: Virginia Woolf, Vanessa Bell, and Painting* and of numerous articles; editor of Woolf's *Roger Fry: A Biography* and of *The Multiple Muses of Virginia Woolf*; and co-editor of Julia Stephen's writings, *Virginia Woolf and the Arts*, and Cicely Hamilton's *Diana of Dobson's*.

Leslie Kathleen Hankins, Professor of English at Cornell College, teaches courses on literature and film. She has presented on Virginia Woolf and the cinema at many of the International Conferences on Virginia Woolf. Recent publications are on Virginia Woolf and Abel Gance's film, *J'accuse*, cinema culture in London in the 1920s, and the holograph drafts of Woolf's essay, "The Cinema."

Notes on Contributors

Kathryn Harvey is currently Head of Archival and Special Collections at the University of Guelph. Prior to this she was Archives Specialist at Dalhousie University Archives and Special Collections (2003-2009). Her recent research focuses on the role of archivists in shaping history and on performing arts archives. Recent publications sole- and co-authored have appeared in *Partnership: The Canadian Journal of Library and Information Practice and Research*, *Archivaria*, and *Journal of Canadian Studies*.

Joyce Kelley is an Assistant Professor of English at Auburn University, Montgomery, specializing in British and transnational modernism. She received her Ph.D. in 2007 from the University of Iowa and spent a year as a postdoctoral fellow at Northwestern University.

Nancy Knowles is Associate Professor of English/Writing at Eastern Oregon University and Director of the Oregon Writing Project at Eastern Oregon University.

Janet M. Manson, Ph.D., is currently teaching classes in American, Middle Eastern, and Latin American History at Warren Wilson College, Asheville, N.C. She is also continuing her research projects on Leonard S. Woolf.

Cheryl Mares is a Professor of English at Sweet Briar College in Virginia. Her research interests focus on works by modernist writers, especially Virginia Woolf and Marcel Proust, on whom she has published a number of articles. Currently, she is working on articles that explore Woolf's relationship with American culture.

Su Reid has taught in the Universities of Aberdeen and Teesside, and until recently she was Director of the School of Arts and Media at Teesside. She lives in North Yorkshire and, as well as writing, is undertaking training for Lay Ministry in the Church of England.

Christine Sizemore is Professor of English at Spelman College in Atlanta, Georgia. She is the author of *A Female Vision of the City: London in the Novels of Five British Women* and *Negotiating Identities in Women's Lives: English Postcolonial and Contemporary British Novels* as well as articles on Woolf and other women writers, most recently Doris Lessing and Zadie Smith.

Nick Smart is Chair of English at The College of New Rochelle. He lives in New York City and writes about Virginia Woolf and Bob Dylan.

Loretta Stec, Professor of English at San Francisco State University, has published articles on modernist figures such as Woolf, West, Lawrence, and Stein, as well as on southern African literature in English.

Tara Surry graduated from the University of Western Australia in 2005, with a Ph.D. on Virginia Woolf's essays and forms of space. She has presented papers at numerous conferences, and has an essay on Woolf, disability and the Gothic being published in a forthcoming collection.

Diana L. Swanson is Associate Professor of English and Women's Studies at Northern Illinois University and served as the founding coordinator of NIU's Lesbian, Gay, Bisexual, Transgender Studies Program. Her publications on Woolf include articles in *Twentieth Century Literature, Woolf Studies Annual, Virginia Woolf Miscellany,* and *Creating Safe Space: Violence and Women's Writing.*

Urszula Terentowicz-Fotyga is a Senior Lecturer in the English Faculty at Maria Curie-Skłodowska University in Lublin, Poland. Her main research interests are culture and theory, semiotics of space, modernist and postmodernist fiction. She is the author of a book on the semiotics of women's space in Virginia Woolf's novels. Currently she is working on a book about the representation of the country house in contemporary noves and culture.

Bibliography

PUBLICATIONS ARISING FROM THE CONFERENCE

Adams, David. "Shadows of a 'Silver Globe': Woolf's Reconfiguration of the Darkness." *Colonial Odysseys: Empire and Epic in the Modernist Novel.* Ithaca: Cornell UP, 2003. Chapter 4.
Banfield, Ann. "Time Passes: Virginia Woolf, Post-Impressionism and Cambridge Time." *Poetics Today* 24.3 (Fall 2003): 471-516.
Bell, Lindsay. "Transmitting the Voyage and the Vision: Adapting Virginia Woolf's *To the Lighthouse* for Radio." *Languages of Theatre Shaped by Women.* Ed. J. de Gay and L. Goodman. Bristol: Intellect, 2003.
Benzel, Kathryn N. "Verbal Painting in Virginia Woolf's Short Fiction: Lyricism in *Monday or Tuesday.*" *Trespassing Boundaries: Virginia Woolf's Short Fiction.* Ed. K.N. Benzel and Ruth Hoberman. New York and Basingstoke: Palgrave Macmillan, 2004.
Blyth, Ian. "A Little 'Einsteinian' Confusion." *Virginia Woolf Bulletin* 9 (2002): 29-33.
Chapman, Wayne C. "Leonard Woolf and the Rowntree Political Monthlies, 1916-1922: With the Irish Rebellion as a Case in Point." *The South Carolina Review* 34.1 (Fall 2001): 165-69.
Clarke, Stuart N. "The Application of Thought to Editing Woolf's Texts." *Virginia Woolf Bulletin* 8 (September 2001): 15-21.
de Gay, Jane. "Tradition and Exploration in *Night and Day.*" *Virginia Woolf's Novels and the Literary Past.* Edinburgh: Edinburgh University Press, 2006. Chapter 2.
Fowler, Rowena. "Virginia Woolf: Lexicographer." *English Language Notes* 39 (2002): 57-73.
Haller, Evelyn. "Alexandria as Envisioned by Virginia Woolf and E.M. Forster: An Essay in Gendered History." *Woolf Studies Annual* 9 (2003): 167-92.
Hoberman, Ruth. "Collecting, Shopping, and Reading: Virginia Woolf's Stories about Objects." *Trespassing Boundaries: Virginia Woolf's Short Fiction.* Ed. Kathryn N. Benzel and Ruth Hoberman. New York and Basingstoke: Palgrave Macmillan, 2004. 81-98.
Hussey, Mark. "Mrs. Thatcher and Mrs. Woolf." *Modern Fiction Studies* 50.1 (Spring 2004): 8-30.
Kitsi-Mitakou, Katerina. "'Let the Poppy Seed Itself and the Carnation Mate with the Cabbage': With Hardy and Woolf at Argiro Mantoglou's *Virginia Woolf Café.*" *Dia-Keimena* [Inter-Texts] 4 (2002): 211-30.
Kosugi, Sei. "Representing Nation and Nature: Woolf, Kelly, White." *Locating Woolf: The Politics of Space and Place.* Ed. Anna Snaith and Michael Whitworth. New York and Basingstoke: Palgrave Macmillan, 2007. 81-97.
Laing, Kathryn. "Virginia Woolf in Ireland: A Short Voyage Out." *South Carolina Review* 34.1 (Fall 2001): 180-87.
Lewty, Jane. "Virginia Woolf and the Synapses of Radio." *Locating Woolf: The Politics of Space and Place.* Ed. Anna Snaith and Michael Whitworth. New York and Basingstoke: Palgrave Macmillan, 2007. 148-65.
Marcus, Jane. "A Very Fine Negress." *Hearts of Darkness: White Women Write Race.* Piscataway, NJ: Rutgers University Press, 2004. Chapter 2.
Marcus, Laura. "The European Dimensions of the Hogarth Press." *The Reception of British Writers in Europe: Virginia Woolf.* Ed. Mary Ann Caws and Nicola Luckhurst. London: Continuum, 2002. 328-56.
—. "Introduction." Translations from the Russian by Virginia Woolf and S.S. Koteliansky. London: Virginia Woolf Society of Great Britain, 2006. vii-xxiv.
McNeillie, Andrew. "Virginia Woolf's America." *Dublin Review* 5 (Winter 2001-2): 41-55.
Oldfield, Sybil. *Afterwords, Letters on the Death of Virginia Woolf.* New York: Columbia UP, and Edinburgh: Edinburgh UP, 2005.
Osborne, Karen Lee. "The Blessed Syncope of Supreme Moments: The Music of Time in AVA." *Casebook on Carole Maso's AVA.* Ed. Monica Berlin. Urbana-Champaign: Dalkey Archive Press, 2001.
Ota, Nobuyoshi. "'Our Commitments to China': Migration and the Geopolitical Unconscious of *The Waves.*" *Locating Woolf: The Politics of Space and Place.* Ed. Anna Snaith and Michael Whitworth. New York and Basingstoke: Palgrave Macmillan, 2007. 167-82.
Peach, Linden. "'Re-reading Sickert's Interiors': Woolf, English Art and the Representation of Domestic Space." *Locating Woolf: The Politics of Space and Place.* Ed. Anna Snaith and Michael Whitworth. New York and Basingstoke: Palgrave Macmillan, 2007. 65-80.
Schröder, Leena Kore. "'Reflections in a Motor Car': Virginia Woolf's Phenomenological Relations of Time and Space." *Locating Woolf: The Politics of Space and Place.* Ed. Anna Snaith and Michael Whitworth. New York and Basingstoke: Palgrave Macmillan, 2007. 131-47.
Seeley, Tracy. "Flights of Fancy: Spatial Digression and Storytelling in A Room of One's Own." *Locating Woolf: The Politics of Space and Place.* Ed. Anna Snaith and Michael Whitworth. New York and Basingstoke: Palgrave Macmillan, 2007. 31-45.

www.ingramcontent.com/pod-product-compliance
Lightning Source LLC
Chambersburg PA
CBHW02193516Ø426
43195CB00011B/1103